GREECE and ITALY

ANCIENT ROOTS & NEW BEGINNINGS

SELECTED ESSAYS FROM THE 33rd ANNUAL CONFERENCE

OF THE

AMERICAN ITALIAN HISTORICAL ASSOCIATION

9 - 11 November 2000
Lowell, Massachusetts

EDITORS

Mario Aste
Sheryl Lynn Postman
Michael Pierson

Founded in 1966, the American Italian Historical Association is an interdisciplinary group of scholars and lay people who share an interest in investigating relationships among Italian Americans, Italy, and the Americas. Its members encourage the collection, preservation, study, and poularization of materials that illuminate the Italian-Amerian experience. The Association promotes research through regional and national activities, including the annual conference and the publication of its proceedings.

American Italian Historical Association. Conference (33rd : 2000 : Lowell, Mass.)
  Greece and Italy : ancient roots & new beginnings : selected essays from the 33rd annual conference of the American Italian Historical Association, 9–11 November 2000, Lowell, Massachusetts / editors, Mario Aste, Sheryl Lynn Postman, Michael Pierson.
  p. cm. (American Italian Historical Association ; volume 33, 2004)
Includes index.
ISBN 0–934675–53–8. – ISBN 0–934765–54–6
  1. Italian Americans—History—Congresses. 2. Italian Americans—Politics and government—Congresses. 3. Italian American arts—Congresses. 4. United States—Civilization—Italian influences—Congresses. 5. United States—Civilization—Greek influences—Congresses. I. Aste, Mario. II. Postman, Sheryl L. (Sheryl Lynn), 1952–. III. Pierson, Michael. IV. Title. V. AIHA (Series) ; 33.

E184.I8A5243 2000
973'.0451—dc22

2005043602

Copyright © 2005 by the American Italian Historical Association. All rights reserved. No part of this book may be reproduced without permission of the publisher.

ISBN: 0-934675-53-8 (soft)
         0-934675-54-6 (hard)
ISSN: 0743-474X

GREECE AND ITALY

Ancient Roots & New Beginnings

Mario Aste
Sheryl Lynn Postman
Michael Pierson

University of Massachusetts Lowell

American Italian Historical Association
Volume 33 • 2004

TABLE OF CONTENTS

Introduction ix

Magna Graecia: The Greek Presence in Southern Italy
ROBERT MARCHISOTTO (1)

"Little Italy" vs "Little Greece": The Selection of Richard Nixon's 1968 Running Mate
STEFANO LUCONI (13)

New York City Italian American Mayors, LaGuardia, Impellitteri and Giuliani: Comparisons, Contrasts and Curiosities
SALVATORE J. LAGUMINA (24)

Governor Charles Poletti
FRANK CAVAIOLI (45)

Henry Molise's Cultural Growth in John Fante's *The Brotherhood of the Grape*
FRANCO MULAS (56)

Little Paul's Psychological Development in Pietro Di Donato's *Christ in Concrete*
MARIA PAOLA MALVA (63)

Triumphs and Tragedies of Ethnicity in America: Italians in the Granite Industry in Barre, Vermont, 1890-1915
ARTHUR PIPPO AND GILLIAN QUINN (72)

Roman Naval Operations During the Second Macedonian War
VALENTINO J. BELFIGLIO (86)

Italian American Voting Preferences
WILLIAM EGELMAN, WILLIAM GRATZER, BRIAN NICKERSON, AND MICHAEL D'ANGELO (94)

Bodies of Nostalgia Shipwrecked in Mediterranean Waters: A "Journey" from Morocco to Naples, "with Bags of Sand and Trunks Full of Fables" told by Tahar Ben Jelloun and Peppe Lanzetta
ROBERTA MOROSINI   (103)

The Italian Contribution to Argentine Popular Culture and Theater
MARÍA TERESA SANHUEZA   (128)

Giorgio Vasari's *The Ages of Life*
LIANA DE GIROLAMI CHENEY   (152)

Ancient History? Sicilians in Gianni Amelio's *Lamerica*
MARISA LABOZZETTA   (174)

Italy and Greece, War, Culture, Religion: Relationships and People in *Mediterraneo* and *Malena*
MARIO ASTE   (180)

A Higher Level of Notation
PAUL MARION   (198)

The Cultural Function and Trickster Figures of Aristophanic Comedy in Fred Gardaphé's *Moustache Pete is Dead / Evviva Baffo Pietro*
PAUL GIAIMO   (200)

Aristotelian Tragedy in *Blue Italian* and *Night Bloom*
MARY ANN MANNINO   (207)

Where It All Began: Tracing the Origins of Cinema to the Mediterranean and the Baroque
JOSEPH GARREAU   (216)

Pirandello e il cinema
MARIA C. PASTORE PASSARO   (225)

The Italian American Press and the 'Woman Question,' 1915-1930
BÉNÉDICT DESCHAMPS (234)

***Virgillia*, or the Contribution of Italian Americans to the United States through Intermarriage**
MARIE-CHRISTINE MICHAUD (245)

Poetry / Poesie
MARIA ROSA CIAVARELLI (255)

The Graeco-Roman Influence in Sicily
ROSEANNA MUELLER (265)

INTRODUCTION

The XXXIII Conference of the American Italian Historical Association was held in Lowell Massachusetts, where Greek immigrants settled at the turn of the century and established a vibrant community. Italians from Calabria, Naples and Sicily soon followed. Throughout the years the two ethnic groups collaborated in many cultural activities, among which the Lowell Opera Company, under the directorship of Vito Selvaggio, originally from "Magna Graecia" in Italy, became a community leader in the cultural life of Lowell. Selvaggio, with his directorship of The Lowell Opera Company, provided a beautiful performance of Italian Operatic pieces to the conference participants.

Regretfully, given the limitation of space and cost, only a selection of papers, through a rigorous, referee process, is published here. The end result is only a selective sample of the papers that provide some of the indication not merely of the work that was presented, but the kind of research, critical analysis, and creative writing in the field of Italian American Studies.

We personally would like to thank all the participants for their contributions in the exploration of the many facets of the field of Italian American Studies and all of the persons and organizations that made the XXXIII AIHA Conference and the publication of these Proceedings possible.

Finally we would like to give special thanks to Provost Robert Wagner for his support and his address to the participants at the Conference and his assistance in obtaining funds for the publication of these Proceedings.

Mario Aste,
Sheryl Lynn Postman,
Michael Pierson.

Keynote Presentation

MAGNA GRAECIA:
THE GREEK PRESENCE IN SOUTHERN ITALY

Robert Marchisotto
PRINCETON RESEARCH FORUM, PRINCETON NJ

In this presentation, we will explore a phase in the development of the Greek civilization that was to have a profound effect on the geopolitical dynamics of the Mediterranean basin and, ultimately, on the rise and ascendancy of Western European culture. We will explore the cause for the massive emigration of the Greeks to southern Italy, where they went and how they got there, whom they encountered there and their successes and failures in these endeavors. We will cover the period beginning with the first Greek settlements in Italy in the eighth century BC, and ending basically with the ascendancy of Rome in 260 BC. Also, we will examine what impact this may have had on the mass migrations from southern Italy to the US in the late nineteenth and early twentieth century.

BACKGROUND AND HISTORICAL PERSPECTIVE

For purposes of this discussion, it is necessary to define the dominant powers in the Mediterranean in the eighth century BC: Greece, prosperous and growing in the eastern Mediterranean; Carthage, a colonial offspring of Phoenicia, located in present-day Tunisia; and the Etruscans, occupying central Italy north of Rome (Maps I, II).

Geographically, the area we are concerned with, southern Italy, is basically the modern-day Mezzogiorno comprising the regions of Sicily, Calabria, Basilicata, Puglia, Campania, Lazio below Rome, Molise and Abruzzi. Magna Graecia is encompassed within this area, but not uniformly, as we shall see presently.

One more clarification: One will sometimes see the term Magna Graecia used only for the mainland portion of southern Italy, excluding Sicily; others use the term inclusively, and I am in that camp. Functionally, all of these regions comprise "greater Greece," because all of the Greek colonists went to these sites on the island and mainland for exactly the same purpose.

Although the historical evidence from the prehistoric period is not entirely clear about the more subtle reasons for Greek emigration, there is no uncertainty about the main reason: it was overpopulation. As prosperity grew, the arable land available for food production could not support the increased numbers of people. While the westward emigration from Greece was an organized movement, armed, equipped and planned by various mother-cities, the effect and intention from the start were not just to colonize but to encourage – if not compel – men to move out permanently to new and independent communities of their own.

WHERE THEY CAME FROM, WHERE THEY WENT, HOW THEY GOT THERE, AND WHO DID THEY FIND THERE?

Although a Greek presence in the western Mediterranean has been well documented by archeological discoveries concerning the Bronze Age (sixteenth to fourteenth centuries BC), it was confined to maritime trading expeditions and, perhaps, the establishment of small trading posts. In any event, Greek seafarers were quite familiar with navigation in the Mediterranean. In fact, the Greeks and their commercial maritime rivals, the Phoenicians, discovered that the Mediterranean was a great sea surrounded by three continents of the ancient inhabited world, with a passage to the ocean. The Greeks called the Mediterranean the inner sea to differentiate it from the outer sea beyond the Straits of Gibraltar. This outer sea the Greeks envisioned would encircle the whole of the inhabited world.

This idea, on the other hand, was virtually unknown to the ancient civilizations of Egypt, Mesopotamia and Anatolia. They had had awareness only of areas of the eastern Mediterranean and, consequently, could never have had any concept of its overall dimension. So when the need arose and Greek emigration was critical, even mandated, it created the conditions necessary for the revival and strengthening of the existing maritime network.

The colonization from these various mother-cities, first from Greece and then by expansion from colonies in Magna Graecia, is a complicated and sometimes obscure picture. Some colonies had one mother-city sponsor, some two or more. So to make more sense of the dynamics of this imbroglio, I have decided to group the colonies with respect to the principal founding mother-city, not necessarily chronologically, and dealing separately with the mainland and Sicily.

It is generally agreed that the first colonies on the mainland were established on the island of Ischia and Cumae near Naples in 750 BC, and at Naxos on Sicily in 735 BC. The last were founded on the mainland at Thurii and on Sicily at Tyndaris at about the same time, 400 BC. Incidentally, all dates cited are, at best, approximations. Interestingly, for reasons that are not entirely clear, the whole area of Greek colonization on mainland Italy lay between the Gulf of Taranto and the Bay of Naples, ignoring the Adriatic coast altogether.

THE COLONIES: MAINLAND (CHART I, MAP I)

Pithecusa, Cumae, and Neapolis – Actually, all three colonies were sponsored, directly or indirectly, by the Euboeans. Pithecusa (Ischia) was settled first, later abandoned and merged with Cumae. Cumae played an important role in spreading Hellenic influence in the west. At the very northern edge of Greek mainland colonization, it inevitably encountered expansion pressure from the powerful Etruscans looking southward. It was finally resolved in 524 BC when the Cumaeans routed a large Etruscan army in a decisive battle. To acquire an adequate harbor, the Cumaeans re-founded an abandoned site on the Bay of Naples and named it Neapolis (Naples). A major Euboean contribution was its alphabet which, when learned by the Etruscans, eventually spread to the Romans and became the base for their alphabet.

Rhegium – was the sole Euboean colony south of Cumae and had great strategic value, by controlling the Straits of Messina along with Zancle, another Euboean colony, on the Sicilian side.

Locri, Sybaris, Croton, Metapontum and Posidonia – Around the toe of Italy from Rhegium to the instep of the foot, the Achaeans founded the first four cities. Their relationships were marked by periods of great wealth followed by precipitous declines in their fortunes. They feuded constantly, alternately making and breaking alliances to further their own agendas. When they were not fighting, culture and the arts flourished. Croton had doctors of the highest repute of the school of Democedes; Pythagoras and his school of mathematicians and philosophers were developed there. In Locri, Zaleucus gave this city a written code of laws, thought to be the first Greek city to do so. As with the previous city-states described, this group also founded colonies all over the peninsula. Sybaris was responsible for Posidonia (Paestum) around 650 BC. During its prosperous but short-lived, three-century existence it produced a series of the most remarkable temples and shrines. They have survived for 2500 years and are in quite good condition.

Elea (Velia) – was founded by the Phocaeans, Greeks from Ionia in Asia Minor, in 535 BC. It fared better than the neighboring Posidonians, who were constantly threatened by the tough Lucanian natives. Their main claim to fame was the development of the Eleatic School of Philosophy.

Taras – Anchoring this string of colonies on the Ionian Sea, nestled in the inner heel of the foot, is Taras (Taranto). It was founded in 706 BC by Spartans, a people not particularly noted for their seafaring skills. The story:

> *While the flower of Spartan manhood was for long years occupied with the conquest of Messenia, their next door neighbors on the Peleponnesus, the Spartan women consoled themselves with those who had been left behind, and the resulting offspring were denied full rights of citizenship by the indignant victors on their return.*

Ergo, it was prudent that they leave town!

INDIGENOUS PEOPLES: MAINLAND

Who were the resident peoples in southern Italy and how did they respond to their new neighbors? Starting at the toe were the Bruttians in Calabria; Lucanians, Samnites and Sabines stretched out from northern Calabria to Lazio; and the Messapians in and about the Ionian colonies. In more ancient times the residents of the Calabrian peninsula were called Itali (better known as Siculi) and ruled by a King Italus from whom, it is believed, the name Italia was derived and, subsequently, Italy. More about the Siculi in the discussion on Sicily.

There was an uneasy and often contentious relationship between the locals and the mainland colonists, much more so than in Sicily. As mentioned previously, there were constant fights among the various colonies, weakening each combatant in the process, and thereby inviting opportunistic and devastating attacks from the locals. Many settlements were decimated or destroyed in the process.

THE COLONIES: SICILY (CHART II, MAP II)

The emigration to Sicily was on a much greater scale and much more successful than those on the mainland: The established city-states became wealthier and more powerful in many cases than the mother-cities from which they emigrated. And they lasted longer than their brethren on the mainland, who by 500 BC had begun a rapid decline.

Starting with *Naxos* first in 735 BC, the Euboeans – in rapid succession in the decade that followed – established colonies in *Zancle (Messina), Katane, and Leontini.* Zancle, coupled with Rhegium four miles across the straits and Cumae further up the coast, gave the Euboeans control of the lucrative metal commerce with the Etruscans.

Syracuse – was founded by the Corinthians in 733 BC. It was the prized site of the Greek diaspora. Blessed with two spectacular natural harbors, it became the most powerful city-state not only in Magna Graecia but in all of the ancient Greek world.

Megara Hyblea and Selinus – were both founded by Megara, the first in 728 BC and the latter a century later in 630 BC. Megara Hyblea was an unwise and ill-advised choice; it was small in size and wedged between the powerful Euboean settlements to the north and Syracuse to the south. Selinus, on the other hand had all that Megara Hyblea did not and developed into a megastar among Sicilian city-states.

Gela and Akragas (Agrigento) – were the next colonies to develop superpower status: Gela was founded jointly by colonists from Rhodes and Crete in 688 BC and – a century later – Rhodes again was involved, with Gela's "cooperation" in giving root to Akragas.

INDIGENOUS PEOPLES: SICILY

Before elaborating on the history and accomplishments of the Greek city-states in Sicily, a look at the peoples they found there would be in order. The eastern two-thirds of the island was populated by the Sicels, derived primarily from the mainland Siculi described previously. Their settlements tended to be more inland and, at first, they seemed to get along with their new Greek neighbors – not unlike our own native Americans and the English colonists. In fact, in all of these colonizations in Magna Graecia, it was men alone who ventured forth. Women did not accompany them. They intermarried with the women of the resident peoples. So, from the very beginning, the ethnic/genetic mix was forever altered in Magna Graecia.

The next largest indigenous group was that of the Sicans, who were believed to have migrated from the Iberian peninsula to the central Italian peninsula and thence to western Sicily. The population there was somewhat sparse in comparison to the Sicels in the east.

The most enigmatic people, the Elymians, occupied the northwest corner of the island. They were thought to be military survivors of the Trojan Wars – both Greeks and Trojans – who, while returning home or escaping, were blown off-course, landed there, and remained.

Lastly, although technically not indigenous to Sicily, were the Carthaginians, who developed into the last superpower to affect Greek expansionist aims. Actually, most historians agree that the Carthaginians preceded the Greeks in Magna Graecia, arriving in western Sicily around 800 BC. They founded colonies at Lilybaeum (Marsala), Motya (San Pantaleo Island), Panormus (Palermo) and Solus (Solunto). Basically, the Carthaginians were Phoenicians who established cities all over the Mediterranean to develop, expand and protect their considerable mercantile sea-trade routes. These were a seafaring people with a trading tradition from time immemorial. More later on their interaction with the Sicilian Greeks.

GROWTH OF THE GREEK SICILIAN CITY-STATES

Syracuse, Gela, Akragas and Selinus developed into the wealthiest and most powerful city-states in all Magna Graecia, with Syracuse becoming the most powerful in all of Greece. Unfortunately, these good conditions were not to last. Some bad habits brought over from Greece proper began to assert themselves, and the Age of Tyrants began in earnest in 505 BC. Except for an uncharacteristic democratic interlude from 466-405 BC, tyrannical rule continued until 215 BC through the Classical and Hellenistic Periods. Not all tyrants were bad; some were scholars, others poets and yet others Olympic athletes, and so on. However, statesmanship and diplomacy were not their strong suit.

Besides the numerous internecine battles they fought amongst themselves for political dominance on the island, the biggest mistake they made was to awaken the Carthaginian giant. The Carthaginians were, like their Phoenician forebears, traders and militarily unaggressive. Tumbling into this arena in the mid-eighth century BC came Greeks hungry for land and trade: Unaggressiveness was not one of their salient national characteristics. The Phoenician communities of western Sicily, and north Africa and Spain, saw that their only hope of survival was to unite under the leadership of their strongest member – Carthage.

Unfortunately for the peace of the western Mediterranean, the Sicilian Greeks found it impossible to live in harmony either with each other or with their "barbarian" neighbors. After a number of small battles and skirmishes, the Carthaginians attacked in great force at Himera in 480 BC, where they were met by forces from Syracuse and Akragas under the tyrants Gelon and Theron, respectively. The Carthaginians suffered a crushing defeat, one of the major conflicts of antiquity, from which they would not soon recover. It was a great day for the Greeks: their mother-cities simultaneously inflicted a tremendous defeat over the Persian fleet at Salamis.

Later in that century Athens, which had not participated materially in the original colonizations in Magna Graecia, became increasingly envious of Syracuse's increasing power and wealth. On the pretext of helping a Sicilian ally, Athens developed a plan to subjugate all Sicily principally through the conquest of Syracuse. From 415-413 BC, Athens launched an enormous invasion of Syracuse which was repulsed with devastating losses. Of the 114 warships and 27,000 men that sailed in 415 BC and of the 71 ships and 15,000 men who tried to salvage the enterprise in 413 BC, very little remained. 7000 survivors were imprisoned in the quarries of Syracuse – an indescribably horrendous fate. The only way out was death or, in the case of a select few, to be chosen as personal teachers for wealthy Syracusans. From this moment, until the ascendancy of Rome in 260 BC, Syracuse was the most powerful city-state in the Greek world.

Returning now to the Carthaginians, they had recovered from their ignominious defeat in 480 and, in 409, invaded Sicily in force laying waste to Selinus and Himera. Continuing battles raged between Carthage and the Sicilian Greeks up until Rome became involved in Sicilian politics as conquerors. All this strife segued directly into the three Punic Wars involving Rome and Carthage.

CULTURE, ARCHITECTURE AND THE ARTS IN SICILY

Despite what appears to a continual state of strife among the Sicilian Greeks and between them and their principal adversary, Carthage, culture and the arts thrived splendidly. Beautiful temples were built in the Doric style in Syracuse, Akragas, Selinus, Segesta and Solus, some of which were among the largest anywhere. Theaters were built all over the island: For example, the one at Syracuse is among the largest in the world; in Segesta it is located on the pristine mountain from which it was carved out; in Taormina it looks down at the Ionian Sea and a volcanic Mt. Etna. Greek plays are still presented in these ancient theaters. The arts and sciences flourished: poets, philosophers and historians were revered and encouraged, as were mathematicians, the most famous of which was Archimedes, a Syracusan; artistically, the coins of Syracuse were the finest and the most prized in the ancient world.

The Emigration to America

Now we take leave of Magna Graecia in the mid-3rd century BC – just as its power and influence are ebbing and being replaced in the region by the new superpower, Rome – and fast-forward to the Mezzogiorno in 1860 AD. Much has happened in the Mezzogiorno – it is no longer referred to as Magna Graecia – in the intervening 2100 years, especially in Sicily. For 500 glorious years Sicily – and to some extent parts of the rest of southern Italy – prospered during the reign of the Arabs and their successors, the Normans. After the death in 1250 AD of Frederick II – who appears to be my ancestor – everything went downhill and in 1860, the year that began a decade of Italian unification, the peasant's hopes were raised that things would finally change for the better.

That was not to happen: The peasants found themselves worse off after 1860 than they were before. This was a bitter pill to swallow: many Sicilians welcomed Garibaldi – when he landed in Marsala in 1860 – and supported and fought for him against the Bourbon tyranny, including my paternal great-grandfather, who was captured and narrowly escaped being hanged for his efforts. By the late 1880s conditions had deteriorated so badly that emigration was the only choice left to many of them.

Who Were These People,
Where Did They Come From and When?

These southern Italians were the descendants, through several iterations, of the Greeks who undertook massive emigrations to Magna

Graecia, now the Mezzogiorno, and were undertaking equally massive emigrations to America 2800 years later. Proportionately, the emigration to Magna Graecia was as massive as that to the United States in the nineteenth and twentieth century. Commenting on the Greek phenomenon, Tomasi Lampedusa, author of the Sicilian classic, *The Leopard*, is quoted thus: "Sicilia quest'America dell'antichità" ["Sicily, this America of ancient times"].

More than 5 million Italians settled in the United States since records have been kept. The great majority of these immigrants, almost 4 million, came between 1880 and 1920. Most were from the Mezzogiorno – 85 to 90%, with some 55% from Sicily alone. It has been estimated that there are about 25 million Americans of Italian origin in the US, which means that there would be 14-15 million of Sicilian background. So, basically, "Italian" emigration was a southern Italian phenomenon.

One final thought; consider this thesis: Those Greeks who left their homelands for Magna Graecia to start anew in a strange land had get-up-and-go qualities – the genetic cream-of-the-crop relative to their less adventurous compatriots. Were these qualities even more selected and present in the successor Mezzogiorno emigrants, even though they were difficult to perceive in a population under such backward conditions? It would be a fascinating study. I believe the DNA technology exists to do this.

CHARTS AND MAPS

PARENT STATE OR REGION	DATE (BC)	COLONY	PRESENT NAME
EUBOEA	750	PITHECUSA	ISCHIA
	735	CUMAE	CUMA
	6th Cent.	NEAPOLIS	NAPLES
	730	RHEGIUM	REGGIO-CALABRIA
ACHAEA	700	LOCRI	LOCRI
	720	SYBARIS	SIBARI
	710	CROTON	CROTONE
	685	METAPONTUM	METAPONTO
	650	POSIDONIA	PAESTUM
PHOCHAEA	535	ELEA	VELIA
SPARTA	706	TARAS	TARANTO

Chart I - MAINLAND ITALY

PARENT STATE OR REGION	DATE (BC)	COLONY	PRESENT NAME
EUBOEA	735	NAXOS	NAXOS
	730	ZANCLE	MESSINA
	728	KATANE	CATANIA
	729	LEONTINI	LENTINI
CORINTH	733	SYRACUSE	SIRACUSA
MEGARA	728	MEGARA HYBLEA	MEGARA HYBLEA
	630	SELINUS	SELINUNTE
RHODES/CRETE	688	GELA	GELA
RHODES/GELA	580	AKRAGAS	AGRIGENTO

Chart II – SICILY

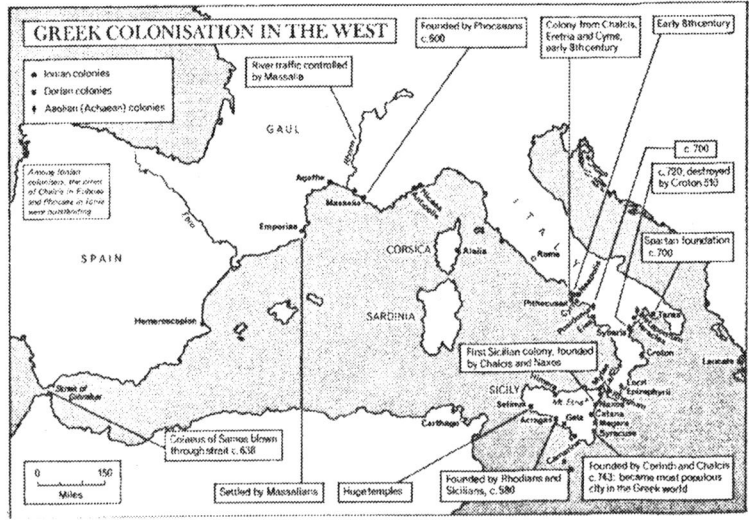

MAP 1 (Grant, *Atlas of Ancient History*)

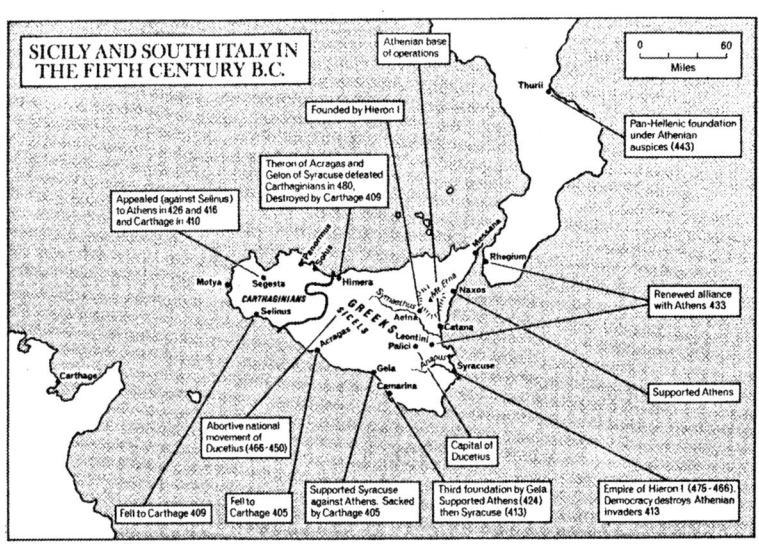

MAP 2 (Grant, *Atlas of Ancient History*)

BIBLIOGRAPHY

Barraclough, Geoffrey. *The Times Concise Atlas of World History*. London: Times, 1982.

Bowra, C. M. *Classical Greece*. New York: Time, 1965.

Carratelli, G. P., ed. *The Greek World: Art and Civilization in Magna Graecia and Sicily*. New York: Rizzoli, 1996.

Caven, Brian. *The Punic Wars*. London: Weidenfeld and Nicolson, 1980.

Durant, Will. *The Story of Civilization: Part II – The Life of Greece*. New York: Simon and Schuster, 1939.

Finley, M. I. *A History of Sicily: Ancient Sicily*. New York: Viking, 1968.

___. *Atlas of Classical Archaeology*. New York: McGraw-Hill, 1977.

Grant, Michael. *Atlas of Ancient History: 1700 BC to 565 AD*. New York: Dorset, 1971.

___, ed. *The Birth of Western Civilization: Greece and Rome*. London: McGraw-Hill, 1964.

Holloway, R. Ross. *The Archaeology of Ancient Sicily*. London: Routledge, 1991.

Johnston, Alan. *The Making of the Past: The Emergence of Greece*. New York: Elsevier, 1976.

Nelson, Nina. *Tunisia*. London: Batsford, 1974.

Randall-MacIver, David. *Greek Cities in Italy and Sicily*. Westport, CT: Greenwood, 1970.

Woodcock, P. G. *Dictionary of Ancient History*. New York: Philosophical Library, 1955.

Woodhead, A. G. *The Greeks in the West*. New York: Praeger, 1966.

"Little Italy" versus "Little Greece": The Selection of Richard Nixon's 1968 Running Mate

Stefano Luconi
UNIVERSITY OF FLORENCE, ITALY

On 8 August 1968, just a few hours after having received the Republican nomination for the White House, Richard M. Nixon announced that his running mate would be Spiro T. Agnew. The governor of Maryland, Agnew was so little known that the *Washington Post* argued that his selection had been "perhaps the most eccentric political appointment since the Roman Emperor Caligula named his horse a consul."[1]

Among those taken aback by Nixon's choice was the second-generation Italian-American governor of Massachusetts, John Anthony Volpe, who thought he was being seriously considered for the vice presidential nomination until Nixon made his final decision. Indeed, Volpe and Agnew ended up being the two surviving contenders for the second spot on the GOP ticket in almost all the meetings that Nixon had with his aides during the National Republican Convention.[2]

Unlike Agnew, who was a first-term governor from a small state, Volpe had a national stature. A self-made construction contractor, after serving as President Dwight D. Eisenhower's first Federal Highway Administrator, a subcabinet position to which he was appointed in 1956, Volpe was elected governor of Massachusetts in 1960 by a vote of 1,269,295 to Democratic candidate Joseph D. Ward's 1,130,810. Defeated by a narrow margin by Endicott Peabody in 1962 (1,053,322 to 1,047,891 votes), he was reelected to the statehouse both in 1964 against Francis X. Bellotti (by a vote of 1,176,462 to 1,153,416) and in 1966 against Edward McCormick. Contrary to the previous ones, this latter was a landslide triumph as Volpe carried the state by 1,227,358 votes to 752,720. His three successful bids for governor in a traditionally Democratic state built up Volpe's reputation as an effective vote-

---

[1] *Washington Post* 25 Sep. 1968. In fact, Caligula named his horse a senator.
[2] Salvatore J. LaGumina, "Case Studies of Ethnicity and Italian-American Politicians," in *The Italian Experience in the United States*, ed. Silvano M. Tomasi and Madeline H. Engel (New York: Center for Migration Studies, 1977), 145; Theodore H. White, *The Making of the President: 1968* (New York: Atheneum, 1969), 251-53.

getter. Indeed, two of his three victories occurred as John F. Kennedy and Lyndon B. Johnson carried Massachusetts and won election to the White House in 1960 and 1964, respectively.[3]

Conventional wisdom has it that Nixon preferred Agnew to Volpe because the Greek-American community committed a contribution of four to five million dollars to Nixon's campaign chest in exchange for Agnew's nomination. The late Monsignor Geno Baroni made a remark to this effect at the 1983 meeting of the American Italian Historical Association. In particular, in their coverage of the Republican convention, the *New York Daily News*, the *Boston Globe*, and the *New York Times* pointed to Boston's Greek-born industrialist and major Republican donor, Thomas A. Pappas, as Agnew's kingmaker. In his controversial biography of Nixon, Anthony Summers has more specifically contended that the 1968 Republican presidential candidate received large sums of money from the recently established Greek military junta through Pappas, and that a vice president of Greek ancestry was part of the strategy to win a more favorable attitude toward the Greek dictatorship from Washington.[4]

Conversely, one can easily contend that Nixon did not choose Agnew as his running mate in order to win the Greek-American vote. A study about the members of this ethnic group in the Norfolk, Virginia, metropolitan area has concluded that a majority of the local Greek-American electorate supported the Republican ticket in 1968. But, with

---

[3] Erik Amfitheatrof, *The Children of Columbus: An Informal History of the Italians in the New World* (Boston: Little, Brown, 1973), 317-18; "Volpe, John A.," *Biographical Directory of the Governors of the United States, 1789-1978*, ed. Robert Sobel and John Raimo, 4 vols. (Westport, CT: Meckler, 1978), 2: 734-35; Anna Maria Martellone, "La presenza del'elemento etnico italiano nella vita politica degli Stati Uniti: Dalla non partecipazione alla post-etnia," in Fondazione Brodolini, *Gli italiani fuori d'Italia: Gli emigrati italiani nei movimenti operai dei paesi d'adozione (1880-1940)*, ed. Bruno Bezza (Milan: Angeli, 1983), 351; Kathleen Kilgore, *John Volpe: The Life of an Immigrant's Son* (Dublin, NH: Yankee, 1987); Jerre Mangione and Ben Morreale, *La Storia: Five Centuries of the Italian American Experience* (New York: Harper Collins, 1992), 403; Frank J. Cavaioli, "Volpe, John A.," in *The Italian American Experience: An Encyclopedia*, ed. Salvatore J. LaGumina et al. (New York: Garland, 2000), 665-66.

[4] Geno Baroni, "An Address by the Rt. Rev. Mons. Geno Baroni," in *Italian and Irish in America*, ed. Francis X. Femminella (Staten Island, NY: AIHA, 1985), 23; *New York Daily News* 9 Aug. 1968; *Boston Globe* 9, 10 Aug. 1968; *New York Times* 10 Aug. 1968; Anthony Summers with Robbyn Swan, *The Arrogance of Power: The Secret World of Richard Nixon* (New York: Viking, 2000), 284-87. For the Greek military junta's perception of Agnew as an ally, see also C.L. Sulzberger, *The World and Richard Nixon* (New York: Prentice Hall, 1987), 147.

as few as 434,571 people of Greek stock in the United States according to the 1970 federal Census, the number of Greek Americans was so small nationwide, that presidential candidates hardly paid attention to them in the 1960s.[5]

While it cannot be denied that donations to Nixon helped place Agnew on the Republican ticket in 1968, they were not the only reason for his selection. Nor were they the one motive for Volpe's dropping.

Even if Agnew was hardly a national figure, he was the governor of a border state with a reputation for supporting civil rights but cracking down on black rioting. Remarkably, when violent disorders broke out in Baltimore following Martin Luther King Jr.'s assassination on 4 April 1968, Agnew summoned the leaders of the city's African American community and publicly reprimanded them for the disturbances. As he put it, outspokenly in front of the press and the television crewmen, the unrest and looting had been triggered off by the "circuit-riding, Hanoi-visiting, caterwauling, riot-inciting, burn-America-down type" of black leadership that had failed to distance itself from such African American radicals as Stokely Carmichael and H. Rap Brown.[6]

Agnew's reaction impressed Nixon and his campaign advisers. It also fit both Nixon's strong stand against lawlessness and his so-called "Southern Strategy" of making inroads into traditionally Democratic southern states by pandering to the backlash of white voters at African American claims and achievements.[7]

While Agnew, who had been elected as a Rockefeller liberal in 1966, adopted a law-and-order approach after taking office, Volpe moved in the opposite direction. In particular, during his third term, besides liberalizing the birth control laws, Volpe had legislation to ban

---

[5] Craig R. Humphrey and Helen Brock Louis, "Assimilation and Voting Behavior: A Study of Greek Americans," *International Migration Review* 7.1 (Spring 1963): 34-45. For the role of Greek Americans in U.S. politics, see, in general, Eleftherios N. Botsas, "The American Hellenes," in *America's Ethnic Politics*, ed. Joseph S. Roucek and Bernard Eisenberg (Westport, CT: Greenwood, 1982), 29-45 (44 for the figure in the text).

[6] *Washington Post* 12 Apr. 1968; Robert Marsh, *Agnew, the Unexamined Man: A Political Profile* (Philadelphia: J.B. Lippincott, 1971), 158-62; James L. Sundquist, *Dynamics of the Party System: Alignment and Realignment of Political Parties in the United States* (Washington, DC: Brookings Institution, 1983), 385; James T. Patterson, *Grand Expectations: The United States, 1945-1974* (New York: Oxford UP, 1996), 700-01.

[7] Stephen E. Ambrose, *Nixon: The Triumph of a Politician, 1962-1972* (New York: Simon and Schuster, 1989), 162-63; Kenneth O'Reilly, *Nixon's Piano: Presidents and Racial Politics from Washington to Clinton* (New York: Free Press, 1995), 296-308.

racial imbalances in schools passed and encouraged affirmative action in both public and private employment in Massachusetts. For instance, he urged Polaroid Corporation to give preference to African Americans in hiring workers for its plants in Cambridge and Waltham. He also came out against Louise Day Hicks because of her opposition to racial integration in Boston's 1967 mayoral campaign and contributed to the election of progressive Democrat Kevin H. White to City Hall by a plurality of roughly 12,000 ballots and approximately 60 percent of the Italian American vote.[8]

With Nixon focusing on the South, unlike Agnew, Volpe was clearly the governor of the wrong state as chief executive of Massachusetts and his record on civil rights issues hardly suited Nixon's prospective electorate. Indeed, Volpe was among the vice presidential hopefuls whom Senator Strom Thurmond vetoed at the final meeting of Republican big shots that led to Agnew's selection. The 1948 white supremacist presidential candidate and a South Carolina Senator, Thurmond had worked on behalf of Nixon's successful bid for the Republican nomination among the southern delegates and clearly realized that Volpe was unable to appeal to the South because of his moderate liberalism in racial matters. Conversely, Agnew's toughness in the wake of the riots that ensued from King's assassination made the Maryland governor a suitable choice for the Southern conservative electorate.[9]

In addition, the 1968 Republican primaries marred Volpe's fame as a proven vote getter. In the effort to position himself to win the vice presidential nomination, Volpe entered the Republican primary in Massachusetts in the hope of going to the GOP national convention as the favorite son of his home state. He was aware that control of a state delegation in a close convention contest had sometimes placed a favorite son in a good bargaining position to be selected as the presidential

---

[8] Jim G. Lucas, *Agnew: Profile in Conflict* (New York: Universal, 1970); Fred Blumenthal, "Gov. John Volpe: He Wants To Be No. 2," *St. Petersburg Times* 25 Feb. 1968, newspaper clipping, John Volpe Papers, box 68, folder "Volpe – V.P.," Snell Library, Northeastern University, Boston, MA; *Post Gazette*, 10 May 1968; Martha Wagner Weinberg, "Boston's Kevin White: A Mayor Who Survives," *Political Science Quarterly* 96.1 (Spring 1981): 89, 91-92.

[9] Gary Wills, *Nixon's Agonistes: The Crisis of the Self-Made Man* (Boston: Houghton Mifflin, 1970), 274-75; Tom Wicker, *One of Us: Richard Nixon and the American Dream* (New York: Random, 1991), 342-43; Mary C. Brennan, *Turning Right in the Sixties: The Conservative Capture of the GOP* (Chapel Hill: U of North Carolina P, 1995), 127.

nominee's running mate. He expected a similar opportunity to arise again to his benefit in 1968.[10]

Volpe's name was the only one printed on the ballot in Massachusetts' GOP primary on 30 April. Yet Volpe was defeated by Governor Nelson A. Rockefeller of New York, who launched a write-in campaign several hours after the Bay State polls had opened. Although voter turnout was only 16 percent in Massachusetts, receiving 29.9 percent of the ballot cast as opposed to the 31.1 percent of Rockefeller and the 26.2 percent of Nixon, Volpe demonstrated that he did not command even the Republican electorate of his home state.[11]

Volpe's allies endeavored to belittle the implications of the primary outcome. For instance, in a letter to the editor of the *New York Times*, former Governor of Massachusetts and U.S. Senator Leverett Saltonstall argued that

> Governor's Volpe vote was about 30 percent of the total cast and must be regarded as an expression of confidence in him, especially when one considers that he was not a presidential candidate, spent not one minute campaigning, and was in Japan as chairman of the National Governors Committee for two weeks prior to April 30.[12]

Still, Nixon himself pointed out in his memoirs that Volpe's defeat had been "embarrassing." Furthermore, that Volpe had shunned the GOP primary in New Hampshire in March after announcing his campaign for Vice President questioned the governor's political following outside Massachusetts. Volpe's decision not to run in New Hampshire was particularly troubling because 43 percent of the state's likely voters thought that the Massachusetts governor would make an excellent candidate according to a mid February poll.[13]

When Nixon asked Volpe for his recommendation on the candidate for Vice President, the Massachusetts governor did not offer his own name. Conversely, he sent Nixon a typewritten study by James F. Collins and Constance S. Collins. Its authors held that the Republican party needed the Catholic vote to win the White House. They added

---

[10] Untitled statement by John Volpe, n.d. [but 10 Jan. 1968], Volpe Papers, box 68, folder "Favorite Son, 1968;" *Worcester Telegram* 11 Jan. 1968.
[11] *Boston Globe* 2 May 1968.
[12] *New York Times* 20 May 1968.
[13] Richard M. Nixon, *RN: The Memoirs of Richard Nixon* (New York: Grosset & Dunlap, 1978), 302; *Boston Herald Traveler* 11 Jan. 1968; *Boston Herald* 12 Feb. 1968.

that Volpe was the vice presidential candidate who could secure the support of the Catholic electorate for the GOP because he was a leading member of the largest Catholic minority in the United States.[14]

After the Massachusetts governor had entered the Republican primary in his home state, an editorial in the *Worcester Telegram* argued that "as an American of immigrant parentage, a Roman Catholic [...], Volpe would add strength in urban voting areas to any ticket the GOP might put forward." James F. Collins and Constance S. Collins further corroborated this view. Volpe had roughly 12,000 copies of their report distributed at the Republican national convention. Still, in spite of the claims of this study, Italian Americans failed to rally unanimously behind Volpe's bid for Vice President.[15]

Many rank-and-file voters of Italian descent, not only from Massachusetts but also from New Jersey, Pennsylvania and New York State, congratulated Volpe on his decision to seek the Republican nomination for Vice President and took pride in such a move by a fellow ethnic. In addition, Republican leaders of Italian ancestry like Anthony A. Maisano, the president of the Columbian Republican League, and Philip A. Guarino, the chairperson of the Italian American Section of the Nationalities Division of the Republican National Committee, mobilized to support Volpe's candidacy in the attempt to empower Italian Americans both within the GOP and in national politics. In particular, Guarino established a committee of fifty prominent Italian Americans to pressure Nixon into choosing Volpe as his running mate.[16]

A few weeks before the Republican National Convention, Americo V. Cortese, the Supreme Venerable of the Pennsylvania Grand Lodge

---

[14] Richard M. Nixon to John Volpe, New York, 26 July 1968; Volpe to Nixon, Boston, MA, 31 July 1968; James F. Collins and Constance S. Collins, "Comments on the Republican Vice-Presidential Nomination, 1968," all in Volpe Papers, box 68, folder "Volpe – V.P."

[15] *Worcester Telegram* 12 Jan. 1968; *Boston Globe* 7 Aug. 1968.

[16] A.J. Caruso to John Volpe, Harrisburg, PA, 27 Feb. 1968; Porfida Stella to Volpe, Staten Island, NY, 28 Feb. 1968; Gus Lombardi, Jr., to Volpe, Boston, MA, 2 Apr. 1968; Dan Montemarano to Volpe, Paterson, NJ, 15 Apr. 1968, all in Volpe Papers, box 68, folder "Volpe – V.P.;" Anthony A. Maisano to Philip A. Guarino, Brooklyn, NY, 20 June 1968, Anthony Maisano Papers, box 4, folder 13, Balch Institute for Ethnic Studies, Philadelphia, PA; *Post-Gazette* 26 July 1968. For Maisano and the Columbian Republican League, see Anna Maria Martellone, "Italian Immigrants, Party Machines, Ethnic Brokers in City Politics, from the 1880s to the 1930s," in *The European Emigrant Experience in the U.S.A.*, ed. Walter Hölbling and Reinhold Wagnleitner (Tübingen: Gunter Narr, 1992), 178-79.

of the Order Sons of Italy in America (OSIA), wrote Volpe and committed this influential Italian American organization to the Massachusetts governor. However, a perusal of the *Sons of Italy Times*, the organ of the OSIA in Pennsylvania, does not show any endorsement of Volpe or any lobbying efforts on behalf of his vice presidential candidacy.[17]

The case of the Boston-based *Post-Gazette* is even more revealing. The major Italian-American newspaper in New England, this weekly not only refused to back Volpe, it even made a point of discrediting his state administration. The *Post-Gazette* accused Volpe of being "a fiscally irresponsible Governor" and held him accountable for both "the tremendous rise" in Massachusetts' tax burden and the state's increasing budget deficit. It specifically criticized Volpe's practice of hiring expensive consultants, his tendency to load the state payroll with political jobholders, and his sponsorship of a 5 percent general sales tax. The *Post-Gazette* also charged Volpe with practicing affirmative action to the benefit of African Americans and the detriment of white people.[18]

In the late 1960s, many Italian Americans began to shift their political allegiance to the GOP out of concerns about the spread of affirmative action and in retaliation for the tax-and-spend policy of the Johnson administration and its encouragement of African American alleged encroachments. Against this backdrop, in view of the criticism of the leading Italian American newspaper in his home state, Volpe could hardly stand out as the more viable vice presidential candidate to lure his fellow ethnics into casting their ballots for the Republican party.[19]

After all, Volpe's record with the Italian American electorate in Massachusetts was troubling. When he ran for governor against fellow-ethnic Democratic candidate Francis X. Bellotti in 1964, he received only 33 percent of the ballots cast by Italian-American voters. Volpe's performances were somehow disappointing also in races against opponents who were not of Italian ancestry. Volpe obtained 54 percent of the Italian American vote in 1960 and 51 percent two years later, although on this latter occasion his opponent was such an old-line Wasp

---

[17] Americo V. Cortese to John Volpe, Philadelphia, PA, 22 July 1968, Volpe Papers, box 68, folder "Volpe – V.P.;" *Sons of Italy Times* 23, 30 July, 7 Aug.1968.
[18] *Post-Gazette* 26 Apr., 10 May, 21 June, 26 July 1968.
[19] Phylis Cancilla Martinelli, "Italian-American Experience," *America's Ethnic Politics*, 224-27; Michael Barone, "Italian Americans and American Politics," in *Beyond the Godfather: Italian American Writers on the Real Italian American Experience*, ed. A. Kenneth Cingoli and Jay Parrini (Hanover: UP of New England, 1997), 244.

as Peabody. It was only in 1966 that Volpe carried the Massachusetts Italian American community with a convincing 66-percent majority. Still this percentage also means that one third of the state's voters from Italian background cast their ballots for Irish-American gubernatorial candidate Edward McCormick. Furthermore, in view of the notorious anti-Irish feelings of Italian Americans in Massachusetts, Volpe's plurality among his fellow ethnics resulted less from their support for the Italian American candidate than from their rejection of his Irish-American challenger.[20]

Volpe's defeat in Massachusetts' Republican primary also affected the standing of the governor at the GOP National Convention. Volpe endorsed Nixon although the state laws compelled him to cast his vote for the winner of the primary election, Rockefeller, on the fist ballot. Conversely, Agnew came to Miami Beach as his home state's favorite son and, by bowing out to the benefit of Nixon on 5 August, secured Nixon eighteen votes of the Maryland delegation. Since Nixon eventually exceeded the 667 votes that he needed for the nomination by twenty-five votes, he would have become the Republican presidential candidate even without Agnew's support. Yet, as Nixon was struggling to get the nomination on the first ballot in order to prevent a possible "draft Rockefeller" movement or a "Reagan-Rockefeller stop Nixon" campaign on the convention floor, Agnew's decision was timely and helped Nixon's candidacy gain momentum and a sense of being inevitable in the eyes of the delegates.[21]

Historian Frank J. Cavaioli has suggested that, if the Massachusetts governor had been named as the 1968 Republican vice presidential candidate, "Volpe might have been the first Italian American president in [U.S.] history" after Nixon resigned following the Watergate scandal. In hindsight, Cavaioli has obviously been right.[22]

---

[20] Mark R. Levy and Michael S. Kramer, *The Ethnic Factor: How America's Minorities Decide Elections* (New York: Simon and Schuster, 1972), 179; Thomas Sowell, *Ethnic America: A History* (New York: Basic, 1981), 128.

[21] "Transcript of Governor John Volpe's News Conference," 27 June 1968, Volpe Papers, box 68, folder "News Conferences;" Joseph Albright, *What Makes Spiro Run: The Life and Times of Spiro Agnew* (New York: Dodd, Mead, 1972), 211-12; Theo Lippman, Jr., *Spiro Agnew's America* (New York: Norton, 1972), 127-29; Jules Witcover, *White Knight: The Rise of Spiro Agnew* (New York: Random, 1972), 222-24.

[22] Frank J. Cavaioli, "Charles Poletti and Fourteen Other Italian-American Governors," in *Italian Americans in Transition*, ed. Joseph V. Scelsa, Salvatore J. LaGumina, and Lydio Tomasi (Staten Island, NY: Italian American Historical Association, 1990), 146.

Yet Volpe did not necessarily miss his opportunity to become President only at the 1968 Republican Convention in Miami Beach. Actually, though to a lesser extent, he had a second chance five years later. Once again, however, the lack of cohesiveness of Italian Americans behind Volpe helped to prevent him from a further rise in politics after he had served as Secretary of Transportation in Nixon's first administration and Ambassador to Italy in the second.[23]

On 10 October 1973, Agnew stepped down from the office of vice president on charges that he had received thousands of dollars in kickbacks on building contracts while county executive of Baltimore and governor of Maryland. Before naming Agnew's successor, Nixon asked Republican Congressmen and national leaders as well as his Cabinet and the White House senior staff about their recommendations.[24]

Among the U.S. representatives and the senator of Italian descent who were polled, only one, Silvio O. Conte from Massachusetts' first district, suggested Volpe. All the others submitted different names spanning from House Minority Leader Gerald R. Ford to New York State Governor Rockefeller and including Barry M. Goldwater, who was the choice of New Mexico's Senator Pete V. Dominici. According to Conte, to the office of Vice President Volpe would bring "a career studded with achievement – successful businessman and civic leader, governor of the Commonwealth of Massachusetts, service in the Nixon Cabinet." Still, despite these outstanding accomplishments, Volpe did

---

[23] Volpe was appointed as U.S. ambassador to Italy after his efforts to diversify forms of transportation in the United States (he was instrumental in the creation of a national railroad, Amtrak, service in 1970), instead of having the nation depend on highways alone, angered the highway lobby that was very influential with Nixon's inner advisers. See Tom Lewis, *Divided Highways: Building the Interstate Highways, Transforming American Life* (New York: Viking Penguin, 1997), 216-18, 230-31. As the U.S. ambassador to Rome between 1973 and 1977, Volpe well represented the staunch anti-Communist stand of both the Nixon and Ford administrations in a country that saw the increasing political influence of the Communist party. See Gian Giacomo Migone, *Dove va l'America: La politica estera degli Stati Uniti e l'Italia durante gli anni Settanta* (Milan: Feltrinelli, 1980), 109; Paul Ginsborg, *A History of Contemporary Italy: Society and Politics, 1943-1988* (Harmondsworth, UK: Penguin, 1990), 374. For a more sympathetic view of Volpe's activities in Rome, stressing his alleged decision to distance the U.S. government from Italy's neo-Fascist groups and his supposed uneasiness with the undercover operations that had characterized the involvement of his predecessor, Graham Martin, in Italian politics, see Kilgore, *John Volpe*, 199-216.

[24] Richard M. Cohen and Jules Witcover, *A Heartbeat Away: The Investigation and Resignation of Vice President Spiro T. Agnew* (New York: Viking, 1974); Stephen E. Ambrose, *Nixon: Ruin and Recovery, 1973-1990* (New York: Simon and Schuster, 1991), 236-37.

not rank first even in Conte's list of prospective Vice Presidents. Indeed, Volpe was Conte's second choice after U.S. Representative Ford.[25]

Italian Americans' half-hearted support for Volpe continued in the following years. The efforts to have President Gerald Ford consider Volpe as vice president in both 1974 and 1976 offer another case in point.

As soon as Nixon resigned and Ford replaced him in the White House on 8 August 1974, Peter D. Gay, the Supreme Venerable of the Order Sons of Italy in America, sent the new President the congratulations of his organization and asked him to nominate Volpe as his Vice President on behalf of the over 250,000 members of the OSIA. Still no major lobbying campaign by the OSIA or other major Italian American association followed suit to support Volpe.[26]

Something similar occurred two years later. The fact that Nixon selected Agnew instead of Volpe as his 1968 running mate made Monsignor Baroni and other Italian-American leaders aware of the lack of voice of their ethnic minority in U.S. politics. As a result, in 1975, they eventually established the National Italian American Foundation (NIAF) for the purpose of advancing the concerns of Americans of Italian descent. Jeno F. Paulucci, a prominent corporation executive and frozen-food king from Minnesota, became the first chairperson of the NIAF. When rumors circulated that President Ford was considering John B. Connally as his 1976 running mate, Paulucci publicly came out against this prospective selection. In his view, as a former Democratic governor of Texas who served as Secretary of Treasury in the Nixon administration, Connally was an opportunist who would discredit the Republican ticket in the eyes of most voters. In a subsequent personal

---

[25] Joseph J. Maraziti to Richard M. Nixon, Washington, DC, 11 Oct. 1973, Richard M. Nixon Presidential Material Project, box 168, folder 1, National Archives II, College Park, MD; Silvio O. Conte to Nixon, Washington, DC, 10 Oct. 1973, ibid. box 168, folder 2; Matthew J. Rinaldo to Nixon, Washington, DC, 11 Oct. 1973, ibid., box 168, folder 4; Angelo D. Roncallo to Nixon, Washington, DC, 11 Oct. 1973, ibid.; Pete V. Domenici to Nixon, Washington, DC, 11 Oct. 1973, ibid., box 169, folder 2.

[26] Peter D. Gay to Gerald R. Ford, Taunton, MA, 10 Aug. 1974, White House Central Files, Subject File, box 16, folder "PL/S-Z," Gerald R. Ford Library, Ann Arbor, MI (research at the Ford Library was made possible by a grant from the Gerald R. Ford Foundation). For Gay, see "Peter B. Gay," in *Guide to the Records of the Order Sons of Italy in America*, ed. John Andreozzi (St. Paul, MN: Immigration History Research Center, 1989), 73.

letter to Ford, Paulucci also submitted the names of three potential vice presidential nominees who would conversely enhance the chances of a GOP success in November. The list included California's Governor Ronald Reagan, Volpe, and Rockefeller in this intentional order. Actually, according to the NIAF chairperson, it was Reagan – not Volpe – who would make, as Paulucci put it, the "best selection."[27]

In his recent autobiography, President William Jefferson Clinton's former Greek-American aide, George Stephanopoulos, has stressed the strong bond of ethnic solidarity within the Greek-American community. As he has pointed out,

> If a Greek like Ike Pappas was on television, all of us watched; if another like Nick Gage wrote a book, all of us read it; when Congressman John Brademas missed the chance to be Speaker of the House, we all felt his loss; when Vice President Agnew resigned, we all felt ashamed.[28]

Italian Americans have hardly experienced such ethnic unity and their response to Volpe's bid for a national office offers a case in point. Along with Volpe's poor showing against a write-in candidate in his home state's Republican primary and his moderate liberalism on race issues, the blatant lack of cohesiveness of Italian American support for the governor of Massachusetts contributed to impairing Volpe's claim that his ethnic background would be an asset for the Republican ticket, and it helped tip the scale for the selection of Nixon's running mate in Agnew's favor.

---

[27] Baroni, "An Address," 23; *St. Paul Pioneer Press* 2 Aug. 1976; Jeno F. Paulucci to Gerald R. Ford, Duluth, MN, 4 Aug. 1976, White House Central Files, Name File, box 2451, folder "Paulucci, Jeno F.," Ford Library. Ironically enough, Paulucci persuaded Volpe to serve as president of the National Italian American Foundation after Volpe had left his post in Rome following President Ford's defeat against Jimmy Carter in the 1976 race for the White House (see Kilgore, *John Volpe*, 216-17). For the National Italian American Foundation, see Frank J. Cavaioli, "The National Italian American Foundation: 1975-1985," in *A. P. Giannini: Banker, Philanthropist, Entrepreneur*, ed. Felice A. Bonadio (Washington, DC: NIAF, 1985), 119-25; Alfred Rotondaro, "National Italian American Foundation," in *The Italian American Experience*, 401-02. For Paulucci, see Frank D. Stella, "Paulucci, Jeno F.," *The Italian American Experience*, 455-56.

[28] George Stephanopoulos, *All Too Human: A Political Education* (Boston: Little, Brown, 1999), 13.

New York City Italian American Mayors, LaGuardia, Impellitteri, and Giuliani: Comparisons, Contrasts and Curiosities

Salvatore J. LaGumina
NASSAU COMMUNITY COLLEGE

The following observations are frankly fragmentary and designed to open inquiry into the subject, rather than a claim to be exhaustive. It is my hope, furthermore, to suggest new lines of investigation with regard to Italian American politicians that will be informative and instructive.

On the threshold of a new century and long after the era of classic mass European immigration, ethnic politics is a subject of continuing fascination. Augmented by large increases in immigration in the latter quarter of the twentieth century from Latin America, especially Mexico, and from Asiatic countries, identifiable ethnic entities dot the geographic and political landscape. From politically active Chinese American enclaves along the West Coast (California) where the Chinese ethnic group organized itself to achieve political prominence in the 1990s, to the knowledgeable, if obvious actions of Miami's Cuban Americans over the Elián González refugee boy controversy, ethnic groups have demonstrated savvy regarding political clout. Speculation continues to abound as to whether newer immigrant groups can attain and maintain the major prize of winning mayoralties in large cities. In some instances, and in partial emulation of earlier immigrant groups, they have already "arrived" such as Cuban Americans in Miami. For other cities such as New York the jury is still out. It is against this background that a study of New York City's Italian American mayors is undertaken.

Recent analysis suggests that whereas it required three decades before Italian Americans were able to sponsor citywide candidates, because of their heterogeneity this may not be the model for current immigrant groups.[1] Simply put, there appears to be too much ethnic diversity for prevailing groups to make the traditional political climb. A

---

[1] *New York Times* 28 Dec. 1999.

review of the careers of Mayors LaGuardia, Impellitteri, and Giuliani may help to shed light on this thesis.

The earliest indication that Italian Americans could be of significance in New York City electoral politics occurred in the 1890s as both the Republican and Democratic parties initiated incipient moves to enlist their support in behalf of traditional party nominees. It was, in effect, a realization that Italian immigration was an increasing phenomenon and that even discounting their relative tardiness in acquiring citizenship, they were, nevertheless, destined to become important factors in elections. By 1900 recognition of the expanding Italian ethnic element had broadened to the point where a scant few Italian Americans became official party nominees for minor posts in city government such as coroner. Needless to say the minimalist apperception failed to satisfy the clamor for more prestigious and powerful positions, chief of which was that of mayor of New York City, a post that has been regarded as second in power only to that of the presidency.

The stage was set for the first serious efforts to obtain this office in the 1920s as Italian Americans became influential in local political clubs that provided important economic assistance and simultaneously served as cohesive political forces. These efforts at political organization intensified in the 1930s with the result that Italian American political clubs comprised the largest number of nationality associations in the city. (Peel 186) When Brooklyn Democrat Assemblyman Jerome Ambro contested and finally toppled a German American club leader in 1932, he set his sights on the mayoralty. Although he commanded support in Brooklyn, he lost the 1933 Democratic nomination to John P. O'Brien. While Ambro's effort proved to be premature, given the prevailing ethnic and political realities within the Democratic party at the time, it nevertheless served as an indication that it would not be too long before the growing Italian American city population would prevail in this regard. For the Democrats the time came in 1950 while for Republicans it arrived much sooner.

BIOGRAPHICAL SKETCHES

Fiorello H. LaGuardia – Born in NYC in 1884, of an Italian Jewish mother and an Italian Catholic father, LaGuardia was brought up a Protestant. Owing to the fact that his father was in the army, young Fiorello spent a major part of his youth in western army camps before returning to New York where he pursued a law degree at New York University. Strongly opposed to the Democratic Party because of its reputation for corruption under the local New York City organization Tammany Hall, LaGuardia became a Progressive Republican. His early experience included working for the United States consular service, interpreter at Ellis Island, election to Congress, president of the Board of Aldermen in New York City and a return to Congress. That he was not content to be just merely another routine member of the House of Representatives but a major role player in vital contemporary issues can be gleaned from the realization that he was the co-author of the pro-labor Norris-LaGuardia Act (1932) that included the significant anti-injunction feature.

In size, personality and appearance LaGuardia seemed incongruous. At 5' 2" he was short, stubby, destined to become corpulent, and the possessor of a squeaky, high pitched voice, he nevertheless, surprisingly became an army flier with the rank of major during the First World War – he was only one of a handful of congressmen who volunteered for service. He could be endearing as when he read comics over the radio during a newspaper strike, but he could also be outrageous in berating and humiliating subordinates. In sum he was a showman the likes of which New York has not seen since his time.

Vincent R. Impellitteri – Born in mountain town of Isnello, Sicily in 1900, Vincent was brought to this country at age one. His family lived for a time in downtown New York, where his father struggled to eke out a living for his large family (wife and eight children). Economic urgency and the presence of many family members in the mid-size industrial town of Ansonia, Connecticut prompted a move to that locale where Impellitteri attended elementary and high schools. Upon graduating the latter, Vincent succumbed to blandishments of patriotism, joined the Navy and saw action during World War I. He then attended Fordham University, from which he received a law degree, where met the son of Governor Al Smith and where his initial interest in partisan politics began. His professional private practice law career included serving as counsel for labor unions – a background that he always highly regarded. His public career found him gaining appointment to Assistant District Attorney of New York, a post that offered the opportunity to demonstrate his ability in high profile cases. Almost completely ignored by historians, the few writers who covered his professional life fail to acknowledge that Impellitteri's work as prosecutor was outstanding. One study of the Manhattan District Attorney's office in which he played a major role as rackets bureau chief, showed that in the 1935-37 period he personally prosecuted 173 felony cases, 170 of which resulted in conviction.[2] So flawless was his performance that it evoked the plaudits of New York District William Crain who observed "If all of the assistants would emulate Impellitteri, I think the District Attorney's office would be a formidable engine of attack against the members of the criminal society in this country."[3] His exemplary work as prosecutor led to speculation in 1937 that young Vincent might succeed to Manhattan District Attorney. Indeed it was this background that commended him to future Mayor William O'Dwyer who, as a judge, was impressed with Impellitteri's professionalism in a case before him. Historians unduly emphasize that it was his Italian ethnicity exclusively that induced O'Dwyer to put Impellitteri on his ticket as City Council President in 1945, completely over-looking his career as prosecutor.

At five foot nine, 172 pounds, with brown eyes and flat black hair that was beginning to gray and thin and parted slightly to the left of center, he presented the visage of a orderly and agreeable man. His facial features somewhat irregular and a trifle rough, were suffused in light olive skin and sincere winning smile that put people at ease. He was clearly a very friendly and likeable man. In a word he had political "sex appeal."

Rudolph W. Giuliani – Born in Brooklyn in 1944, Rudolph studied at Catholic schools, attended Manhattan College, and received a law degree from New York University. His professional work included clerking for a federal judge, serving as a prosecutor in the Justice Department, assistant United States attorney in New York and assistant to the deputy Attorney General in the Gerald Ford administration. In 1983 he was named to head the United States attorney's office in the New York Southern District.

Giuliani proffers the image of an intense man who tries to smile even while he is scolding. His physical visage lends itself to unusual caricature. Studying him as he sought the Republican mayoral nomina-

---

[2] Letter in behalf of election of Hastings, Nov. 1937, *Impellitteri Papers*, Municipal Archives, New York City.
[3] Salvatore J. LaGumina, *New York at Mid Century, The Impellitteri Years* (Westport, CT: Greenwood), 69.

tion in 1989, journalist Joe Klein depicted him as an "odd-looking man ... his severe medieval face, deathly pale... his ill-fitting jacket a temporary restraint on his chunky body... on his forehead, matting the tortured contrivance that is his hair."[4]

Giuliani came to public attention as an aggressive prosecuting attorney. A former Democrat, he became a Republican following the 1972 McGovern campaign and at age 38 was appointed to the Justice Department and subsequently United States Attorney for New York by President Ronald Reagan, continuing in the latter position under President George H. Bush. Clearly ambitious, he maneuvered to obtain high profile cases that brought banner headlines and wide acclaim. Giuliani's spectacular and successful prosecution of organized crime, and of political corruption traced to leading politicians in Mayor Koch's administration, as well as of important Wall Street figures, elicited widespread praise. In February 1986 students at John Jay College of Criminal Justice voted him man of the year.[5] Notwithstanding criticism for using roughshod methods and disregarding the rights of innocent individuals unfortunate enough to be caught in his wide net, comparison to Thomas E. Dewey, whose career path as New York governor and presidential candidate began as a prosecutor, was inevitable. He clearly made an impact opined a *Newsday* editorial because he was "unquestionably a terrific prosecutor... has already made his mark – by etching a new performance standard for federal prosecutors yet to come."[6]

ELECTED MAYOR

LaGuardia – Italian Americans' first success in attaining the New York City mayoralty came via the Republican Party that nominated Fiorello H. LaGuardia for mayor in 1929. Defeated by popular Democratic incumbent Jimmy Walker, LaGuardia would not stay down, running again as a Republican as well as a Fusion Party candidate – this time successfully – in 1933, and again in 1937, and 1941. Given the reputation LaGuardia was eventually to earn as New York City's finest 20th-century mayor, it might be somewhat of a surprise to learn that he

---

[4] Joe Klein, "Ready for Rudy," *New Yorker* 6 March 1989.
[5] *New York Daily News* 25 Feb. 1986.
[6] *Newsday* 11 Jan. 1989.

won his first mayoralty race because of a three-way split between Democrats Joseph V. McKee and John O'Brien.

With regard to his support within the Italian ethnic community, it can be demonstrated that he was indeed the pride of Italian Americans and that fellow nationality members undoubtedly crossed party lines to back him. Thus in 1933 it is estimated that he received 62.2 % of the Italian American vote.[7] One study that sampled Italian American election districts in resolutely Democratic assembly districts that had voted heavily for Democrat President Franklin D. Roosevelt in 1932, shows the extent of ethnic support for LaGuardia in 1933. In three such districts in Brooklyn, for example, LaGuardia swamped his rivals by garnering 80 to 90% of the vote.[8] Italian Americans, moreover, voted in greater numbers than in previous elections. Although Italian American support for LaGuardia continued in 1937, it fell notably to 46.1 % in 1941, a development attributable to LaGuardia's criticism of the Italian Mussolini government and isolation sentiment among Italians.[9]

Impellitteri – Comparison regarding Italian ethnic support for Impellitteri and Giuliani presents peculiar challenges. Whereas LaGuardia's opponents were of non-Italian background, Impellitteri's main adversaries, Ferdinand Pecora and Edward Corsi were also of Italian heritage, and indeed selected because of that background, thereby seeming to render moot measurement of the degree of ethnic backing. Incontrovertibly, the fact that the three main candidates for mayor in 1950 were all Italian-born ipso facto argues forcefully about the saliency of Italian ethnic political power. It might be said of the 1950 election, "only in America" could one witness a public election for what is arguably the second most powerful and prestigious position in which major candidates were foreign born. Two Sicilian born contestants, Pecora on the Democratic ticket, and Impellitteri of the Experience Party, in addition to a third candidate Republican Corsi, born in Capistrano, Italy, as the three main nominees for mayor, found Italian American voters fractionalized. Each aspirant offered powerful credentials. Pecora brought forth an estimable reputation as an eminent justice following national attention as counsel to the Senate Investigations

---

[7] Ronald Bayor, *Neighbors in Conflict* (Baltimore: Johns Hopkins UP, 1978), 130.
[8] Arthur Mann, *La Guardia Comes to Power: 1933* (Philadelphia: Lippincott, 1965), 132-34.
[9] Bayor 143-44.

Committee that led to the creation of the Security and Exchange Commission. Corsi had served with distinction as U.S. Commissioner of Immigration under Republican President Herbert Hoover and Democrat President Franklin D. Roosevelt, in addition to being New York City Relief Commissioner. Impellitteri offered a good record as a popular president of the City Council of New York in addition to serving as Acting Mayor. Each could claim his share of ethnic endorsement because of his activity in behalf of Italian Americans, thus they balanced each other out. Impellitteri's special appeal that comported well with his manifestly friendly, affable, clean cut, and amiable image, was his feistiness in refusing to surrender to Democratic power bosses who preferred Pecora.

There has been somewhat of a decrease in the city's Italian American population in the 1990s in comparison to its proportion of the electorate in LaGuardia's elections of 1933, 1937, and 1941 or in Impellitteri's victory in 1950. Nevertheless they still constituted a crucial portion of city voters in 1993, and 1997, particularly in Brooklyn, Queens and Staten Island. Political observers noted that in 1989 Italian Americans made up 7% of probable voters in the Democratic Party primary but 17% of the probable voters in the Republican Party. Although a thorough analysis is absent, the impresssion, gleaned from reporters' accounts in traditionally Italian neighborhoods like Bensonhurst and Howard Beach, indicated they soundly supported Giuliani.[10] It was not surprising to find enthusiastic crowds at St. Frances Cabrini Club in Bensonhurst greet Giuliani as a "folk hero."[11] A Bronx Democratic leader predicted his Italian areas would give Giuliani strong backing against David Dinkins predicting that fewer than 2 of 10 would vote for Dinkins. The same could be said regarding the concentration of Italian Americans in Staten Island.

Upon his resignation as federal prosecutor, Giuliani lost little time in obtaining the nomination for mayor in 1989. Promoting his candidacy was Liberal Party leader Ray Harding, who soft-pedaled the "litmus test" issues: abortion, death penalty, and tuition tax credits. Giuliani then gained the Republican Party nomination thereby terminating speculation that he might run for statewide office as senator or gover-

---

[10] *New York Times* 3 Oct. 1989.
[11] *New York Times* 6 July 1989.

nor especially because of a long history that the mayoralty was a dead end for one's political career. Early polling indicated Giuliani, running as a "law and order" candidate, was very popular and could defeat Koch and Dinkins, the African American who would win the Democratic Party nomination.

That Giuliani made a serious blunder in designating comedian Jackie Mason his liaison to the Jewish community was apparent when Mason joked about Dinkins with remarks that were insensitive to African Americans. Respected journalist Murray Kempton asserted that in choosing Mason, Giuliani "blundered grievously from his ignorance of the nuances of conscience in politics."[12] Although Giuliani separated himself from Mason some damage was done and despite an impressive showing in a city with overwhelming Democrat registration, he nevertheless lost to Dinkins by 47,000 votes.

In 1993 Giuliani once again threw his mayoral hat into the ring. Benefiting from the 1989 experience and from continued public exposure, he was especially the beneficiary of a city populace anxious to have the city restored to a safer and more positive cosmopolitan center. City residents sought a return to an image of civic pride and responsibility that seemed wanting under Dinkins. Remarkably this time Giuliani defeated Dinkins by 50,000. A vote analysis yielded evidence that suggested an increase for Giuliani in mostly white Staten Island, within orthodox Jewish districts in Brooklyn, among Asian Americans and some liberal districts. In addition, there was a small slippage for Dinkins support among African Americans and Hispanics.[13] Giuliani's election was greeted with promise both within and without the city. The Florida newspaper *Sun Sentinel* opined that former residents of New York who love the city "should be encouraged by the theme of hope and determination sounded by incoming Mayor Rudolph Giuliani."[14] The editorial proclaimed that the new mayor was on target in demonstrating that big cities can be made to work. Albeit he inherited a city racially bifurcated, with a deteriorating tax base and a nearly 2 billion dollar deficit, the former prosecutor energetically took on the challenge and soon began to demonstrate a determination to stop the free fall and turn things around. The first seemingly small steps such as removing

---

[12] *Newsday* 8 Oct. 1989.
[13] *New York Times* 27 Dec. 1993.
[14] *Sun Sentinel* 6 Jan. 1994.

nuisance and intimidating window washers from street intersections, followed by tough police action in apprehending perpetrators of violence against Hasidic Jews, were in stark contrast to the forbearance in similar matters that characterized the administration of his predecessor.

ITALIAN AMERICANS IN PUBLIC LIFE

Did election of Italian Americans as mayor open doors for other Italian Americans to play an important role in city government? Were they to be placed in prominent municipal government positions commensurate with their percentage of the city population? Although this has not been extensively analyzed, a preliminary assessment based on impressions can be attempted. With respect to LaGuardia, it can definitely be said that his victory helped uncover doors for Italian Americans to play a more influential role in city government. This is not to say that he appointed an excessive number from his ethnic group to cabinet posts and commissioners in his administration, because in fact they remained limited in number causing one historian to maintain that only about 5 % of appointments went to Italian Americans; they nevertheless became more visible.[15] In this consideration all things are relative since as circumscribed as was the 5 %, it looms larger when compared to 1 to 3 % Italian Americans appointees under Mayors Walker and O'Brien. Interestingly in 1937 Democrats sought to make an issue that LaGuardia was not providing sufficient political positions for the Italian community.[16] The LaGuardia years also saw Italian Americans become more prominent as candidates for elective office. For the next third of a century beginning with LaGuardia, Italian Americans became fixtures on tickets of the two major parties for one of three most important elective positions in city government: mayor, city council president, comptroller.

Italian American names in public life continued to be of consequence in the Impellitteri administration. Nevertheless in 1950 there was criticism from a Pecora supporter who assailed Impellitteri for failing to make sufficient appointments of Italian Americans during his tenure as Acting Mayor.[17] This may be attributed to election cam-

---
[15] Bayor 35.
[16] Bayor 137.
[17] "Box 48 Mayoralty Campaign, 1950," *Impellitteri Papers*.

paigning hyperbole, although definitive investigation of the subject remains to be done.

In the absence of in depth research it may be a similar story for the Giuliani administration. What can be said in this regard is that a number of his more prominent advisors bore Italian names: Lategano, Mastro. The absence of nepotism appears to be an incidental fact for all three Italian American mayors. Simply put, their mayoralties did not result in an immediate opening of doors for family members.

CRIME

LaGuardia – LaGuardia took an aggressive stand against crime, even personally leading raids on illegal alcohol stills in which he wielded an axe to destroy unlawful alcohol. He also launched a war against slot machine operators. "From his first day in the Mayor's office, LaGuardia reinforced by his passionate hatred of crime, made war upon the underworld with all the power at his command." In addition, he fully cooperated with District Attorney Thomas Dewey in his fight against notorious gangsters.[18] Notwithstanding his zealousness against gambling that sometimes led to a disregard for individual rights, LaGuardia's crusade against gambling and prostitution would ultimately fail, although he enjoyed a bit more success in countering racketeering in public markets.[19]

Impellitteri – The incidence of crime reduction during the Impellitteri years may not seem so apparent because of a public preoccupation with scandals then making headlines that were simultaneously becoming television staples. For example, the early 1950s saw the Special Senate Investigating Committee on Organized Crime familiarize the public with nefarious criminal activity, much of it traceable to New York City during the administration of former Mayor O'Dwyer. There was also the uncovering of a notorious gambling gang led by Harry Gross that involved high police officials during O'Dwyer's tenure. Impellitteri, however, was never implicated in criminal activity either personally or as part of an administration. Indeed the only major scandal to surface while he was mayor revolved around a sewer project in Queens to which he responded forcefully by meeting it head on personally vis-

---

[18] Charles Garrett, *The La Guardia Years: Machine and Reform Politics in New York City* (New Brunswick, N.J.: Rutgers UP, 1961), 159.
[19] Garrett 162.

iting the scandal site and vigorously supporting allocation of funds that led to conviction of the perpetrators.

Giuliani – Rudolph Giuliani came to public attention as an aggressive and successful crime fighter. He continued in this vein as mayor, as for instance, tackling abiding corruption in the Fulton Fish Market that had stymied previous mayors. He also waged war against minor irritating crime and public nuisances such as uninvited windshield washers who harassed drivers waiting for streetlights to change or annoyance attributed to homeless groups. So impressive was Giuliani's war against crime that police departments from around the country came to New York to see this archetype model of how to combat the drug menace and thereby reduce crime. The institution of a Model Block Program, for example, was regarded a major influence in combating the drug trade.[20] In addition, the police department's severity with which it fought crime led inevitably to considerable criticism, namely that in his fight against crime he was overzealous with the result that he inflicted harm to innocent minority peoples. This was clearly the reaction to his unconditional defense of the police department's handling of the Amadou Diallo and Patrick Dorismond cases, that by mid 2000 elicited admission that he should have expressed his error in not being more understanding and sympathetic to the families of these men. For most observers the Giuliani years were associated with dramatic drops in crimes of violence as year after year showed sharp decreases in homicides, shootings, robberies and auto theft.[21] Notwithstanding his reputation for law and order, Giuliani demurred when it came to cracking down on illegal aliens, thereby taking sharp issue with Washington. His sterling defense in behalf of immigrants won plaudits as illustrated in a *New York Times* editorial. "Mayor Rudolph Giuliani struck a blow for decency and common sense when he criticized Congress' proposed crackdown on both legal and illegal immigrants."[22] On balance, all three Italian American mayors were exemplary when it came to refusing to tolerate crime.

---

[20] Peter Maas, *Parade Magazine* 10 May 1998.
[21] *New York Times* 3 Jan. 1995.
[22] *New York Times* 27 Aug. 1995.

LABOR

LaGuardia – Assessment of how each dealt with organized labor has to take into account the forces and times involved. Sympathetic to organized labor, having served as counsel to a labor union early in his career and a noted defender of labor during his congressional years (Norris-LaGuardia Act, 1932), LaGuardia's administration was definitely pro-labor. The strong support rendered him by the American Labor Party (ALP) in 1937 that delivered 500,000 votes to him attests to the reciprocal appreciation of the newly organized labor political party.[23] Conscious of the devastating blow working people suffered during the Great Depression LaGuardia's pro-labor leanings were in New York City akin to that of the pro-labor New Deal in Washington. His dealings with the Transport Workers Union (TWU) was a notable exception. Representing the combined union employees of three previously private transportation systems that had become unified during his tenure, LaGuardia rejected their right to strike, thereby indicating a difference in outlook when negotiating with city employees. There would be no succumbing to union demands as was to take place under future Mayor John Lindsay. On balance, however, LaGuardia presided over a staunchly pro-labor administration.

Impellitteri – Although economic conditions had improved since the worst days of the Depression, working people still sought improvement of their positions. For the most part Impellitteri was sympathetic. Like LaGuardia his early experience in representing labor unions rendered him favorably disposed to working people including city employees. In appreciation of Impellitteri's interest in labor, a number of union locals bucked their organization to support him in the 1950 election. As mayor, Impellitteri approved a modest across the board wage increase for city workers and authorized an agreement that would gradually give many of them, for the first time, a 40-hour week as a standard. Justifying a move that would augment the city budget with requisite tax increases, he explained, "The forty-hour week is well established in government and private industry and should no longer be

---

[23] Foster Rhea Dulles and Melvyn Dubofsky, *Labor in America: A History* (Wheeling, IL: Harlan Davidson, 1966), 36.

postponed."[24] Simultaneously he did not cow tow to all union demands. While he moved to expedite police retirement benefits, for example, he rejected the notion of police unionization. Accordingly, he successfully resisted pressure from sanitation workers that utilized slowdown methods to try to obtain wage increases and reduction of hours. Likewise, he met head on the severe test by the Transport Workers Union led by wily and resourceful Michael Quill who called his bus drivers out in an effort to coerce the city administration to increase wages and shorten the work week. Unable to move Impellitteri, Quill ended the walkout earning the mayor praise for standing up for the innocent bystander... more than 3,000,000 daily bus riders.[25]

Giuliani – It is of course impossible to make an equitable comparison between Giuliani's administration and the administrations of LaGuardia and Impellitteri, given the differences in times and the progress labor has made over the years. Giuliani's adamantine reputation as mayor carried into his transactions with city labor unions and became part of his determination to do what was deemed necessary to insure the economic well being of the city. In short, he was resolved to demonstrate that he could work with labor (83 city workers unions) and yet secure large dollar savings concessions from them.[26]

Giuliani's dealings with labor during his administrations provide contrasting examples of strident rhetorical hardness on the one hand and cooperation on the other hand. Because, with the exception of the firefighters, correction officers and policemen, he won the 1993 election without labor union support that had backed Democrat Dinkins, Giuliani, not beholden to labor, moved resolutely to pare down the municipal payroll even obtaining the collaboration of union leadership.[27] There was a consequential reduction of the city workforce, however, it was achieved largely without massive layoffs, relying instead on early retirement incentives and concessions that allowed redeployment of workers from one city agency to another. Despite fierce rhetoric, there was accommodation between city unions and Giuliani, since no union

---

[24] "Address by Mayor Vincent R. Impellitteri Before the Chamber of Commerce of the State of New York," January 7, 1952, *Impellitteri Papers*, file "Speeches and Addresses," Municipal Archives, City Hall.
[25] *New York Daily Mirror* 30 Jan. 1953.
[26] *New York Times* 23 Oct. 1995.
[27] *New York Times* 3 Feb. 1994.

members were actually laid off.[28] Another instance of Giuliani's resistance to municipal labor union demands was his threat not only to use the state Taylor Law, but also to levy huge fines against transit workers union leaders in 1999 that resulted in a return to work by employees.[29] Denounced for resorting to such aggressive steps, he nevertheless received organized labor backing in his 1997 reelection bid because unions did not want to be perceived as opposing his likely victory that would surely place them in an adverse position.[30] By 2000, on the other hand, labor support for Giuliani seemed to be wavering on the eve of his withdrawal from an expected race against Hillary Clinton for the New York United States Senate seat.

CURIOSITIES

Mayoral aspirants – Among Italian Americans who made serious but abortive efforts to become New York City mayors were Jerome Ambro, Vito Marcantonio, Mario Proccaccino, John Marchi, Mario Biaggi, Frank Screvane, Mario Cuomo, and Vito Battista. Some like Ambro, Screvane, Biaggi, and Cuomo tried but failed to obtain the Democratic nomination; while Battista, ran on an independent line, and two, Proccaccino and Marchi, received the Democratic and Republican nominations respectively, only to split the Italian American vote that enabled John Lindsay to win.

Mayoral tenures – From 1929, the first time an Italian American ran for New York City mayor, until the end of the century, a total of 71years, Italian American mayors have served a total of 22 years, or approximately 36 % of the time. This would seem to be positive from a proportional representation perspective.

Marriage facts – All three mayors married non-Italian American women (LaGuardia's first wife was Italian, and his second wife was of German heritage; Impellitteri's wife was of Irish background; Giuliani's first marriage to an Italian American was annulled, and his second wife was of Polish ancestry). Impellitteri was spared the trauma of the death of a spouse that befell LaGuardia, as well as the broken marriages that became the lot of Giuliani. All had small families: LaGuardia's first child died of illness; he had two adopted children

---

[28] *New York Times* 25 July 1995.
[29] *Newsday* 15 Dec. 1999.
[30] *New York Times* 9 Sep. 1999.

with his second wife. The Impellitteris were childless, and Giuliani has two children. This may be the reason why they have not led to the establishment of political dynasties as, for example, Baltimore where Thomas D'Alessandro and his son Thomas Jr. became mayors and a daughter, Nancy Pelosi, is currently a member of Congress from California.

Generations – Impellitteri was a first-generation Italian American, while LaGuardia and Giuliani were second generation. Impellitteri's election is somewhat at variance with the previously referred to *New York Times* analysis of December 29, 1999 that inferred mayoral success for contemporary immigrant groups would not transpire with the first generation.

Ages – LaGuardia and Impellitteri were in their fifties when elected mayor, while Giuliani was in his forties.

Post mayoral careers – "Curse" of mayor's office seems to apply in that none succeeded to higher office after tenure as mayor. LaGuardia's hopes for vice-presidency or appointment as general were not realized. Impellitteri became a city judge. It is still too early to tell about Giuliani in view of the commotion that surrounded his entry and later withdrawal from the Senate race in 2000, his health and marital problems. Current speculation about Giuliani running for higher office on a national or state scale does not seem on the immediate horizon, although that could change in the future.

EVALUATIONS

Preliminary observations – There is substantial literature, including doctoral dissertations, biographies and incisive articles on LaGuardia, rendering him perhaps the most studied of all Italian American political figures. By contrast, although there is a growing body of literature on Giuliani, there is a paucity of penetrating research on Impellitteri with the result that we know a great deal about LaGuardia, have only slightly less information but still substantial knowledge about Giuliani, and yet possess relatively little knowledge about Impellitteri. It can be said that with regard to Impellitteri piercing investigation and analysis are relatively minuscule. The simple fact is that Impellitteri has been the subject of very few comprehensive works thus leaving us with observations that can be regarded as a regurgitation of critical stereotypes and perpetuation of hackneyed images and shibboleths that were registered early in his mayoralty. These were, for the most part, not completely impartial nor subject to attenuated scrutiny, thereby fostering negative evaluations of Impellitteri.

With regard to achievements and accomplishments, of the three mayors, LaGuardia stands out as the most remarkable because he served in the midst of the country's worst depression as well as while the nation was engulfed in World War II. More so than the other mayors under review, he confronted desperate issues of relief, utilizing the government WPA program, organizing the city for defense in wartime, promoting the war effort, obtaining a greater voice in Washington, D.C., and fostering pride in cleaning up the city.[31] This is not to say that he was devoid of fault, or that he did not have to deal with huge psychological issues as, for instance, in the wake of the death of his first wife and child, his pre-occupation with politics notwithstanding his remarriage, or for the seeming lack of concern for the welfare of his sister who was in a concentration camp.[32] He likewise has been criticized for trying to do everything himself not being inclined to delegate authority. However, as Thomas Kessner, one of his most recent biographers shows, his mayoralty was one of the finest the city has experienced, warts and all.[33]

Compared to LaGuardia, Impellitteri was less vigorous and less charismatic, although the most friendly and affable of the three. Impellitteri was rightly criticized for promoting fewer initiatives than LaGuardia, a stance that may have been in part due to the absence of crisis situations of depression and war that were previously present. He appeared not to be as resourceful or imaginative. It may be that the consequence of not having to deal with the challenges of guiding the city during a major economic downturn nor during a hot, shooting war rendered him less imaginative. If so he would understandably pale in comparison.

Notwithstanding the different milieu in which Impellitteri and LaGuardia operated, and conceding Impellitteri's relative weakness in comparison to LaGuardia, Impellitteri acquitted himself respectfully, if

---

[31] See Sayre and Kaufman, *Governing New York City: Politics in the Metropolis* (New York: Russell Sage Foundation, 1960), 680-97.
[32] Thomas Kessner, *Fiorello H. LaGuardia and the Making of Modern New York* (New York: Penguin, 1989), 81.
[33] Kessner 590-91.

not spectacularly. Impellitteri's aversion to assert the full panoply of mayoral prerogatives was due in large part to his self-imposed view that the proper mayoral role was that of sharing power with the Board of Estimate and the City Council. Possibly because of his previous tenure in the City Council, he concluded that power sharing was desirable. "I am only one of eight members of the Board of Estimate which governs this City. I can enunciate a program but I must have the wholehearted support of my elected associates to carry it out. The City Charter provides for a government of checks and balances, and determine the rules by a which the Mayor must abide."[34] Clearly a more democratic approach to mayoral powers than one espoused by LaGuardia and Giuliani, Impellitteri nevertheless seemed to ignore the reality that although the Council and the Board of Estimate are vested with legislative powers according to the city charter, they usually follow the lead of the administration.

Giuliani, the most controversial of the three, is widely credited with restoring New York City to a position of distinction as the nation's premier urban center. Even if grudgingly, many of his detractors credit Giuliani with sharply turning around the city's reputation concerning crime, economic health, and the power of labor. It was the public perception of Giuliani presiding over a city flying high, a city which once again was the magnet for business, a city where real estate values flourished and a city that had regained its international stature, that commended him to a wider public. By 1998 there was open speculation that he could aspire to higher office, even the presidency because of his New York performance.

While he won widespread acclaim for his management and improvement of the city, he was not above criticism, especially for his style. Bob Herbert of the *New York Times,* for example, berated him for his bullying treatment of Schools Chancellor Ramon Cortines, whom the mayor blamed for dismal status of the Board of Education finances. Herbert attributed Giuliani's nasty behavior to a basic inability to control his temper.[35] By and large, however, Giuliani moved in the right direction with regard to presenting a realistic budget that emphasized safe, clean streets and fighting fires rather than social programs. He was

---

[34] "Address by Mayor Vincent R. Impellitteri Before the Chamber of Commerce of the State of New York," 7 Jan. 1952, *Impellitteri Papers*.

[35] *New York Times* 13 Apr. 1994.

determined in tackling unpopular issues as, for example, when he refused to be intimidated by a strike threat issued by Legal Aid Society lawyers.[36] He took an equally tough stand against the stranglehold that school custodians had long exercised over the cost of school maintenance.[37] As mayor, Giuliani demonstrated competent ability to administer the city effectively, notwithstanding his overly tough and abrasive style, and his growing alienation of city minorities, especially African Americans. The latter point was exacerbated particularly after horrific actions, death and violence were perpetrated by New York City policemen against members of their race. At one point Italian American City Councilman Alphonse Stabile denounced him for wanting "to be another Mussolini." Christine Lategano, Giuliani's spokesperson, in turn criticized Stabile for using offensive and painful anti Italian remarks.[38] That Giuliani was in a strong position for re-election in 1997 was evident in the results that showed a majority of voters, impressed by his first-term success at curbing crime, cutting taxes and moving people off welfare, heavily endorsed him over liberal Democrat Ruth Messinger by a 17 point plurality. The victory was so impressive that exuberant but unrealistic talk of Giuliani for president emanated.[39] He became the hottest speaker in the Republican Party's fund-raising circuit giving political speeches from New Hampshire to South Carolina.[40] If a contest for the presidency was heady talk, a race for New York Governor or the United States Senate was not. By mid 1999 it was becoming clear that he had set his sights on the Senate seat held by retiring Democrat Senator Daniel P. Moynihan thereby setting up the prospect of a heated race between the feisty mayor and First Lady Hillary Clinton. However, as the year 2000 unfolded so did his candidacy as the Mayor acknowledged the need to deal with health and marital problems. At this writing Giuliani continues his mayoral term that will terminate at the end of 2001.

---

[36] *New York Times* 6 Oct. 1994.
[37] *New York Times* 15 Oct. 1994.
[38] *New York Times* 13 Dec. 1994.
[39] "Rudolph W. Giuliani," *People* (25 Dec. 1997-5 Jan. 1998), 62-63.
[40] *New York Times Magazine* 6 Dec. 1998: 72-76.

OVERALL CONCLUSION

On balance, all three Italian American mayors carried out their responsibilities creditably – LaGuardia, by bringing the city out of depression, by instilling a can-do philosophy, by taking on power wielders, became the standard by which all twentieth-century mayors were judged. Although some censured the attempt, it is not surprising to find that Giuliani looked to him as his model and that he attempted to wrap himself in the LaGuardia mantle.[41] Impellitteri was perhaps not as energetic, imaginative or resourceful as the other two, but he was far from reactionary; he undertook some responsible initiatives and certainly did not disgrace the office. He was, in addition, most pleasant and likeable. Although there is still some time remaining in the Giuliani tenure as mayor, the overall consensus is that he deserves major credit for bringing the city back to its position as the nation's premiere municipality.[*]

LESSONS

Bifurcation – With regard to the *New York Times* 1999 observation that before contemporary ethnic groups can make major political impact they must end bifurcation, it is instructive to see that this somewhat paralleled Italian Americans of the immigrant generation who also had to overcome a bifurcation based on regionalism. They much more strongly identified themselves as Neapolitans, Calabrese, Sicilians, etc. rather than Italians, gradually realizing that only by subscribing to the latter term could they hope to develop effective solidarity. Likewise "Hispanics" is an umbrella term that obscures divisions within multiple groups: Cubans, Puerto Ricans, Dominicans, Colombians, etc. If the Italian model is taken as a guide, then it would probably require a couple of generations for the influence of separate backgrounds to diminish, especially since with Hispanics, one must contend with exceptional

---

[41] *Newsday* 14 May 1989.

[*] EDITORS' NOTE: This essay was written in the fall of 2000. Since that time, the United States, and especially New York, under the governance of Mayor Giuliani, have literally pulled themselves out of the ashes. The horrific attacks of September 11, 2001, could have left the cosmopolitan center devastated and a wasteland. Giuliani, calling on his civic pride, guided the city from its infernal state to a new beginning. Giuliani is recognized as a hero to the people of New York, the United States, and the world. Queen Elizabeth II of Great Britian has bestowed upon him the title of Knighthood, and the former mayor is now affectionately known as "Sir Rudy."

factors, including enduring nations, histories, and ethnic characteristics. Even among African Americans, divisions persist. (One recent example manifested itself in a primary in 2000 that pitted African American Representative Major Owens versus a West Indies black against whom there was resentment within the African American community.) Immigrants from India also must deal with backgrounds based on regional differences in language, dialect, and religion. The point is that it takes some time before the attainment of a substantial degree of unified outlooks and agendas become strong enough to establish political clout.

Transitory Stay – When one adds the factor of the temporary aspect of immigration, which was characteristic of first-generation Italians, many of whom did not expect to become permanent residents, then one can understand why they were less likely to establish political roots. It helps account also for low rates of citizenship. Even those inclined toward a permanent stay were initially primarily pre-occupied with earning a living, in addition to having to deal with language difficulties and unfamiliar customs and laws. These background factors apply in part to African Americans, and even more so to Hispanics and Asians.

Finances – To be effective in politics ethnic groups need access to substantial capital, much of it expected from within group. For Italian Americans it took some time – perhaps a couple of generations. There is also some evidence that in part financial backing came from criminal elements.[42] The background related suggests, therefore, that as economic conditions improve, the entry of newer ethnic groups into elective politics will likewise improve. Asians will probably achieve earlier success in this regard.

Education – Jefferson's dictum regarding the essentiality of an educated public to a successful democracy has applicability. Dropout statistics before high school graduation indicate that first generation Italian Americans lagged behind others regarding formal education, a development partially explained by the need to work. It can also be argued that in the pre-1920s a livelihood could be earned without as extensive an education as is required in the present. While Asian Americans present a generally favorable picture in educational attain-

---

[42] Gay Talese, "The Ethnics of Frank Costello," *Esquire* 56 (Sep. 1961): 72-74+.

ment, there is some cause for concern regarding higher rates of quitting school by African Americans and Hispanics.

In summation, there are a number of areas wherein the course of political behavior of recently arrived ethnic groups in New York City parallels the Italian American experience and for which the latter may serve as a useful model. It is also true that there must be allowance for the uniqueness of each group, as well as for differences in time and circumstances. What has been offered is an opportunity to explore Italian American political history to see how and where its study can be utilized to consider the contemporary scene.

GOVERNOR CHALES POLETI

FRANK CAVAIOLI
POMPANO BEACH, FLORIDA

The political career of Charles Poletti illustrates the remarkable progress made by second generation Italian Americans who helped to lay the foundation upon which later generations could succeed in public life. The highest public office Poletti held was of governor of New York State, for a period of twenty-nine days from December 2, 1942 to January 1, 1943. Poletti had been lieutenant governor and he thereby completed the term of Governor Herbert H. Lehman who resigned to assume the position of United States Director of Foreign Relief during World War II.

The great pivotal event for the economic, social, and political advancement of Italian Americans was World War II. The structural insularity of foreign-stock Italians weakened as they entered military service of their adopted country. Inroads were made on their community's cultural lifestyle as young people left home for extended tours of duty. Upon returning, with higher expectations and greater sophistication, they eagerly sought to seize the opportunities available to them in the larger society. For example, the passage of the GI Bill of Rights in 1944 hastened social change. Italian Americans and others took advantage of the benefits offered by this law: low cost mortages, life insurance, tax benefits, medical care, and educational subsidies. They also faced less discrimination, and as they merged into the larger society accelerating the Americanization process, they successfully applied their skills and knowledge to the demands of the host society. The career of Charles Poletti bridged the pre- and post-World War II political experience of Italian Americans. He provided an excellent role model for the next generation.

Chales Poletti was born in Barre, Vermont, on July 2, 1903, to Dino, a granite cutter, and Caroline Gervasini Poletti, both of whom were immigrants and Protestants. His father came from Piedmont and his mother came from Lombardy, Italy. He overcame the challenges of an immigrant youth as he excelled academically in public school while working on a farm, in a bakery, and at a grocery store owned by the stonecutter's association. Later in life, Poletti said, "he learned at first hand" while in school the problems of the poor and the underprivileged. Encouraged by his high school principal, he decided to go to Harvard. He received a scholarship to attend Harvard and supported himself by waiting on tables, washing dishes, delivering newspapers, and tutoring students. He was elected to Phi Beta Kappa and graduated *summa cum laude* in 1924 with a bachelor's degree in political science and history. Poletti received an Eleanora Duse scholarship to study at the University of Rome for one year. He also studied at the University of Madrid in 1928. In both instances he perfected his fluency in Italian and Spanish. He completed his formal studies at Harvard Law School in 1928.

While he attended Harvard, Poletti came under the influence of Professor Frank Taussig, an outstanding economist, who advised his brilliant young student to study law. Poletti was impressed by the writings of former President Woodrow Wilson. He also admired Governor Alfred E. Smith of New York, whom he regarded as the ideal role model in American democracy. Poletti said of Smith, "I liked his record as Governor. I liked the way he was fighting for improvement of the conditions of the common man. It was Al Smith and Woodrow Wilson who made me a Democrat."

After he received his law degree in 1928, Poletti joined the New York law firm of Davis, Polk, Wardell, and Reed. John W. Davis, a principal in this law firm, had been the 1924 Democratic presidential candidate. While serving with this firm Poletti also became the legal assistant to the St. Lawrence Power Development Commission in 1930. In an article published in *The New Republic* (4 August 1941), he continued to be a strong advocate of this public energy venture.

> The outlines for the Administration's [President Franklin D. Roosevelt] were foreshowed by the President during the 1932 campaign in a series of speeches that were remarkable for their vigor and clarity. Four great publicly owned power "yardsticks" were promised – the TVA, Bouler Dam, the Columbia River development centering on the Bonneville and Grand Coulee, and the St. Lawrence project. And the failure to build the St. Lawrence can in no way be ascribed to the Administration. On the contrary, the fact that we are denied the use of the St. Lawrence power at a time when we need every available

kilowatt can be laid, in large measure, at the door of a group of interests unalterably opposed to cheap, publicly own power.

It was on April 25, 1959, during President Dwight D. Eisenhower's administration, that the St. Lawrence Seaway became a reality and opened to allow ocean ships to reach the mid-western part of the United States. The St. Lawrence Seaway and power projects cleared the way for the North Country to expand industrially and give New York State a second seacoast. Thanks to Poletti, and others like him, the St. Lawrence project was realized. Ealier, in 1941, while serving as lieutenant governor, Poletti had stated, "The St. Lawrence project is a natural, like the Suez and Panama Canals." From 1955 to 1960 he served as a trustee of the Power Authority of the State of New York, which constructed the electric power projects on the St. Lawrence River and at Niagara.

In 1932 he began his public career when he became General Counsel to the National Democratic Committee, serving in the post until May, 1937. Poletti became counsel to New York State Governor Herbert Lehman, a position that lasted to 1937. Lehman had been elected governor the year before. Harvard Law Professor Felix Frankfurter, who later became a U.S. Supreme Court Justice, had recommended his former student to Governor Lehman as a person who had a "disciplined and inventive mind." Frankfurter understood Poletti's commitment to put the law to social use. At the age of thirty Poletti moved to Albany to write speeches, draft legislation, recommend patronage appointments, lobbied for the state's Little New Deal, and serve as Governor Lehman's confidante. He also was appointed Chairman of Governor Lehman's Conference of Crime, the Criminal and Society, and as Chairman of a special committee to prepare a program to combat racketeering. From 1936 to the middle of 1937, he was a member of the State Board of Social Welfare. With this education and legal training, Poletti responded to the social upheaval caused by the Great Depression of the 1930s. Other factors that motivated his social conscience were his immigrant parents, hardships experienced by his father in the granite industry, and the economic disadvantages he faced as a youth.

In 1937 Governor Lehman appointed Poletti to fill a vacancy on the State Supreme Court. Six months later he was elected on his own to a fourteen-year term to this position. In July, 1937, he served as Chairman of the New York State Constitutional Convention. The committee produced a twelve-volume report. In November, 1937, he was elected as a Delegate-at-Large for the Convention.

Governor Lehman, after having won two-year terms, reluctantly decided to run in 1938 for the newly established four-year gubernatorial term, a decision prompted by the news that the popular Thomas E. Dewey was about to receive the Republican party nomination. He told Jim Farley and Ed Flynn that "we must protect our social gains in this state." Lehman insisted he had to have an able and effective running mate as lieutenant governor to lighten the burden of executive responsibility. Being dissatisfied with incumbent Lieutenant Governor Bill Bray, whom he considered to be a drag on the administration and allied to the Utica and Tammany Hall political machines, he maneuvered Poletti into the party nomination for this position. Lehman wanted Poletti to act as "his good right arm" as lieutenant governor, and he vetoed a suggestion that Poletti run for state attorney general. With Poletti on the ticket, the influential American Labor Party now supported the Lehman-Poletti ticket. Luigi Antonini, American Labor Party Chairman, placed Poletti's name in nomination at its convention, emphasizing the latter's Italian roots and his outstanding record. Poletti thus resigned from the secure judgeship that paid $25,000.00 a year to risk his chances in the political arena for the lieutenant governorship that paid only $10,000.00 salary. From Washington, D.C., President Roosevelt praised the Democratic ticket whose platform greatly resembled the New Deal program.

Poletti made his initial campaign appearance at Morris High School in the Bronx addressing the county convention of the American Labor Party. Responding to some friendly jibes for giving up his $25,000.00 salary to run for office, he said:

> But those who know me do not consider anything strange about it. As lieutenant governor with Lehman as my chief, I think the opportunity will be extended to me to render greater service to the people of New York than I can render on the bench. Surely there's something more important in America than seeing how much money one can make. There are many things more important than a salary of $25,000, $50,000, or any sum you may choose.

In the contest for state executive leadership Dewey conducted a tough campaign. He proved to be a formidable opponent. Born in Owosso, Michigan, he received a bachelor's degree from the University of Michigan (1923), a law degree from Columbia University (1925), and practiced law in New York City. He was Special Prosecutor of the Investigation of Organized Crime in New York, 1935-1937, and then was elected District Attorney for New York County in 1937. He gained an enviable reputation for fighting crime and corruption. In his book, *The Case Against the New Deal* (1940), can be seen Dewey's political philosophy. During the campaign he demonstrated fairness in repudiating the religious prejudice that arose over Poletti's renunciation of Catholicism and adoption of Protestantism. Bray was a Catholic and in some upstate districts there was resentment for dropping him as Lehman's running mate. Dewey stated, "I condemn and despise any support based on racial and religious prejudice."

Nevertheless, the Reverend Edward Lodge Curran, President of the International Catholic Truth Society, based in Brooklyn, had questioned Poletti about his beliefs. Religious tensions surfaced, but Poletti quickly confronted the issue by responding to Father Curran in a letter dated October 18, 1938. Poletti's response was unequivocal in stating his political philosophy. Here are his salient points:

- I always have been a Democrat.
- As a Democrat I stand on the democratic platform and no other.
- As a Democrat I favor the election of all the candidates on the Democratic ticket.
- I believe in progressive and humane government under the American Constitution.
- I believe in helping the workingman, the poor and underprivileged. I favor economic and social justice-principles nobly expounded in the encyclicals of Pope Leo XIII and Pope Pius XI.
- I am opposed to both reactionary and radical government.
- I believe in preserving the American form of government. In mind and soul, I have always been and am opposed to Communism and other forms of government and other forms of dictatorships.
- I believe in the right of every citizen to the equal protection of the law.

- I believe in protecting the civil and religious liberties granted to each citizen by the American Constitution.
- I shall continue to oppose any act of discrimination on the grounds of race, color or religion.

Poletti went on to explain how he was baptized as a young boy in the Baptist Church in Barre, Vermont and that later he and his wife became members of the Riverside Church in New York City where they were married in 1934. He provided more autobiographical details.

> My father was an Italian stonecutter who came to America in 1890 to improve his economic condition. My mother, an Italian woman of peasant origin, came to this country with her sister who was married to an Italian stonecutter. Around 1900 they went to Barre, Vermont, where granite quarries were being developed. I was born there in 1903…
>
> We lived across the railroad tracks near the stone cutting plants. I was brought up with working men and women. In our home we had several working men as boarders. I began work at an early age.
>
> Unfortunately, neither myself nor the neighbors' children ever received religious instruction at home. These working people spoke no English. They were foreigners in a strange land. No one went to church. Theirs was a bitter struggle for existence. They made no contacts with the prior residents. There was no neighboring church and they ceased to be a religious people.
>
> Around the age of twelve a few of us boys became acquainted with an Italian Baptist missionary. He invited us to join a boy's club at the mission in another part of the city. We did and soon some of us were attending Sunday school. And some time thereafter we were baptized in that church. Then during my school days I taught Sunday school there.
>
> At public high school I was awarded a scholarship to Harvard College. During my early years in college my father and mother both died. I have no relatives in this country…
>
> I am certain you and I agree that America means a people who do not classify public officials or citizens according to their religion. We believe that any citizen, no matter what his religion, has the right to aspire to the highest office in the nation. It was because of that

> conviction that in 1928 I labored wholeheartedly for the election of Governor Alfred E. Smith as President of the United States.
>
> In the light of what has and is transpiring in some countries of the Old World, I shall devote myself to preserving America as the land of the free, the land of opportunity, the land where every citizen enjoys freedom of religious worship and where neither race, color or religion will determine the rights of a citizen, or open or close to him the door of election to public office.
>
> I am an American. Believe me that I shall always do all in my power to protect and preserve the American form of government which alone made it possible for me to rise from the most humble surroundings to my present position. I have been nominated for a most important elective office. I seek the votes of my fellow citizens not as a protestant, not as a person of Italian descent, but as a free-born American who feels that his record of achievement, his character and attainments qualify him for office....

This statement of Poletti's Americanism more than satisfied Reverend Curran who stated that "Judge Poletti's reply is not merely satisfactory but is most inspiring as coming from one so willing to discuss who he is and what he stands for the public life of our great state." He congratulated Poletti upon his realization of the needs of all classes of the population. Father Curran said his original request was "not an attack but a desire to secure the information that he has so graciously given." One may wonder whether it may have been Poletti's Italianness, as well as his Protestantism, that was being questioned at a time when Italians had not yet fully entered the American mainstream and prejudice remained strong. Nevertheless, Poletti's humble but straightforward statement demonstrated a total loyalty and commitment to the American creed.

In the election of 1938 Lehman and Poletti defeated the Republican slate. Poletti's hard campaigning actually had him running ahead of Lehman in the popular vote. Lehman was described by Robert O. Ingalls in *Herbert H. Lehman and New York's Little New Deal (1975)* as "humorless and colorless" whose "popularity rested on his strikingly apolitical qualities" but was "devoted to the public interest." Poletti had gained a reputation for being affable and exuberant, a "one-man brain trust" who complemented the persona of Lehman.

Warren Moscow, an expert on New York politics and author of *Politics in the Empire State* (1948), said that Poletti has handled the religious issue effectively. He also observed that Italian Americans were a force to be reckoned with in New York elections; neither party could claim them. They were clannish in their voting as they usually voted as a bloc for Italian American candidates. Leaders learned this fact in the successes of Fiorello LaGuardia, Vito Marcantonio, and Poletti himself. Moscow said that New York Italians tended to support Republican candidates, but they began to support the Democratic Party during the rise of Franklin Delano Roosevelt in the 1930s. As lieutenant governor of New York state, Poletti astutely extended his view to national and international developments. He criticized Nazi and Fascist propaganda that was emerging in the United States. He advocated a "campaign to stress what democracy really means. . . American citizens, be they first generation or descendants of the founders of our country, can have no divided allegiance." As the federal government's defense efforts expanded, Governor Lehman appointed a State Council of National Defense in August, 1940, to coordinate preparations for possible United States involvement and to advise him on all points where national and state cooperation was needed. The Governor designated Poletti as general coordinator of this group. This council advised railroads, power companies, factories, municipalities, and other groups to protect their property against sabotage. Plans for evacuation of children were laid out. All aspects of war production, vocational training for specific industries, medical services, and selective service administration were outlined. Historian Allan Nevins pointed out in his book, *Herbert Lehman and His Era* (1963), that New York thus became a model state when the United States entered the war in December, 1941. In 1940 Poletti resigned from the National Lawyers Guild because he questioned the loyalty of this group. He said "some members of the Guild were more interested in Communism than anything else." In October, 1940, he made a patriotic Columbus Day address:

> We must strengthen our democracy by preserving the ideals of liberty, justice and tolerance that are its very cornerstone. Each of us, no matter of what racial strain, has a great responsibility to keep his thoughts and actions thoroughly American.

Fulfilling his mandate as the state's defense coordinator, he sought to revive the 150 idle manufacturing plants, urged the training of skilled workers, and admonished manufacturers to "avoid racial discrimination in selecting their employees." He acknowledged progress as the state met its wartime goals by early 1942. He was critical of "obstructionists and defeatists" and urged their defeat at the polls. "It is to labor and all other liberal Americans that we must look for constant vigilance against the isolationists." On October 13, 1942, Poletti joined Governor Lehman and Mayor LaGuardia at the Columbus Day ceremonies at Columbus Circle in praising the contributions of Italian Americans in fighting for freedom in World War II. He called for tolerance of all minorities. He expressed pride in his Italian heritage, contending that Italian Americans are "second to none" in their loyalty, patriotism, and devotion to the United States. He said 10 percent of the five million members in the armed forces were Italian Americans.

At the same time, U.S. Attorney General Nicholas Biddle, with the approval of President Roosevelt, announced that 600,000 Italians living in the United States were to be freed from the stigma of "enemy aliens" status. They would be allowed to travel freely, possess firearms, carry cameras, be out of the curfew, and not worry about carrying identification cards. Biddle said they earned this by their loyalty. In just the first ten months of war time vigilance, fewer than 1/20 of 1 percent, or 228, Italians had been interned, that is, taken into custody. In the election of November, 1942, Republican Thomas E. Dewey was the "outstanding favorite" to defeat Democrat John J. Bennett, Jr., for governor. Poletti was not able to receive the nomination for governor because the party leaders of the Democratic party did not support him; however, he was renominated for lieutenant governor and ran against Republican candidate Thomas W. Wallace. Dewey defeated Bennett for governor, while Wallace narrowly defeated Poletti for lieutenant governor by 20,000 votes. It was a sweep for the Republicans who won all state offices and who increased their majorities in both houses of the state legislature. In the post-election lame duck period, Governor Lehman resigned as governor on December 2, 1942, to take a new post as U.S. Director of Foreign Relief. In a simple ceremony in the executive chamber in Albany Poletti was sworn in as governor to complete the last twenty-nine days of Lehman's gubernatorial term, until January 1, 1943, when Dewey would take office. On this occasion Poletti said:

> It is a great honor to be, even for a short while, Governor of the State of New York. That honor I shall assume with a deep sense of gratitude and a deep sense of responsibility. Mrs. Poletti appreciates the great honor of being the First Lady of the State. In my opinion, she will be a very attractive First Lady.

Adding a serious note to the assumption of his new position Governor Poletti added, "We must carry on and make decisions in the month of December as we would in the month of March." The twenty-nine days that Poletti spent as governor were busy ones. Deeply concerned about intolerance, he ordered an investigation of the "desecration and destruction" of Jewish religious property at Lake Placid and Saranac Lake. As shortages of war materials became acute at the end of 1942, Governor Poletti ordered state institutions to be self-sufficient regarding food consumption, and that all state fans and all state acreage be put to full and efficient use. On his last day in office he proposed an extensive agenda for social legislation under the aegis of a "Beverage Commission." His proposal included state health insurance, improvement of unemployment insurance, construction of low rent housing, money for financing child relief, development of the St. Lawrence water power resources under state ownership, and lowering the voting age to eighteen in New York. It was believed that Poletti was setting a platform to run for the governorship in 1946, something which never developed because of his participation in World War II. At the very least, it revealed his adherence to the New Deal program. It also placed him in the camp of Mayor LaGuardia's compassionate public agenda in New York City. It even resembled much of the political philosophy of radical Congressman Vito Marcantonio. Poletti was a progressive and social activist. Four days before leaving office, Governor Poletti made a special appeal, in Italian, over shortwave radio to the people of Italy to overthrow their Fascist leaders. Within three days of leaving office, and Dewey's inauguration as governor, Poletti was appointed special assistant to Secretary of War Henry L. Stimson, receiving a commission of lieutenant colonel assigned to the civil affairs division of the section on military government of occupied countries. From 1943 to 1946 he served as Allied Military Governor in Italy (Sicily, 1943; Naples, 1944; Rome, 1944-1945; Milan, 1945-1946). Among the many honors he received were the Legion of Merit (United States), Officer of the Order of the British Empire, Knight Cross of the Order of the Crown of Italy, Commander of the Papal Order of St. Gregory the Great, First Order of the Star of Jordan, Grand Officer of the Order of St. Agatha (San Marino), Gold Medal of the City of Rome, and Honorary Citizen of Naples, Rome, and Milan. He served in various capacities when called upon. He was a member of the Harvard Board of Overseers, Cornell University Board of Trustees, and Syracuse University Board of Directors. He returned to law practice as part of the legal firm of Poletti, Fredikin, Praskner & Gartner (1966-1985). He served as counsel to the New York State Commission on Educational Finances (1955-1956); was a trustee of the Power Authority of New York State (1955-1960); was in charge of International Relations and Exhibits of the New York World's Fair (1960-1965). For many years he was a participant and leader in the Italian Welfare League; Council Against Intolerance in America; Council of Foreign Relations; and the National Urban League. Charles Poletti was one of twenty governors whose ethnic heritage was partially or totally Italian. The other Italian American governors were Caesar Rodney, William Paca, Andrew Houston Longino, Alfred E. Smith, John O. Pastore, Foster J. Furcolo, Albert D. Rossellini, Michael V. DiSalle, Christopher Del Sesto, John A. Notte, John A. Volpe, Philip. W. Noel, Ella Tambussi Grasso, Richard F. Celeste, Mario M. Cuomo, Edward D. DiPrete, James J. Florio, George E. Pataki, and Angelo Paul Cellucci. Though Poletti's tenure as governor was only twenty-nine days, his public and private achievements were remarkable. Through hard work, he realized the American dream, always marveling at the opportunities a free society offered. As a child of Italian immigrants who arrived in the United States with millions of other Europeans seeking economic well being, he was driven by ambition to develop his talents. He symbolized the American success story and helped to break down barriers in making it easier for other Italian Americans to succeed in public and private life.

HENRY MOLISE'S CULTURAL GROWTH IN JOHN FANTE'S
THE BROTHERHOOD OF THE GRAPE

Franco Mulas
UNIVERSITY OF SASSARI, ITALY

*T*he Brotherhood of the Grape, Fante's last and perhaps best portrayal of the Italian immigrant's struggle for identity, is in one context a novel of return, of reunion and of personal redemption. As such it is clearly his final autobiographical statement. But it is also, and almost more importantly, a novel about alliance and solidarity. In developing this theme Fante focuses on the colorful and often boisterous world of Nick Molise, a hard-headed bricklayer from Abruzzi, and his circle of family and friends. In this world the center is always a table and the centerpiece a jug of wine, though at times the wine may give way to a 'trippa milanese' prepared with "rice, bell peppers and tomato sauce, sprinkled with parmesan cheese and seasoned butter and spices" (145). The two themes come together dramatically when Henry, Nick Molise's self-exiled son, returns home in a regenerating visit during which the aging father passes away:

> The kitchen. *La cucina*, the true mother country, this warm cave of the good witch deep in the desolate land of loneliness, with pots of sweet potions bubbling over the fire, a cavern of magic herbs, rosemary and thyme and sage and oregano, balm of lotus that brought sanity to lunatics, peace to the troubled, joy to the joyless, this small twenty-by-twenty world, the altar a kitchen range, the magic circle a checkered tablecloth where the children fed, the old children, lured back to their beginnings, the taste of mother's milk still haunting their memories, fragrance in the nostrils, eyes brightening, the wicked world receding as the old mother witch sheltered her brood from the wolves outside.[1]

Food and wine are always the primary elements for the Molise family. Mrs. Molise still prepares a great deal of food on special

---

[1] John Fante, *The Brotherhood of the Grape* (New York: Bantam, 1977). All references to the text are from this edition.

occasions although none of her four children lives in the household any longer. When Henry, just returned home, asks his mother who is going to eat all the food she has prepared, she answers:

> "Everybody."
> "You invited everybody."
> "No, but they will come anyway." (49)

The ritual of the meal stirs the emotions through memory:

> The baked eggplant took me back to the childhood of my life... The thin slices of veal had me fighting tears again as I washed them down with Joe Musso's magnificent wine... And the gnocchi prepared in butter and milk finally did it. I covered my eyes over the plate and wept with joy. (51)

But it is wine that has always been the regenerating force in the family and thus "easily the most important commodity in the house" (49). Without it Henry acknowledges that his father "would quickly dry out and fade away" (49). But it also works on the spirit. In the darkness of the evening, with a glass of wine in his hands, Henry feels the bitter taste of the passing of time and experiences a chilling sense of his father's imminent death:

> A lonesome town (San Elmo). All the valley towns were like it, desolate, mystically impermanent, enclaves of human existence, people clustered behind small fences and flimsy stucco walls, barricated against the darkness, waiting. I...felt grief seeping into my bones, grief for man and the pain of loneliness in the house of my mother and father, aging, waiting, marking time. (51)

Most significantly for Henry, however, wine brings companionship between he and his father. It is the one element that can clear all cultural obstacles between him and his old man, giving to both of them that freedom which allows them to abandon themselves to their true feelings:

> Flopping down beside him, I took the jug. That wine! It renewed my mouth, my flesh my skin, my heart and soul, and I thanked God for Angelo Musso's hills. We sprawled in silence, listening to the birds, passing the jug. (117)

Later, while working together, Henry ponders:

> I crushed the rock and he did the wall. We did fine. When tired, he called for wine. He could not straighten up, so he stood like an ape as he drank. When he began to sweat the blotches on his back and under his arms were rose-colored. I thought what the hell, it's nutritious, it's grape sugar, energy, and drank with him every time. We were doing fine, fine. (119)

While it is easy to see in Nick a biographical portrait of Fante's own father, it is important to appreciate him as the prototypical Italian-American father, first generation. He is an aging laborer, a flesh-and-blood survivor of the quest for at least a small share of the American Dream, and he is at the end of his days. He spends these mostly with his old paesani, engaging in the everyday ritual of passing a large bottle of wine. At such times he and his friends attempt to bring meaning to their life's struggle, that of the outsider in a cold, often forbidding land of seeming opportunity.

The story of Nick Molise and his friends unfolds along clearly biblical lines. Their diaspora is of enormous proportions, considering the tragic consequences it implies for the millions they are here called to represent. Their disenchantment can clearly be read in their tired faces and witnessed in their low speeches and defiant silence when dealing with people outside the Brotherhood. All have seen the hope of returning to their place of birth shatter with the realization that the promised land has yielded little more than a place to work and grow old. We experience their sadness and bitterness, but it is a sadness leavened with pride and a bitterness free of any cynical edge. They have been doubly defeated, on the one hand by not being able to return triumphant to Italy, and on the other by failing to gain what some people perceive as true success in the New World. Yet Nick proudly shows off his achievements to his youthful American born descendents:

It was the Grand Tour, the complete works of Nick Molise... My father's first stop on the tour was across town in the neighborhood of the rich, where the public library was situated, a white brick structure, pure New England, with four stone columns above a cascade of red sandstone steps.

Pausing across the street, hands on hips, his face softened reverently as he stared at the building.
"There she is, kid. Isn't she pretty? You know who built her?" "You did, Papa."
"Not bad. Not bad at all."
"It's a beauty, Papa."
"Lasts a thousand years."
"At least." (22)

The Brotherhood of the Grape in some ways exposes the conflict between the feelings of pride in the pioneering accomplishments of expatriation, however undervalued, and the need for cultural identification with the Old World. To feel convincingly redeemed a man must see himself as useful in the present but at peace with what he has left behind. Settling in a new land is one of the most radical experiences imaginable. It is, as we have come to say, broadening, mind-shatteringly so, and as such it is treacherous. In the words of Dante:

> Tu proverai sì come sa di sale
> lo pane altrui, e come è duro calle
> lo scendere e 'l salir per l'altrui scale.
>
> [Thou shalt learn how salty tastes
> the bread of others and how hard a road it is
> to go down and up another's stairs].[2]

Nick Molise has suffered the humiliating wounds of social rejection, but as to whether he should be seen as a defeated man, the answer (as Henry comes to realize upon his return) is a definite "no".

---

[2] Dante, *Paradiso,* Canto XVII, ll, 58-60.

The dominant culture has not been able to bend him. His kitchen still smells of the rich spicy Italian cooking and his cellar of home made wine. Now at the end of his life he feels more Italian than ever.

Nick Molise, however, is also a father, and although he does not seem to understand his children, they have perhaps begun to understand him. It is the special message of this novel that there comes a point in the life of second-generation descendants when they need to reconnect with that old-world parental figure whom they so agonizingly tried to escape.

So the novel is also about Henry, the elder of Nick's sons who, upon returning to San Elmo, his place of birth, slowly rediscovers his ethnic origin. Through his aging, dying father (whom we have considered the main protagonist of the story) Henry comes to experience his own Italianità.

Back home again, after many years of absence, he immediately senses great change. The old neighborhood is dying and with it the soul of a culture that he and his contemporaries had been quick to abandon. There are few people left in San Elmo now who can still bring significance to Chianti drinking, and they are old like Nick Molise. They spend the last days of their lives at the Cafe Roma or at Angelo Musso's vineyard, which have become virtual shrines to the past. Henry realizes that he is an outsider, for he has broken ties with this world, "too Italian" as far as he was concerned, with its poverty and social exclusion. Now we see him seeking his own redemption which, however, requires a certain rite of initiation:

> Like all the rooms in that old house, my mother's bedroom was small. The bed was still warm from the heat of the day as I slipped naked beneath a sheet and down into a cradle in the mattress that measured the contours of my mother's body ... In the pillow my nostrils drew the sweet, earthly odor of my mother's hair, pulling me back to other times, when I was not yet twenty and sought to run away. Yes, I got away. I made it when I was not yet twenty. (61)

The process starts with a vivid remembrance of the past, evoked by the presence of his mother: the Italian food, the smell of spices on her hair and on the bed which, like a cradle, accepts him and takes him back in time to the days when he dreamt of running away from poverty and isolation and primarily from his father. Now the true ritual of initiation begins as he puts on some of his old clothes saved by his mother when he left the family and the town. To be fully accepted, however, he must first undergo the wine-drinking ritual as well, for it is the wine, Angelo Musso's Chianti, that has always been the main ingredient of unification. Henry will perhaps be the last member to join the Brotherhood.

Once into the vivifying power of the wine, Henry begins to feel happy and at peace with himself and the others: "It renewed my mouth, my flesh, my skin, my heart and soul" (117). All this leads to his inevitable identification with his father; "An ill-fated mason who had struggled all his life for a bit of space on earth. Like father, like son" (137). This revelation takes place just before his ailing father chooses to die eating and drinking wine at Angelo Musso's vineyard. Among his paesani, the priest Angelo Musso, like a sybil, declares openly that, "it is better to die of drink than to die of thirst. It is better to die among friends than to die among doctors" (159-60), placing in the hands of his old friend a straw-wrapped bottle of Chianti as if it were a rosary.

With Nick Molise goes another part of San Elmo, and his old friends will soon be gone as well, taking with them a past which Henry would like now to preserve. Nick remains for Henry: "a lightening that illuminated my life... a nimbus around me, my own flesh and blood, a poet asserting his will to live" (154), leaving him two precious gifts: love and respect for his cultural roots, and the strength to go on in life.

BIBLIOGRAPHY

Aste, M. "Sacco e Vanzetti: Italian Filmic Images." Aste et al.

Aste, M., J. Krase, L. Napolitano, and J. E. Worrall, eds. *Industry, Technology, Labor and the Italian-American Communities.* Staten Island, NY: AIHA, 1997.

Cammet, J. M., ed. *The Italian American Novel.* Staten Island, NY: AIHA, 1969.

Caporale, R., ed. *The Italian Americans Through the Generations,* Staten Island, NY: AIHA, 1986.

DeSena, J. N., ed. *Italian Americans in a Multicultural Society,* Stony Brook, N.Y.: Forum Italicum, 1994.

Fante, J. *Dago Red* (Short Stories). New York: Viking, 1940.

___. *Wait Until Spring, Bandini.* Santa Barbara, CA: Black Sparrow, 1983 [1938].

___. *Ask the Dust*. Santa Barbara, CA: Black Sparrow, 1982 [1939].

___. *Full of Life*. Santa Barbara, CA: Black Sparrow, 1988 [1952].

___. *Dreams from Bunker Hill*. Santa Barbara, CA: Black Sparrow, 1982.

___. *The Brotherhood of the Grape*. Santa Barbara, CA: Black Sparrow, 1988 [1977].

Gambino, R. *Blood of My Blood: The Dilemma of the Italian Americans*. Garden City, NY: Doubleday, 1974.

Gardaphé, F. L. "Continuity in Concrete: (Re) Constructing Italian/American Writers." Aste et al.

Malva, M. P. *Arturo Bandini in John Fante's Wait Until Spring, Bandini*. Sassari: Centro Stampa, University of Sassari, 1999.

Mangione, J. "My Experience as an Italian American Writer." *Italy and Italians in America, R.S.A. Rivista di Studi Americani* 3.4-5. Abano Terme: Piovan, 1985.

Mulas, F. *Studies on Italian-American Literature*. Staten Island, NY: Center for Migration Studies, 1995.

Napolitano, L. "The Bittersweet Promise of America in Selected Works of Italian-American Fiction." *Italian Americans in a Multicultural Society*. Ed. J. Krase and J. N. DeSena. Stony Brook, NY: Forum Italicum, 1994.

Tomasi, L. E. *Italian Americans: New Perspectives in Italian Immigration and Ethnicity*. Staten Island, NY: Center for Migration Studies, 1985.

Unali, L. "Silence of the Ethnic Cradle, the Noise of America, the Control of the Noise." *RSA, Rivista di studi anglo-americani* 10 Supernova (1994): 459-65.

Vecoli, R., ed. "The Italian Americans." *The Center Magazine* 7.4 (July-August 1974): 31-43.

Viscusi, R. "What is Italian American Literature?" *Italian Ethnics: Their Languages, Literature and Lives*. Ed. D. Candeloro, F. L. Gardaphé, and P. A. Giordano. Staten Island, NY: AIHA, 1990.

Little Paul's Psychological Development in Pietro Di Donato's *Christ in Concrete*

Maria Paola Malva
UNIVERSITY OF SASSARI, ITALY

> *O God how it hurts – but I must not
> let them see I have hurt myself
> already – I must lay brick!*

Chirst in Concrete, Pietro Di Donato's autobiographical novel, focuses on the development of Little Paul's character, a twelve-year-old boy who is forced to leave the world of childhood and start work to support his family after his father's death in a construction accident. This can be considered a novel of "Education" as F. Rosengarten states,[1] mainly for the different forms of experiences through which Little Paul acquires a universal sort of tragic knowledge, namely the nonexistence of God.

Our purpose here, besides pointing out how the young protagonist builds up a new vision of the world and life in general, is to discuss how the author emphasizes the intergenerational conflict, and whether in this 'case' too, as in the case of Annunziata's and Geremio's family, the second generation's estrangement from the parents' Old World heritage is expressed through the rejection of religious values. Our thesis implies also that the alienation from the culture of the first generation by the second one is combined with the desire manifested by the latter to be assimilated by the American society. However, as we shall see in our analysis, although Little Paul is depicted in his progression toward a kind of partial atheism, his 'learning' is not paralleled by any identification with or acceptance of the American social and economic system. On the contrary, his rebellion against the Catholic religion could be explained, at least in part, by his rebellion against the very structure of American society. Actually, we do not think that *Christ in Concrete* could be limited by any interpretation based upon a particular place, period or consideration of characters as

---

[1] Frank Rosengarten, "Alienation: The Quest for Identity and Social Conflict," in *The Italian American Novel*, Proceedings of the Second Annual Conference, 25 Oct.1969, ed. Cammett J. M. (New York: AIHA, 1969), 14.

members of an ethnic group on the American soil. This, we believe, is because the content of the novel leads the reader to reflect about his own position in the world, his vision of life as it is or should be, in relation to the existence or the nonexistence of God. Thus, the subject-matter of the novel goes beyond its relative setting of time and space as well as the characterization of the people. Consequently, Little Paul's experience of life and his view of the world in America, after his father's and godfather's deaths, transcend both the value system of his parents' generation as well as the experience of the immigrants to America at the turn of the century, to embrace universal themes such as that of God and man's relation to Him. Considering this aspect of *Christ in Concrete,* the best definition that could be applied to it, in terms of ethnic literature, is the concept proposed by Rose Basile Green's regarding Italian-American literature, according to which, "literature must project consistent and continuing values that are unique to the group in question."[2]

This opinion certainly contributes to place Di Donato's novel in the appropriate literary context. Indeed, Little Paul, the son of immigrants from Abruzzi, acknowledges social injustices that often reach the level of crime, and rebels against the exploitation of the immigrants and above all the hypocrisy, embodied by the Church and its clergy, as exemplified by Father John's behavior. Little Paul's gradual realization of his father's distress, as well as that of all the other Italian immigrants and the laboring masses in general, who suffered heavy injustices at the hands of the rich, is depicted in the novel against the ethnic background of Southern Italian family life. His disenchantment with the American economic structure, its class system and Catholicism, since he can no longer believe in God who allows such injustices to happen, represent the two central points of the novel.

Little Paul's disclosure of the tragic universal reality, namely that he "has been cheated" (303), as his father had been in the past, is illustrated in different phases through two important characters: Louis Molov, the Jewish boy who lives in the same tenement as Paul's, and Nazone, his godfather. Louis attitude towards life and Nazone's daily experience at work among his *paesani*, help Little Paul gain a different

---

[2] Robert J. Pietro and E. Ifkovic, "Introduction," in *Ethnic Perspectives in American Literatures* (New York: The Modern Language Association of America, 1983), p. 12.

vision of life from that of his parents, as shown in the first part of the novel.

Indeed, the novel starts by emphasizing the optimistic expectations of the two Italian immigrants, Geremio and Annunziata, concerning their future in the land of their dreams, before Geremio is killed in the crash of a building constructed with inferior materials owing to the boss's cynical profiteering. Annunziata's happiness, for the house she and her husband are going to buy and their eighth child about to be born, as well as her trust in America, is expressed in her words addressed to Geremio, first by saying, "The children are so happy, Geremio; let them be, for even I would dance a Tarantella," and then prospecting a joyful future, she adds, "Our children will dance for us… in the American style someday" (16). Geremio's trust in America is recalled, and even more emphasized by Little Paul himself when he approaches "the men at Job," hoping desperately that they will give him the chance to work so that his fatherless family will be saved from starvation:

> Paul recognized some of the faces… faces he had seen at the great street feasts of Saint Joseph, faces that had visited the house and drunk muscatel and alicante wine, faces he had seen at baptisms and weddings, faces he had seen at the Liberty Loan benefit in the Bricklayers's Local the time of the War with the Huns, the time they had beer and sandwiches and prize fights and when his father put him high on his shoulder and told him to sing *America I Raised a Boy for You* and *The Sunshine of Your Smile* and they threw pennies to him that glorious time he would never forget… They were faces that had stood by and attended his father in coffin with severe eyes and lowered chins. (89)

Initially Little Paul, like his mother and father, places his hopes and trust in America. Talking to Louis Molov, he is willing to bet that his Jewish parents will like America, for he says, "…It's the best country in the world" (164). At Job, Little Paul is accepted by all the *paesani,* in the same way his father had been, and each of them offers him part of his lunch, repeating spontaneously and unconsciously the main action of the Last Supper, when Christ broke the bread and gave it to his disciples. Thus, the bricklayers, poor and exploited to the point of losing their own lives, perform in their workday routine one of the main symbolic deeds upon which the Christian belief is based: the act of renunciation for another human being, a 'brother.' This scene is dramatized in its meaning and effects, compared to the previous one, in which Little Paul goes to talk to Father John, who being at supper refuses to see him. Only after the insistence of Donna Katarina, who though an "old gypsy woman" gives him "a round loaf of bread" (79), Paul is finally admitted to Father John's presence as well as to a:

> ...long table reaching away beautifully lit with slim candles throwing warm glow on shiny porcelain plates containing baked potatoes and cuts of brown dripping lamb and fresh peas and platters of hot food, cool food, hard food, soft food... (81)

In contrast with the bricklayers, who each gave Little Paul part of their meal, the priest refuses him every kind of help pointing out that: "I have nothing to do with the Charities. There is a board of trustees who confer and pass on every expenditure, do you understand?" (83), indirectly suggesting to the little boy to sell his nice little overcoat! Previous to this scene, where the priest's un-Christian attitude is highly emphasized, the author depicts the most appalling moment, when Paul tries to explain to the "old-old face who appeared through the half-opened door" (79) that "father died under a building. We are eight and mother. We need help. We will suffer..." (80), and the man replies: "This is a *church*!" (80).

The author's ferocious attack on the Church is echoed in Nazone's following remark about American society when Paul goes to Job to see if he can work there as a bricklayer:

> Nazone said to Paul in under-voice:
> 'Would you wish to become a master-builder of walls like the good spirit of your father?
> 'I ...have this trowel with me.'
> 'Bless God,' said Nazone to the men, 'and why shouldn't the son of a bricklayer learn the art and bring food to his family? Is the school going to satisfy their needs? The Police? The Army? Or Navy? The Church? Or the City Hall stinking with thieves?' (93)

Paul already had the proof that Nazone's words were true because the priest, who should be considered as the example of a real 'Christian,' to be followed by other Christians, not only did not help him but openly revealed his hypocrisy. Nazone's argument to convince the other bricklayers to give Little Paul the opportunity to work, even though he is only twelve years old, in order to support his family, shifts from religious or sentimental reasons to social justice, namely from the irrational to the rational: "It is not a fact of heart," said Nazone, "It is the right of a bricklayer's family to live. It is the right of a bricklayer's son to follow the art of his father" (94), Nazone's belief, that it is "...the crime of corporations about the right of a bricklayer's son to support his family" (101), convinces him that Paul *must* have the chance to work despite his young age.

As soon as Paul enters the adults' world as a worker, he learns the workers' condition and exploitation, but above all he learns "the way the world is" (130), as Mr. Rinaldi answers him when Paul objects to his boss that his pay is not proportionate to his immense efforts and hard work. Nevertheless, the real crime is committed by the Corporation personified by Mr. Murdin, Geremio's 'Boss,' who at the Compensation Bureau accuses him of being directly responsible for the accident, thus for his own death, by not following the orders he gave him to safely underpin the scaffold. "The case is adjourned for further investigation," giving the Baldwin Insurance Company the necessary time "to fully substantiate the disclaiming of all or any liability" (175). Meanwhile, Little Paul tries to support his family by working as much as his body and physical strength allow him, as long as Mr. Rinaldi gives him the opportunity to work on his job despite his age. When his pay arrives, only five dollars for the entire week, Little Paul cries: "What had I failed to do?" (118). This feeling is echoed by Annunziata's brother Luigi, whose leg is cut on a construction accident and on whom Annunziata relied for economic support after her husband's death: "...But tell me, sister what have I done?" (121). After the visit at the Compensation Bureau,

> That night was passed in uncertainty, in the feeling that for some reason the family of Geremio was wrong, that the meek fearful faces in the corridors of Workmen's Compensation were wrong, that the people who lived about them in careers of fits and starts were wrong,

that the man who sweated and cursed on Job were wrong, that they
were cheap, immoral, a weight of charity and wrong to the
mysterious winning forces of right.
And Paul clutched his pillow.
O God above, what world and country are we in? We did not mean to
be wrong.
And toward dawn Annunziata also went into sleep wondering of her
wrongness. (177-78)

From the very beginning, after Geremio's death, Little Paul's view of the world begins to shake: "Dear mother, is not all this a wrong story?" (47). And indeed, this sense of 'wrongness' pervades the whole novel. Immediately after the scene at the Compensation Bureau follows that of the Memorial Day celebration when Louis Molov reveals Little Paul that for him, "...there is no God" (185). Louis's brother was shot by the Czar's soldiers in Russia, because:

'During the World War he tried to organize the peasants against war'... 'He made a great speech against the Czar and his war. He made the people cry. He did it even though father was making a lot of money by the war. He hated money and war and cruel people. The crowds carried him on their shoulders. I'll never forget.' (165)

Although his brother had the opportunity to run away, after he was arrested, he did not, "...because he said he had done nothing wrong and was afraid of no one" (166). If Louis's brother's fault in the Russian Empire was that of being a Jew against the Czar, "money, war and cruel people" and that the revolution carried by the "spirit of Louis's brother ideals," came and avenged him, then Little Paul's and his family's fault in the America is that of being poor.

Little Paul's complete "Education" will be achieved only when he becomes conscious of class conflicts, stressed in the text at the moment he realizes that "The scaffolds are not safe, for the rich must ever profit more" (301). He begins to acquire consciousness of his condition in the world when his godfather Nazone dies, falling from the scaffold pushed by a tub thrown violently to him by the foreman Jones. From that moment on, Little Paul acknowledges that "not to die" on the Job is the exception: " 'Boys,' said the foreman, 'that's all there is, there ain't no more!' Today he did not die. Perhaps somewhere tomorrow. And he left Job grimly with level and tool bag" (302). Therefore, Little Paul becomes aware that he, as a human being, and his life, do not depend on God, or Jesus Christ, but on the structure and system of the society where he lives, namely the American society, where the immigrant workers are exploited to death by the few.

Actually, Di Donato's denunciation of the immigrant workers' reality and living conditions is not limited to Southern Italian immigrants. Indeed, as workers of different nationalities appear in the quotation concerning the scene where the bricklayers are in competition for an award, the author's criticism against America would apply to all those who emigrated there from all over the world:

> I must win the award! Said Dave the only Jew bricklayer – said Frank the Scotchman – said Barney the Irishman – said Tommy the Englishman – said Hand the German said Grogan the 'real' American – said they all.
>
> I must win! prayed Paul. (237)

Within the novel, the paragraph preceding this quotation mentions another worker's ethnic origin and depicts another accident:

> A Swedish carpenter was coming down slowly and holding up his right hand. It looked like a ghastly dripping rose. The four fingers had been shorn off to the palm and the mangled remains ran red faucets. (236)

In our opinion, the immigrant workers' real tragedy, when accidents occurred on the Job, lies in their awareness that they have crossed the Atlantic Ocean hoping for a better life and instead could only find misery and degradation if not death. In other tragic cases, for example unemployment, or the crash of 1929 and all its consequences, America is seen, according to Nazone's own words, as "...a soil that has contradicted itself" (278). Therefore:

> ...what is going on today in this America is not a thing of temperament, it is something we cannot understand, it is the beginning, and all shall be shut to the hands that labor. It is like the

war that brings itself and for us only suffering awaits... Discovered by an Italian-named from Italian – But oh, that I may leave this land of disillusion! (279)

Nazone's severe judgement of America and his attack on its economic system is extended by Little Paul, after his godfather's brutal death, to a general reflection on the condition of men, on their relationships with one another, on the issue of the very essence and purpose of human life and ultimately a reflection on the question of the existence of God. When Little Paul becomes aware that God does not control the lives of human beings, because the 'Padrone' together with the American social system do so. When he later realizes that God does not even exist, otherwise He would have not allowed pain and suffering inhabit the world and man's heart, he becomes the master of his own life and destiny. At this point, we come to the conclusion that he rejects religious values because of America's cruel social reality. Paradoxically, by condemning and rejecting America, he frees himself from the beliefs in the Southern Italian notion of destiny – the sense of fate beyond human control – which represents the most significant achievement in his process of "Americanization," as said in his own words: "I want justice here! I want happiness here! I want life here!" (304). Only at this point, Little Paul's view of the world changes from a passive acceptance of fate to a total control of his life, a process which could be considered as an affirmation of the individual self-consonant with America's celebration of individual achievement.

BIBLIOGRAPHY

Aste, M. "Sacco e Vanzetti: Italian Filmic Images." Aste et al.

Aste, M., J. Krase, L. Napolitano, and J. E. Worrall, eds. *Industry, Technology, Labor and The Italian-American Communities.* Staten Island, NY: AIHA, 1997.

Boelhower, W. "The Immigrant Novel as Genre." *MELUS* 8.1 (Spring 1981):

Cammet, J. M., ed. *The Italian American Novel.* Staten Island, NY: AIHA, 1969.

Caporale, R., ed. *The Italian Americans Through the Generations.* Staten Island, NY: AIHA 1986.

DeSena, J. N., ed. *Italian Americans in a Multicultural Society.* Stony Brook, NY: Forum Italicum, 1994.

Fante, J. *Dago Red.* New York: Viking, 1940.

___. *Wait Until Spring, Bandini*. Santa Barbara, CA: Black Sparrow, 1983 [1938].
___. *Ask the Dust*. Santa Barbara, CA: Black Sparrow, 1982 [1939].
___. *Full of Life*. Santa Barbara, CA: Black Sparrow, 1988 [1952].
___. *Dreams from Bunker Hill*. Santa Barbara, CA: Black Sparrow, 1982.
___. *The Brotherhood of the Grape*. Santa Barbara, CA: Black Sparrow, 1988 [1977].
Gambino, R., *Blood of My Blood: The Dilemma of the Italian Americans*, Garden City, N.Y.: Doubleday, 1974.
Gardaphé, F. L. "Continuity in Concrete: (Re) Constructing Italian/American Writers." Aste et al.
Krase, J. and Egelman W., eds. *The Melting Pot and Beyond: Italian Americans in the Year 2000*. Staten Island, NY: AIHA, 1987.
Krase, J., and J. N. DeSena, eds. *Italian Americans in a Multicultural Society*. Stony Brook, NY: Forum Italicum, 1994.
Malva, M. P. *Arturo Bandini in John Fante's Wait Until Spring, Bandini*. Sassari: Centro Stampa, University of Sassari, 1999.
Mangione, J. "My Experience as an Italian American Writer." *Italy and Italians in America, R.S.A. Rivista di Studi Americani* 3.4-5. Abano Terme: Piovan, 1985.
Mulas, F. *Studies on Italian-American Literature*. Staten Island, NY: Center for Migration Studies, 1995.
___. "Jews in the Italian-American Novel." Krase and DeSena.
Napolitano, L. "The Bittersweet Promise of America in Selected Works of Italian-American Fiction." Krase and DeSena
Tomasi, L. E., *Italian Americans: New Perspectives in Italian Immigration and Ethnicity*, Staten Island, N. Y.: Center for Migration Studies, 1985.
Unali, L. "Silence of the Ethnic Cradle, the Noise of America, the Control of the Noise." *RSA, Rivista di studi anglo-americani* 10 Supernova (1994): 459-65.
Vecoli, R., ed. "The Italian Americans." *The Center Magazine* 7.4 (July-August 1974): 31-43.
Viscusi, R. "What is Italian American Literature?" *Italian Ethnics: Their Languages, Literature and Lives*. Ed. D. Candeloro, F. L. Gardaphé, and P. A. Giordano. Staten Island, NY: AIHA, 1990.

Triumphs and Tragedies of Ethnicity in America: Italians in the Granite Industry in Barre, Vermont, 1890-1915

Arthur Pippo
MASSACHUSETTS TEACHERS ASSOCIATION

Gillian Quinn
MASSACHUSETTS TEACHERS ASSOCIATION

During the first half of the twentieth century, vast numbers of immigrants came to America to work in its various industries. Many historians have assumed that these "diverse groups eventually discarded their pre-immigration behavior... and merged into the larger community" (Bodnar, *Immigration* xiv). However, more recently, other historians, among them John Bodnar, have concluded that the social processes of industrialization did not promote assimilation, but caused "ethnic alignments to be more pronounced" (Bodnar, *Immigration* xv). These historians believe that rather than adopting a working-class consciousness, these immigrant workers maintained an ethnic consciousness throughout the first decades of the twentieth century and relied on their own political philosophies and social institutions in order to adapt to their new home. Bodnar believes that "rank and file [immigrant] workers at this time were not preoccupied with the desire to regulate access to employment," but rather these newcomers embraced the labor movement in order "to impart human and moral values to a society dominated by commercial ones" (Bodnar, *Workers World* 5). The Italian granite workers in the late 1800s and early 1900s in Barre, Vermont prove this point. This paper examines the characteristics, political philosophies, and social institutions of these people. This paper will show that even though they represented perhaps the most sophisticated and lively participants in labor politics in the early twentieth century, the Barre Italians were not interested in the politics of the Barre labor unions, rather, they relied on their own ethnic politics and social institutions to help them adjust to life in the United States. [Picture 1]

The abundance of granite in Barre and the expansion of the railroad in the last two decades of the nineteenth century, which made transporting granite pieces easy, sparked the immigration of skilled Italian stone cutters to Barre, Vermont (Richardson 7). The Italian immigration began in the late 1890s and continued at a rapid pace until 1910 (Serota-Winston 32). By 1910, the Italians in Barre made up about 30% of the 12,000 inhabitants of the small town. Italians outnumbered all other ethnic groups, except for the Scots who also made up 30% of the population. The remaining ethnic distribution was: Native-born Americans constituted 25% of the population, Scandinavians constituted 10% of the population and Irish and other Europeans constituted 5% of the population (Serota-Winston 32). Sixty-one percent of the Italian immigrants were male (Serota-Winston 32) and, unlike many other immigrants of the time, they were extremely well educated. Ninety-eight percent of the Barre Italians were literate in their native language (Serota-Winston 32).

A beneficial by-product of coming to America, as far as the Barre Italians were concerned, was that they were finally free of the influence of the Catholic Church and the Vatican's efforts to stamp out the Socialist philosophy these workers held dear (McNeil 91). The Italians were not only very anti-Catholic, but anti-religion, in general. "'Neither God nor Master' was the motto which guided many (McNeil 98)." Some Italians went so far as to name their children "Ateo," which means Atheist. Protestant groups attempted to attract the Italians to the Protestants' more politically liberal denominations. This didn't work. While the Italians were content to take advantage of the play groups for Italian children and other social services established by the Protestant sects, the Italians shunned all other efforts by the Protestants to convert them (McNeil 98).

Bodnar's study of the immigrant workers in the steel mills in Steelton, Pennsylvania suggests that the ethnic isolation and resistance to unionization of those workers was due, in part, to the fact that they were unskilled and uneducated (Bodnar, *Immigration* xv-xvi). If this were so, the literacy, marketable skills and Socialist philosophy of the Barre Italians would seem to provide all of the elements necessary for a successful labor movement. Indeed, among the most significant figures in radical labor politics turned their faces away from the cities to cast a glance at the little town of Barre. This is so, undoubtedly, because

Barre was known for being the home of the *Cronica Subversiva* (Subversive Chronicles), the largest Italian-American anarchist journal, and its editor Luigi Galleani. Galleani was described as "one of the greatest radical orators of his time..." (Serota-Winston 37). Galleani arrived in America after he was forced to leave Italy, France, Switzerland and England. He got into legal trouble for inciting labor riots and strikes, such as the Patterson Silk Strike in 1902. Galleani fled to Canada, but finally returned to live in Barre. Galleani represented the ideals of anarchism that were "driven to destroy all forms of hierarchical social organization" (Serota-Winston 38). The presence of Galleani made Barre, itself, prestigious in the radical labor movement.

Emma Goldman, another famous labor radical, visited Barre and, with Galleani, addressed a crowd at the Opera House in Barre, in February 1907 (Falk 7). She is considered to be one of the most important female activists in the United States between the late 1800s and the early 1900s. She immigrated to the United States from an oppressive Russia and "[s]he was eager to settle into America... a free democratic society" (Gay and Gay 8-9). However, when she arrived in the United States, she was shocked by the horrible working conditions in the factories. She became active in the radical labor movement, advocating for the eight-hour workday and the improvement of working conditions. Goldman had many loyal followers. However, because of her wildly radical views on free love, free speech, and the draft, as well as labor, and her willingness to speak openly about them in public, she also had many enemies. She was even suspected in the conspiracy to assassinate President McKinley in 1901 (Gay and Gay 8-9).

Emma Goldman's trip to Barre had quite an impact on its citizens. In a personal interview with one Barre citizen named Cornelius Granai, Sr. (Mr. Granai), he recalled, that "the hall [where she spoke] would hold two hundred if you really squeezed together; the [rest of the] multitude was out on the sidewalk and in the road." Three years later in 1910, Eugene Debs, the father of the American Socialist Party, "urged a Barre audience to 'unite in one great union. Then you can accomplish something' " (Collins 3).

The prominence of Barre as a labor center was recognized by other workers in the Northeast. In January of 1912, striking textile workers in Lawrence, Massachusetts "adopted the European practice of sending their children to families out of town" (Juravich, Hartford, and Green

83). This practice conserved resources for the workers and kept their children safe. Some of the strikers' children were sent to Barre. In a personal interview with Barre citizen, Alma Bianchi Fisher (Ms. Fisher), she recalled a photograph of the Lawrence children that was sent to their parents to reassure the strikers that their children were safe. [Picture 2] The fact that Barre was selected as a safe harbor for the children of the "Bread and Roses" strikers underscores its prominence in the labor community, despite its tiny size, as most of the children were sent to big urban centers such as New York and Philadelphia (Juravich, Hartford, and Green 86).

The Barre workers were called upon to assist in other labor causes as well. In his personal interview, Mr. Granai recalled that in the 1920s, the lawyer for Nicola Sacco and Bartolomeo Vanzetti, who were followers of Galleani, came to Barre to raise money for their murder trial.

Another visitor to Barre, William D. Haywood, the head of the radical labor organization, the Industrial Workers of the World (the Wobblies), observed that "the Italians have through force of character taken a place in the front ranks of the revolutionary [union] movement" (Buhle 270).

Thus, the Barre Italians were a sophisticated, literate people with a good grasp of the radical union principles who could attract the attention of union activists of national stature. Nevertheless, even though Bodnar would have predicted that only unskilled and uneducated immigrants would reject a working-class consciousness in favor of ethnic consciousness, the Barre Italians also preferred their own social institutions and politics to the organized Barre unions:

> Italian class-consciousness sought expression in areas where Italians could organize [as an ethnic group], to improve the Barre Italian community through mutual aid. As such, these efforts generally were not predicated or based on the organization of the granite workers as granite workers..." (Serota-Winston 34)

For example, the Barre Italians started a mutual aid group called the Mutuo Succorso. The Mutuo Succorso hosted many radical speakers as well as fundraisers and dances every week. In her personal interview, Ms. Fisher confirmed there was no connection between

"Mutuo" and the unions. The Mutuo was "just a separate Italian lodge, like the Elks, you know... they used to pay you so much when you were sick." Ms. Fisher recalls attending Mutuo picnics, dances and a winter banquet that would be attended by the whole family. [Picture 3] Another social institution organized at the time was sports teams, including a semi-professional baseball team (McNeil 66). Two former Italian stone cutters even went on to play professional baseball with the New York Yankees (McNeil 66).

Another important center of social activity for Barre Italians was the Socialist Block, upon which was located a large hall called the Granite Hall. The Granite Hall housed food co-operatives where the Italians shopped. In a personal interview with Barre citizen Bella Webster, she remembers that she "used to go down and get Gorgonzola cheese."

Part of the adherence to an ethnic consciousness, as opposed to an economically-driven class consciousness, was intentional and was derived from the uncompromisingly, radical philosophy left over from the repression the Italian workers had suffered in Italy. These Old World grudges were carried by the Galleanists who "forswore permanent organization, and defended individual violence against tyrants, and continually called for general strikes and labor uprisings" (Buhle 273). Mr. Granai commented that the Barre radicals were "radicals against the government; not the American government but where they came from; they were anti-monarchy, anti-clerical, anti-padrone (boss)." This distrust of permanent organizations was not limited to the owners of the sheds, but extended to Scottish leadership of the unions, as well. Paul Buhle, who studied the failure of the union movement among radical Italian workers at the turn of the century in Westerly, Rhode Island, observed a similar distrust by Italian radicals of mainstream union participants:

> The radicals had been unable to make the turn away from the old ultra-radicalism to a more calculated politics... The continuing isolation of the self-styled revolutionary vanguard led to a sense of absolute distance from the majority who followed the orders of the factory owner. (287)

There was, however, another reason for the Italians' failure to assimilate into a working-class community; this was the racism they suffered. In his case study of workers in the steel mills of Steelton, Pennsylvania in the early twentieth century, Bodnar observed that while the immigrants did not make an effort to assimilate, it would have been nearly impossible, anyway, due to the fact that the "Old Stock" Anglo-Saxon elite, employers and union leaders alike, were threatened by the new comers and openly shunned them (Bodnar, *Immigration* 76). Racial epithets were common (Bodnar, *Immigration* 77-78). This was so in Barre, as well. Ms. Fisher recalled that Saturday night dances at the Granite Hall were called "Guinea Hops." "They used to call [us] Guineas. Have you ever heard of that?"

Some examples of racism are not so amusing. One of these examples is the silicosis epidemic that plagued the Italian granite workers. Virtually every Italian man in Barre worked in the granite quarries. [Picture 4] The cold Vermont climate made it impossible for the stonecutters to work outside, as they had in Italy, so they were forced to do all of their work inside. The fact that the workers were forced indoors, along with the use of new pneumatic tools, made the deadly granite dust more abundant in American sheds than it had been in the Italian workplace (Richardson 7). It was consistently announced by the Anglo-Saxon establishment, however, that the reason for the illness was the poor hygiene of the Italian workers. The working conditions in the sheds, for which the shed owners would be responsible, were not blamed (Richardson 13). It was also published in local magazines that tuberculosis was found in the homes of those who were "poor and careless" (Richardson 14). The view that it was the workers' sloppy habits that caused silicosis was discarded in 1909 by a Barre doctor, D.C. Jarvis, who concluded that the disease that the cutters were victim of was a form of tuberculosis caused by the granite dust (Richardson 17). While the medical view was more enlightened, the prejudice remained, however. Dr. Jarvis recommended that the shed owners conduct mandatory medical examinations of the workers in order to differentiate between those nationalities that would fall prey to the disease and those that wouldn't. Employers did not want to invest time in a worker who would get sick and not be able to work (Richardson 17). With no medical basis for his opinion, Jarvis concluded that Italians, more than any other nationality, were able to withstand the disease (Richardson 17). Jarvis also preached that the dust settled into the lungs of the workers and caused an "adaptation" in the respiratory tract. He said that if the workers were idle due to striking, they would lose this "adaptation" and would be more likely to develop tuberculosis when they returned to the quarries (Richardson 20). The racist views held by the native-born ruling class guaranteed that practically every Italian "pneumatic tool operator could be expected to develop the disease after fifteen years of exposure to granite dust" (Rosner 43). Certainly, by refusing to take measures to stamp out silicosis, the ruling class in Barre ensured that this widespread, deadly illness would render the Italians physically and emotionally unable to take charge of the political processes in the town. [Picture 5]

The Italians' ethnic consciousness as opposed to a general working class consciousness is most dramatically illustrated by the strike of 1915. The Italians thought unions were important as a moral force, not an economic one. The Italian view of the philosophical differences between the Italian approach to the strike and that of the Scottish union leadership was stated in an October 5, 1915 edition of the Italian syndicalist journal *Lo Scalpellino* (The Stonecutter) published in Barre:

> What enormous difference exists between this American proletariat and the Italian one... the Italian goes on strike through solidarity, without a penny compensation but only because he feels that his generous hearts beat together with those of the rest of the exploited... But has the other proletariat, the American one, ever seen to hold a strike of solidarity. Never!

While the leadership of the union was eventually willing to accept the management proposal, the Italians were not satisfied and insisted that the union's acceptance of the proposal be by a show of hands (Serota-Wilson 43). The show of hands vote appealed to the Italians because they believed in public individual accountability and strongly distrusted the labor leaders and felt that with the public vote, there was less of a chance for the labor leaders to unfairly influence the outcome. The union leadership insisted upon holding a secret ballot vote. The Italians were so angry, 1,000 of them marched on the Barre Opera House where the vote was being taken, stole the ballot box and ran off with it (Serota-Wilson 43). [Picture 6] However, this did not prevent the other union members from acting. The vote was held anyway without the input of the Italians, and the management proposal carried.

Although it was natural and comfortable for the Barre Italians to revert to familiar customs in the face of a somewhat hostile new home, refusing assimilation hurt them in the end. The Italians refused to take part in the union process and, by doing this, they never took advantage of the opportunity to give input into any decisions the union, or those in charge of Barre politics, made. Thus, decisions about the Italians' own working and living conditions were made without them.

There are people in the world presently who decide not to vote because they disapprove of the government. However, by not participating in the existing political process, they do not make a difference in the government about which they are complaining.

ILLUSTRATIONS

Picture 1

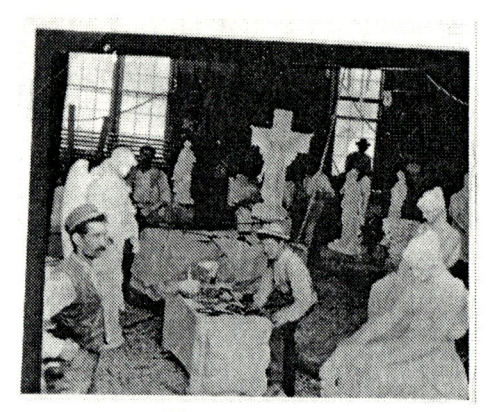

Picture 1A

Picture 2

Picture 3

Picture 5

Picture 6

Picture 7

Picture 8

Picture 9

Picture 10

Picture 11

Picture 12

Picture 13

Picture 14

References

Books

Avrich, Paul. *Anarchist Voices.* Princeton: Princeton UP, 1994.

Bodnar, John. *Immigration and Industrialization: Ethnicity in an American Mill Town, 1870-1940.* Pittsburgh: U of Pittsburgh P, 1977.

___. *Workers' World: Kinship, Community, and Protest in an Industrial Society, 1900-1940.* Baltimore: Johns Hopkins UP. 1982.

Buhle, Paul. "Italian-American Radicals and Labor in Rhode Island, 1905-30." *The New England Working Class and the New Labor History*. Ed. Herbert G. Gutman and Donald H. Bell. New York: Knopf, 1976.

Gay, Kathlyn, and Martin Gay. *The Importance of Emma Goldman*. San Diego: Lucent, 1977.

Juravich, Tom, William F. Hartford, and James R. Green. *Commonwealth of Toil*. Amherst: U of Massachusetts P, 1996.

Montgomery, David. *Workers' Control in America*. Cambridge: Cambridge UP, 1987.

Rosner, David, and Gerald Markowitz. *Deadly Dust: Silicosis and the Politics of Occupational Disease in Twentieth-Century America*. Princeton: Princeton UP, 1991.

Solomon, Martha. *Emma Goldman*. Boston: Twayne, 1987.

Articles

Collins, Ben. "Barre's Labor Socialist Tradition Has Deep Roots." *The Sunday Rutland Herald and The Sunday Times Argus* 4 Sep. 1977, sec. 3: 3.

Lo Scalpellino 5 Oct. 1915.

Richardson, Wendy. "The Curse of Our Trade: Occupational Disease in a Vermont Granite Town." *Vermont Historical Society* 60.1 (1992): 5-27.

Unpublished Papers

McNeil, Charles A. "Carved From Stone? Community Life and Work in Barre, Vermont, 1900-1922." Diss. McGill U, 1989.

Serota-Winston, Jason. "I Can Laugh at the Granite: Class, Ethnicity, and Ideology Among the Scottish and Italian Stonecutters, Barre, Vermont, 1880-1915." Diss. Carleton U, 1995.

Interviews

Aldrich Public Library Oral History Project. Barre, Vermont.

Fisher, Alma Bianchi. Personal interview. 27 June 1978.

Granai, Cornelius Sr. Personal interview. 7 April 1978.

Webster, Bella. Personal interview. 17 Aug. 1976.

Other

Falk, Candace. "Emma Goldman: A Guide to Her Life and Documentary Sources." *Emma Goldman Papers*. 53 p. Online. Berkeley Digital Lib. Internet. (undated). Available: http://sunsite.berkeley.edu.

Roman Naval Operations
During the Second Macedonian War

Valentino J. Belfiglio
TEXAS WOMAN'S UNIVERSITY

> "Come over into Macedonia, and help us."
> Holy Bible, *The Acts of the Apostles*, xvi. 9

INTRODUCTION

After the Second Punic War (219-202 BC), Rome controlled Corsica, Sicily, Sardinia, Further Spain, Hither Spain, and Africa. The army of Philip V of Macedonia, in alliance with the military forces of Antiochus III of Seleucid, Syria was one of the last barriers to Roman domination of the Mediterranean. After the indecisive First Macedonian War (215-205 BC), Philip moved to control Greece, Thrace, and the Aegean coast of Asia Minor. Many Roman Senators felt that Philip had not been sufficiently punished for his alliance with Hannibal. Others saw a war with Macedonia as an opportunity to plunder and refill the treasury of Rome. Rome responded to appeals for help from Pergamum, Rhodes, and Athens by declaring war on Macedonia in 200 BC. The official pretext for entering the war was the protection of Greek states from Macedonian imperialism.[1] Nabis, king of Sparta, allied with Philip and conflict erupted.[2]

THE BATTLE OF CHIOS

During autumn of 201 BC, the combined fleets of Pergamum and Rhodes had engaged the Macedonian navy in a battle off Chios, an Aegean island five miles west of Asia Minor. Philip's ships, commanded by Admiral Democrates, consisted of 53 warships and 150 galleys. The enemy had 53 warships and an undisclosed number of other vessels, commanded by King Attalus I of Pergamum, and Admiral Theophiliscus of Rhodes. The antagonists relied primarily upon the tactic of ramming enemy warships. The superior seamanship of the Rhodians

---

[1] Charles Freeman, *Egypt, Greece and Rome: Civilizations of the Ancient Mediterrancean* (New York: Oxford UP, 1996), 327.
[2] Victor Duruy, *History of Rome, and of the Roman People* (Boston: Estes and Lauriat, 1884), 78-90.

gave the allies a victory; and Philip lost nearly half of his fleet. Thus, the allies of Rome paved the way for Roman domination of the sea lanes around Greece.[3]

ROME MOVES TO CONTROL THE SEAS BORDERING GREECE

Roman leaders had learned during the First Punic War (264-241 BC), that control over the seas, and especially of strategically important narrow waterways, was crucial to the defeat of Carthage. They would use the same strategy in their war with Macedonia. In preparation for war Propraetor Marcus Valerius Laevinius deployed 38 ships from Vibo, a town on the coast of Bruttium in Italy, and sailed to Macedonia in 201 BC.[4] After a Declaration of War by the Roman Senate in 200 BC, Consul Publius Sulpicius set sail from Brundisium towards the end of autumn with two legions, and arrived in Macedonia two days later. He ordered Legatus Gaius Claudius Cento to sail to Athens with 20 warships and 1,000 soldiers.[5] Sulpicius established his base of operations at Apollonia, a town in north Epirus, and spent the winter there. Meanwhile, Cento secured the island of Corcyra, located in the Ionian Sea near the coast of Epirus. From there he and his forces cruised to Piraeus, the port of Athens in east central Greece, and took control of this important waterway.[6]

During the summer, a fleet commanded by Legate Lucius Apustius, left Corcyra, rounded Cape Malea, and joined Attalus off Syllaeum, in the region of Hermione.[7] The fleets of Apustius and Attalus set out on a series of amphibious raids and assaults against Andros, Cythnos, the lands of the Carystii, Cassandrea, and Acanthus. After the execution of these naval operations, they situated their main fleets at Euboea, an Aegean island in east central Greece, north of Attica.[8] Troops from Rome, Pergamum and Rhodes laid siege to and captured Oreus on the northwest part of the island. It was around September 23, and the end of the sailing season. The allied naval forces

---

[3] Polybius, *The Histories*, trans. W.R. Paton (London: Heinemann, 1926), 16.2-10.
[4] Livy, *History of Rome*, trans. B.O. Foster, E.T. Sage, and A.C. Schlesinger, Books 31-35 (Cambridge, MA: Harvard UP, 1919-1957), 31.3.8-10.
[5] Livy, *History of Rome*, 31.8.16-17; 31.14.5-9; 32.16; 32.19.6-8; 32.23.
[6] Livy, *History of Rome*, 31.22.9-16.
[7] Livy, *History of Rome*, 31.44.1-5.
[8] Livy, *History of Rome*, 31.45.

returned to Piraeus and Corcyra to pass the winter and plan for a spring campaign.[9]

On March 15, 199 BC, the Roman Senate appointed Publius Villius as consul, and authorized him to take command of the army of Sulpicius in Macedonia.[10] Titus Livius (Livy) wrote that Philip was already experiencing concern over "the constant pressure of the enemy by land and sea."[11] The Macedonian king acted to strengthen his alliance with the Achaeans, and to fortify strategic passes in northern Epirus.[12] A year of inconclusive operations followed. During the winter of 198 BC, Titus Quinctius Flaminius became consul; and the Senate placed him in charge of the Macedonian campaign.[13]

ROME LAUNCHES A MAJOR OFFENSIVE

While Roman forces engaged Philip's militia in a series of skirmishes, raids, and diversionary operations between 200 and 198 BC, the navies of Rome and its allies gained control of strategically important narrow waterways in the Ionian and Aegean seas in and around Greece. The Roman military then prepared to launch a major invasion of Macedonia. The commander the Senate chose for this task was Titus Flaminius, a very able general. He had served with valor and distinction as a tribune in the war against Hannibal, under Consul Marcus Marcellus.[14] Titus possessed extraordinary diplomatic skills. Plutarch wrote that he was a man of "persuasion and friendly intercourse."[15] Titus received permission from the Senate to give command of the Roman fleet to his brother, Lucius Flaminus. Lucius had served as *curule aedile* (patrician aedile) in 200 BC, and as *praetor* (judicial magistrate) in 199 BC.[16]

In 198 BC, a Roman assault force of 8,000 infantry, and 800 cavalry, assembled at Brundisium and sailed to Corcyra. After arrival, Titus cruised to Epirus in a quinquereme and traveled on land to the

---

[9] Livy, *History of Rome*, 31.46-47.
[10] Livy, *History of Rome*, 32.1.3, 6-8.
[11] Livy, *History of Rome*, 32.5.6.
[12] Livy, *History of Rome*, 32.5.
[13] Livy, *History of Rome*, 32.6.13-15.
[14] Plutarch, "Titus Flaminius," *Plutarch's Lives*, trans. Bernadotte Perrin (London: Heinemann, 1921), 1.28-30.
[15] Plutarch, "Titus Flaminius," 2.21-22.
[16] Plutarch, "Titus Flaminius," 3.17-19.

Roman camp.[17] Meanwhile, Lucius rendezvoused with the fleets of Attalus and Acesimbrotus – admiral of the Rhodian navy. The entire flotilla of 82 warships laid siege to and took possession of the city of Eretria in south central Euboea. After subduing all of Euboea, the allied navy returned to the west coast of Greece to conduct an amphibious raid of Cenchreae, the harbor of Corinth.[18] One of Lucius's greatest contributions to the war effort was persuading the Achaean League, a confederation of 10 principal cities in north Peloponnesus on the Gulf of Corinth, to side with the Romans.[19]

In the meantime, Titus made Epirus his base of operations, and prepared to cross the Pindus mountains and invade Macedonia. During the summer a shepherd showed him a path around Philip's position through a gorge of the Aous River.[20] The Roman general moved his army through the path, to outflank the Macedonian army, and attacked them from behind. The Romans killed 2,000 men and drove the rest into Thessaly.[21] Flaminius's legions pursued their enemy and overran Thessaly and Central Greece. However, they made little progress against towns held by Macedonian garrisons, while Philip's army conducted forced, retrograde operations.[22] Nevertheless, Roman land and naval forces had made significant gains as both armies settled down for the winter.

In 197 BC, the Roman Senate directed Titus and Lucius Flaminius to continue their campaign against Macedonia. With the war going badly for him, Philip attempted to gain some advantages through diplomacy. Titus and Philip met on the shore of the Malian gulf near Nicaea during the winter for three days of negotiations. The Roman commander was in no mood to compromise. He issued an ultimatum: "The king must withdraw his garrisons from all the states of Greece, give back the captives and deserters to the allies of the Roman people, and restore to the Romans those districts of Illyricum which had been seized after the conclusion of peace in Episus."[23] Philip refused to

---

[17] Livy, *History of Rome*, 32.9.20-24.
[18] Dio Cassius Cocceianus, *Roman History*, trans. Earnest Cary (London: Heinemann, 1917), 18.16.16-31.
[19] Dio, *History of Rome*, 18.16.16-31.
[20] Livy, *History of Rome*, 32.11.1-7.
[21] Livy, *History of Rome*, 32.12.
[22] Livy, *History of Rome*, 32.15, 18, 25.
[23] Livy, *History of Rome*, 32.33.7-10.

abide by these terms. He and Titus then sent representatives to Rome to appeal to the Senate. The Senate refused all efforts of compromise, and dismissed the king's delegates: the war would continue.[24]

Bent upon a strategy of *divide et empera* (divide and rule), Titus met with Nabis, the Spartan king, at Mycenica. He persuaded Nabis to sever the Spartan alliance with Macedonia. The Spartan king also agreed to supply 600 Cretans for the Roman army.[25] Then Titus went to Thebes and forged an alliance with Boeotia.[26] Philip was then in a desperate situation. He had suffered heavy casualties in his war with the Romans.[27] With the Macedonian army reduced to 26,000 men, and increasing odds against him, Philip decided to take the risks of a decisive battle. He reentered Thessaly and forced an encounter on the field of Cynoscephalae.

THE BATTLE OF CYNOSCEPHALAE

Roman and Macedonian officers ordered an arrangement of their troops for combat. The center of gravity of the Macedonian army was its phalanx of 16,000 men.[28] Its critical vulnerability was a lack of flexibility. The center of gravity of the Roman army was its two legions. Its critical vulnerability was long logistics routes and lines of communication with Brundisium.[29] Both armies were equal in strength – about 26,000 each.[30]

The day of the battle was foggy, and the terrain uneven. The Macedonian army held the high ground. Skirmishing units of cavalry and light-armored infantry clashed in the mist to gain tactical intelligence-information required for planning tactical operations. Macedonian soldiers had an edge in the fighting until Roman forces pushed back their lines. Philip's cavalry and mercenaries entered the fray, and the Romans conducted a withdrawal. The main armies then made movements to contact. The Macedonian phalanx and Philip's Thracian allies engaged the rightward Roman legion. Titus ordered the legion to hold its ground and led the left wing of his army and allied

---

[24] Livy, *History of Rome*, 32.7.12-13.
[25] Livy, *History of Rome*, 32.40.11-13.
[26] Livy, *History of Rome*, 33.2.11-15.
[27] Livy, *History of Rome*, 33.3.6-8.
[28] Livy, *History of Rome*, 33.4.10-11.
[29] Dio, *Roman History*, 18.1-2.
[30] Plutarch, "Titus Flaminius," 7.14-17.

forces to relieve his lightly armored troops. Light infantry on both sides retired through their lines.[31]

The two armies reorganized for the decisive engagement. Philip ordered his phalanx and peltasts to double depth, halving its front to leave room for his left wing, which hastened up in column. With uproarious shouts and cries, the Macedonian army thrust downhill to force back the Roman lines. The tightly packed Macedonian pikemen could move in only one direction – forward. Philip's left wing deployed across a ridge. Titus ordered his rightward legion and 20 elephants to attack. The Romans used smaller, more mobile units. They exploited gaps in the phalanx. Once inside, they bumped their enemies with their large shields, and thrust with their short swords. The spectacle was terrifying and exhilarating. The Macedonian left wing foundered, but the Roman left was losing ground. Seeing this, a tribune led 20 maniples (3,200 men) and attacked the phalanx from behind. The phalanx broke down; and the Macedonians retreated. The Romans executed exploitation and pursuit. They killed 8,000 of the enemy, captured 5,000, and suffered 700 casualties.[32]

THE AFTERMATH

The peace terms included the loss of most of Philip's navy, payment of 1,000 talents of silver to Rome, and the loss of all Macedonian territories outside of Macedonia.[33] Rome subsequently established a benevolent protectorate over Greece. Philip's son and successsor, Perseus, formed alliances with several Greek city-states, and aroused the displeasure of Roman officials. The Third Macedonian War (171-168 BC), ended when the Roman army of Lucius Aemilius Paullus defeated Perseus's forces at the Battle of Pydna. Finally, the Roman praeter Quintus Metellus crushed a Macedonian rebellion in 148 BC. Two years later, Macedonia became a Roman province, and Roman culture began to displace Greek culture throughout the Mediterranean region.[34]

---

[31] Polybius, *The Histories*, 18.21-23.
[32] Polybius, *The Histories*, 18.24-27; Livy, *History of Rome*, 33.7-10.
[33] Appian, *Wars of the Romans*, trans. Horace White (London: Heinemann, 1912), 9.3.
[34] M. Cary, *A History of the Greek World From 323 to 146 BC* (London: Methuen, 1951), 200-05.

CONCLUSION

During the Second Macedonian War, Philip's army was the primary strategic objective of Roman military operations. The land forces of Titus Flaminius and Rome's allies were critical for victory. So too were the diplomatic successes of Titus and Lucius Flaminius in manipulating the balance of power against Philip's regime by organizing hostile coalitions among his Greek neighbors. However, Roman command of the sea through naval superiority was a significant factor that many have not been sufficiently appreciated. Roman mastery of the Greek shores and strategic waterways of the Aegean and Ionian seas was important to the maintenance of logistical lines of communication with Brundisium. Tactical maneuvers by the Roman navy also prevented the strategic deployment of the Macedonian navy. Philip's fleet had been so weakened during the naval battle near Chios that it did not often venture from its fortified base at Demetrias. Allied ships sailed freely, protected allied trade, and brought supplies by sea to the nearest points where they could be utilized by the legionnaires. How different the outcome might have been if the Macedonian navy controlled the seas, and Philip was able to invade Italy.

Titus Flaminius was a man of great military ability, consummate tact, and a skillful diplomat. An artisan engraved his likeness on a Roman coin after the war. The depiction has a jutting chin covered by a trim beard. Its intense eyes beneath wavy hair, rugged features, and Roman nose give an impression of physical and emotional strength. What a face! Titus seems determined and stalwart-ready for anything which might confront him on the battlefield. The image engenders an aura of old-Roman virtues – *gravitas* (seriousness), *dignitas* (dignity), and *fides* (trust).

Nevertheless, Titus's campaign lacked the amphibious strategy of Scipio Africanus Major's operations during the Second Punic War. Scipio conducted a well-planned amphibious assault of Utica, in north Africa, in 204 BC.[35] Unlike Scipio, Titus deployed his army and navy independently of one another. Roman forces could have opened a second front against the Macedonians through a carefully coordinated, synchronized attack; employing naval surface fire, ship-to-shore

---

[35]Valentino J. Belfiglio, "Ancient Roman Amphibious and Offensive Sea-Ground Task Force Operations," *Military and Naval History Journal* 5 (March 1997): 11-18.

movement, landings, operations inland, and assault from ground forces against Pydna.[36] Roman forces then could have moved along the Axius or Haliacmon rivers to confront the Macedonian army in a pincer attack from the southwest and southeast.

---

[36] Pydna – a town in southern Macedonia, near the Gulf of Thermaic.

Italian American Voting Preferences

William Egelman
William Gratzer
IONA COLLEGE

Brian Nickerson
PACE UNIVERSITY

Michael D'Angelo
ROCKLAND COUNTY, DEPARTMENT OF PLANNING

INTRODUCTION

Assimilation involves adapting to a variety of institutional settings in the area of destination. These include adapting to the economic, the social, and the political environment. This paper will first examine the political adaptation of Italian immigrants to the American political system and develop some expectations or hypotheses about their political preferences. The next section of the paper presents collected data regarding Italian American political preferences in Westchester County, New York.

The major period of Italian immigration to the United States was from the mid-1880s until approximately 1930. While some of the immigrants were from northern Italy and came from middle class and even upper class backgrounds, most Italian immigrants came from the Mezzogiorno, that area of Italy south of Rome. Most of these immigrants were from the lower end of the social class spectrum. Some were skilled artisans, but many were of peasant background.

The southern Italy they came from was still largely a feudal state in the nineteenth century. There was little tradition of participatory democracy. Southern Italy had a long history of being ruled by foreign powers, and after the Risorgimento, by the political élites of the northern Italy. Therefore, the immigrants arrived with little background or understanding of the American brand of politics. In addition, unlike the earlier Irish immigrants, the Italians arrived without knowledge of English. Both factors contributed to their relatively slow adaptation to the American political process. A third factor may be added. Many Italian immigrants were "birds of passage." They arrived, planned to stay a relatively short period of time, and then, they would return to Italy. Such a pattern would not involve a long-term investment in American society. Many immigrants did not intend to make the United States their home. Therefore, any thought of political involvement would have been pointless (see LaGumina, 2000; Lopreato, 1970).

For those who did intend to stay, there was a fourth factor that may have contributed to their slow integration into the political system, and that was the immediate economic exigencies that existed. Many of the Italian immigrants fit the classic image of the immigrant. They were poor and largely uneducated. They took jobs at the lowest end of the economic ladder. Michael Eula (1993) points out that during the early period of immigration most of the immigrants were in unskilled or semi-skilled work categories. They were more concerned with surviving than with getting ahead. For them, the major concern was living day by day. Mangione and Morreale (1992) make a similar point when they note that the Italian immigrants did much of the "dirty work." This dirty work "entailed a variety of unskilled jobs such as sewer laying, tunneling, subway construction, street grading, general construction, and street cleaning…" (138-39). The overall concern with economic survival was a major factor in limiting the interest in politics.

A fifth factor that may have contributed to the slow process of political assimilation was the lack of a cohesive group identity (see Sowell, 1981:128). Italy, as a nation-state, was formed in the latter part of the nineteenth century. In Italy itself, individuals did not generally identify with the nation-state; rather, their identities were tied to family, village, and perhaps region. Ironically, these immigrants became "Italian" in the immigration process. That is, others came to see them as Italian, being ignorant of the regional diversity of the newcomers. This Italian identity took root in the United States when it never existed in Italy. This lack of a cohesive identity served as a barrier for the formation of a true ethnic voting bloc. Unlike the Irish, and their fellow immigrants the Jews, the Italians were somewhat slow to realize the efficacy of ethnic politics.

Another factor that may have played a role in the slow process of political assimilation was the role of the ethnic community. While all ethnic-immigrants groups formed their own ethnic neighborhoods, Italian immigrants tended to remain in their neighborhoods for a longer period of time than did other European immigrant groups. The ethnic neighborhood did serve as a buffer between the immigrant and the new and dramatically different society called America. Within the community, the immigrant could find housing, jobs, and everyday social intercourse. More so than other European groups, the Italians' social world came to be embedded in the community. There was little need to look outward. Therefore, interest in or concern for politics, in the larger sense of the term, or in the larger political realm, that lying outside the community was generally lacking.

Aguirre and Turner (1998: 215-16) point out another factor that limited access to the political process. They argue that in addition to the economic issues, and the general lack of trust of government, Italian immigrants also faced a certain degree of discrimination. Anti-immigrant feelings coupled with anti-Catholic feelings may have inhibited Italian American participation, at least on a national level. This was not entirely true with respect to their role in local politics where a number of Italian Americans held public office prior to World War II. The authors go on to suggest that the national antipathy toward Italian American office holders is on the wane, and since World War II there is a greater presence of Italian Americans on the national level.

On the local level, however, many urban politicians came to view immigrants as a new and potentially powerful source of votes. New immigrants, including Italians, were mobilized politically and eventually became one of the primary components of the "urban ethnics" who were a foundation of the Democratic Party coalition that President Franklin D. Roosevelt forged in the 1930s (Janda, 2000: 148). As part of this new and powerful political force, Italians as well as other ethnic immigrants often supported more liberal causes and candidates than traditional Anglo-Saxons (Glazer, 1988: 4).

As with other groups, Italian Americans seem unable to resist the powerful forces of assimilation. Over time, Italian Americans came to be political in the same manner as did the descendents of other immigrant groups. Along with educational change, shifting occupational patterns, and a slow dispersion from the urban ethnic neighborhoods of settlement, Italian Americans have come more and more to resemble the larger American population (see Egelman, 2000). Recent studies of public opinion demonstrate that the attachments of the "old" ethnicity of early immigrants, particularly Democratic Party affiliation and support of liberal conciliates and causes, is giving way to "new" ethnicity based on race whereby descendents of Italian immigrants are becoming more conservative in their political preferences (see Erikson, 1998).

Consequently, based upon the Italian American experience with immigration and eventual assimilation, several hypotheses concerning the political and voting preferences of today's Italian Americans can be formulated. First, although historically associated with the Democratic Party, it is plausible that assimilation has resulted in Italian Americans identifying with the Republican Party and supporting its candidates. Second, Italian Americans should also identify more conservative social issues – crime, and the state of the economy – as more pressing than other liberally oriented issues, such as the environment and health care.

THE STUDY

In order to examine Italian American political attitudes this paper will utilize data drawn from the *Iona College Center for Social Research*. Once a year the Center undertakes a survey of Westchester County residents. Westchester County is a relatively wealthy suburban county bordering on New York City in the State of New York.

In October 2000, 614 randomly selected subjects were asked a variety of questions including questions on political affiliation and voting preferences. It is these data that will serve as the basis for our analysis of Italian American voting preferences. Of the 614 subjects surveyed, 119, or 19.4 percent of the total sample, identified themselves as Italian American. Thirty-two percent of the sample was male, and 68 percent were female. This distribution was practically the same for Italians and non-Italians (non-Italians were 33 percent male and 67 percent female). The educational achievement levels were much higher for both groups than for the nation overall. Fifty-eight percent of the non-Italians and 39 percent of the Italians had at least a college diploma. The age distribution for both groups had a similar profile with Italian Americans having a slightly more aged population (see Table 1).

Table 1: Age Distribution of Italian and non-Italians

Age	Italian	Non-Italian
18-29	13.4	13.9
30-49	39.5	43.0
50-64	24.4	26.1
65 and over	22.7	14.9
No Response		2.0
Total	100.0 (119)	100.0 (495)

The Italian Americans in Westchester County have a larger percent affiliated in the Republican Party than those who affiliate with the Democratic Party. Table 2 presents data on the political affiliation of the sample.

Table 2: Party Affiliation by Political Party

Political Affiliation	Italians	Non-Italians
Democratic	26.3	42.8
Republican	37.3	19.6
Independent	11.9	13.5
None	16.9	11.7
Other	3.4	2.0
No Response	4.2	10.3
Total	100.0 (118)	100.0 (495)

While two out of five non-Italian persons are affiliated with the Democratic Party, for Italians it is about one out of four persons. Traditionally, Italian Americans have been seen as part of the urban working classes that have strong linkages to the Democratic Party. These data may reflect changes that come about with the suburbanization of urban-ethnic communities. As ethnic-immigrant groups experience the assimilation process, with greater levels of educational attainment, and with it the accompanying increase in occupational status and income there appears to be a move away from their working class roots and movement toward a more conservative ideology.

This change seems to be reflected in their preferences for presidential candidates. Table 3 presents data on presidential preferences for the two major candidates. While neither candidate holds a clear majority for either of the sub-samples, clearly a larger percent of Italian Americans favor George W. Bush. Only a little less than one-third of the Italian Americans would vote for Al Gore.

Table 3: Presidential Preferences*

Presidential Candidate	Italian	Non-Italian
George W. Bush	40.3	20.6
Al Gore	30.3	47.9
Undecided	21.0	14.7
Total	100.0 (119)	100.0 (495)

*Missing data are either votes for minor candidates or No Response

This preference for George Bush carries over even if one controls for sex. Table 4 presents data on voting preference by sex. Among Italian Americans, both males and females prefer Bush, although Bush is less favored by Italian females. Even in the female category, however, Italian females favor Bush at over twice the level of non-Italians, 37 percent to 15 percent, respectively. A cautionary note must be added insofar as the Italian American males sub-sample has an N of only 38.

Table 4: Presidential Voting Preferences by Ethnic Group and Sex.*

	Italian		Non-Italian	
Candidate	Male	Female	Male	Female
George W. Bush	47.4	37.0	20.4	14.7
Al Gore	23.7	33.3	34.3	40.6
Undecided	21.1	21.0	10.9	12.5

*Missing data are either votes for minor candidates or No Response

The survey also included questions on preferences for the senatorial candidates from New York. Table 5 presents data on the results of this question.

Table 5: Senate Voting Preferences by Ethnic Group: New York State

	Italian	Non-Italian
Hillary Clinton	22.7	43.0
Rick Lazio	56.3	30.3
Undecided	15.1	16.6
No Response	5.9	10.1
Total	100.0 (119)	100.0 (495)

As the data indicate, Rick Lazio is the overwhelming favorite of Italian residents. His margin is two and one-half times that of Hillary Clinton. Non-Italians favor Mrs. Clinton by almost thirteen percentage points. Lazio even outperforms Governor Bush among the Italian-Americans by some 16-percentage points.

How does gender influence this voting pattern? Table 6 reflects voting preferences by ethnic group and sex.

Table 6: Senatorial Voting Preferences by Ethnic Group and Sex: New York State

	Italian		Non-Italian	
Candidate	**Male**	**Female**	**Male**	**Female**
Hillary Clinton	15.8	25.9	44.2	42.4
Rick Lazio	65.8	51.9	34.4	28.4
Undecided	13.2	16.0	11.0	19.5
No Resp.	5.3	6.2	10.4	9.8
Total	100.0 (38)	100.0 (81)	100.0 (163)	100.0 (328)

Rick Lazio is the strongest candidate among the Italian sub-sample. For both males and females he beats Hillary Clinton by a substantial margin. Whether this is due to their Republican affiliation, their conservative views, or Lazio's Italian last name is unclear. However, Italian Americans retain a relatively stronger attachment to ethnicity than other groups and will often rely on personal identification, including ethnic surname of an individual candidate, to make political choices.

The survey also included a series of questions on political attitudes. More specifically, respondents were asked to answer the following question: "On a scale of 1 to 5, with 1 being the least concerned and 5 being the most concerned, how concerned are you with each of the following issues facing the country?" Table 7 presents data comparing the responses of Italians and non-Italians. The results include all those who responded with a 4, or a 5. These responses indicate a strong concern with the specific issue listed.

Table 7: Political attitudes for those most concerned with specific issues

Issue	Italians	Non-Italians
Crime	73.1	60.0
Education	84.9	80.2
Environment	62.2	67.9
World Affairs	53.8	55.2
Health Care	76.5	76.8
The Economy	66.4	65.3

There are no significant differences in attitudes between Italians and non-Italians with the exception of the issue of crime. It is difficult to assess why the difference in the concern for crime appears. This may be due to some vestige of concern for crime that stems from their urban past. It may be due to the specific neighborhoods within Westchester where the Italian sub-sample resides. It is possible that the Italian sub-sample reside in the more "urbanized" areas of the suburban county, areas that may have higher crime rates. This can only be inferred at this point, as the researchers did not undertake an analysis of neighborhoods. Strikingly, for all the other issues, the results are almost identical.

CONCLUSIONS

These data reflect some interesting patterns among Italian Americans. Clearly, they favor the Republican candidates over the Democratic candidates for the presidential election and the election for New York State senator. While Lazio's Italian surname may have influenced the results in his favor, the favorable vote for George Bush may indicate the influence of suburbanization, and a more conservative perspective on American politics. This appears to confirm our first hypothesis. In a largely Democratic county, more Italian Americans identify themselves as Republican than those who identify themselves as members of the Democratic Party.

The second hypothesis cannot be confirmed by the data. The only issue where Italian Americans have a greater concern is that of crime. The fact that political attitudes across a variety of issues show very little variation between Italian Americans and non-Italian Americans is perhaps the greatest clue that these data may reflect broad influences on the Italian American experience. The similarity of responses may indicate that it is the process of suburbanization that may have the greatest impact on the perception and concern with specific social issues. Along with suburbanization, these data may indicate that the process of political assimilation is well underway in the Italian American community.

References

Aguiree, Jr., Adalberto, and Jonathan Turner. *American Ethnicity: The Dynamics and Consequences of Discrimination.* 2nd ed. Boston: McGraw Hill, 1998.

Egelman, William. "Traditional Roles and Modern Work Patterns of Italian American Women in New York City." *Italian Americana* 18 (Summer 2000): 188-96.

Erikson, Robert, et. al. *American Public Opinion.* 3rd ed. New York: Macmillan, 1998

Eula, Michael J. *Between Peasant and Urban Villager: Italian Americans of New Jersey and New York: 1880-1980: The Structure of Counter Discourse.* New York: Lang, 1993.

Glazer, Nathan. "The Structure of Ethnicity." *Public Opinion* 7 (Oct./Nov. 1984): 1-15.

Janda, Kenneth, et. al. *The Challenge of Democracy.* 6th ed. Boston: Houghton-Mifflin, 2000.

LaGumina, Salvatore. "Politics." *The Italian American Experience: An Encyclopedia.* Ed. Salvatore LaGumina, et. al. New York: Garland, 2000. 480-86.

Lopreato, Joseph. *Italian Americans.* New York: Random, 1970.

Mangione, Jerre, and Ben Morreale. *La Storia: Five Centuries of Italian American Experience.* New York: Harper Collins, 1992.

Sowell, Thomas. *Ethnic America: A History.* New York: Basic Books, 1981.

Bodies of Nostalgia Shipwrecked in Mediterranean Waters: A 'Journey' from Morocco to Naples, "with Bags of Sand and Trunks Full of Fables" told by Tahar Ben Jelloun and Peppe Lanzetta

Roberta Morosini
WAKE FOREST UNIVERSITY

> "il cerchio del mondo è bello/ l'ossi-geno delle stelle/ e la poesia dei ritorni, di emigranti e di isole/cercando l'invisibile: l'appartenenza."
> (Gianmaria Testa and Pier M. Giovannone, *Il La valse d'un jour / Il valzer di un giorno*)

*L*abyrinthe des sentiments and *Albergo dei poveri*[1] are two novels by the Maghrebian writer Tahar Ben Jelloun. Both are set in Naples, but tell also of Morocco, Ben Jelloun's native country. In *Labyrinthe des sentiments,* the protagonist Garhib goes to Naples to give a conference. Here he meets Wahida, whose name means "one and only." A Moroccan who thought she would find a better life in Naples, but who has become trapped in prostitution, Wahida is the Morocco that does not change except for the new destination of the displacement of its people: once France and now Italy, but with a difference. France in fact has had rather dramatic historical ties with certain countries of emigration, and they have passed from colonization to immigration. Italy, instead, does not have this type of problem since it has changed from being a country of emigration to one of immigration and this with many illegal immigrants.[2]

Garhib's reflections are melancholic, whether they be about Morocco or about the possibility of coming to terms with one own's past and that for him is analogous to his ability to change.[3] Garhib signifi-

---

[1] Here and elsewhere I quote from the French *Labyrinthe des sentiments* (Paris: Stock, 1999) with drawings by Ernest Pignon-Ernest, and from the Italian edition of *Albergo dei poveri* (Torino: Einaudi, 1999).
[2] Tahar Ben Jelloun, *L'estrema solitudine* (Milano: Bompiani, 1999) 11-12.
[3] "History weighs on me as does the passage of time and my inability to change" says Bidoun in *Albergo dei poveri* 110. Bidoun's thoughts on the past remind one of James Joyce's character Stephen's reflection when he says "History is a nightmare from which I

cantly means exile or solitude in Arabic; he goes to Naples with the pretext of exorcising the past and he succeeds.[4] In *Albergo dei poveri*, Naples is constructed as a space where a person can exorcise the past. Bidoun, the protagonist and the writer's *alter ego*, travels to Naples in order to forget: "to leave one's home where nothing happens anymore, and to recreate Joyce's character Larbi Bennya, a Moroccan Leopold Bloom in a Moroccan version of Ulysses. But rather than Joyce's Ulysses it is the homeric hero that Bidoun's character evokes.[5] The novel is completely constructed on nostalgia and correlated themes of exile,[6] memory and the exercise of memory through the "revocation of memory" as Milan Kundera eloquently puts in *L'ignoranza*. In this novel Kundera treats themes as Ben Jelloun but in a Prague before and after Communism.[7] More explicitly than Ben Jelloun, Kundera closely links the themes of absence, nostalgia and identity to the experience of Homer's Ulysses, "the greatest adventurer of all times, but also the most nostalgic".

---

am trying to awake." Tahar Ben Jelloun's use of Joyce in his writing of *Albergo dei poveri* and *Labyrinthe des sentiments* takes two directions: a reflection on the irreversibility of time and the Homeric theme of return. I will not dwell at length on *Labyrinthe* as I have already discussed in "A Sud: tra pescatori di nuvole, cacciatori di elefanti e ladri di ricordi. Viaggio nel pianeta sottosopra con Erri De Luca e Gesualdo Bufalino. *Scrivere nella polvere: saggi su Erri De Luca* edited by Myriam S. Ruthenberg (Pisa: E.T.S., 2001).

[4] At the end of the novel, "with the very strong impression that [he] was reliving a situation identical to that of April 1967. The eternal return was not an image in a book, it was a mirror, an old mirror sending back to him a portrait of himself a few decades younger (*Labyrinthe* 146). See Morosini, "A Sud....".

[5] Stephanie Nelson, "Calypso Choice: Immortality and Heroic Striving in the *Odyssey* and *Ulysses*," *Literary Imagination, Ancient and Modern. Essays in Honor of David Grene*, ed. Todd Breyfogle (Chicago: The University of Chicago Press, 1999). One could say that the Bidoun and Garhib's vicissitudes in *Labyrinthe des sentiments*, like Bloom's, evolve around time and its irreversibility. See Nelson 79-81.

[6] For an overview of the discussion on these themes see P. Carravetta, "Viaggio," *Segnalibro.Voci da un dizionario della contemporaneità* a cura di Lucio Saviani (Napoli: Liguori, 1995) 205-256 e dello stesso autore "L'esilio come certezza. La ricerca dell'identità culturale italiana dalla rivoluzione francese ai nostri giorni," *Con/texts....* by A. Ciccarelli & P. Giordano (W. Lafayette: Bordighera, 1998) 246-83; Cristina Perissinotto, "Polo, Paolini e Venezia: riflessioni lagunari" and her notes 6 and 8 in *Looking for Nanaï* ed. by R. Morosini and A. Vitti. Accepted for publication by De Soto Press.

[7] There is no English translation of Kundera's last novel yet. I used the Italian edition translated by Giorgio Pinotti, L'ignoranza (Milano: Adelphi, 2001). I quote here and elsewhere from the Spanish edition translated from French by Beatriz de Moura, *Ignorancia* (Barcelona:Tusquets Editores, 2000) 13.

In *Albergo dei poveri*, the protagonist eloquently calls himself Bidoun in memory of a horrible 1975 voyage to Kuwait, where he discovered a camp in which the Kuwaiti government gathered illegal immigrants and those of uncertain nationality, the ones who destroyed their identification documents so as not to be expelled. They were called in Arabic the Bidoun, the 'without,' the ones without a homeland, shadows of men deprived of their identity and of their past. Bidoun, a fifty-year-old professor, lives in a tired Morocco, worn out by a wearing and asphyxiating power that has thrown the country into a state of resigned "boredom," and utterly dismayed by a marriage "without sparks," he decides to leave for Naples, as he has won a literary competition promoted by the Neapolitan Mayor Antonio Bassolino, Sant'Antonio as he ironically calls him. Ben Jelloun's story begins in Morocco, in Marrakech. From there we are led to Naples where writers from the world over have been invited to write about the city (how they have dreamed of Naples, how they see it, what they have heard). Bidoun arrives in Naples and receives a phone call from a mysterious woman who invites him to meet at the "Albergo dei poveri," the inn of the poor. This building is a great and disturbing monument to misery constructed by Charles the Third of Bourbon in 1860. It still stands today, a witness to the "the fall of utopia,"[8]

> a forgotten manuscript, or rather one that was lost in the basement of a memory full of holes, rags, and mute paper [...] of bags of dust for counting the time [...] a shelter for solitude soaked in hard liquor and bad wine, for the improbable adepts of a brotherhood of beings [...] pillaged by life, ruined before their time, deserted by glory, by love, and above all, by money, all of these things generate a society without subtlety, without tenderness, of people who insult or greet each other in an exaggerated manner, with broad gestures, as if in a theatre.[9]

---

[8] The inn was meant to host 8000 people, separated according to sex and age. It stands today as an example of what Foucault would call "existence correctionelle."As Ben Jelloun writes, the 5,600 wretches are welcomed into a place built to console the guilty conscience of a king who gave shelter to the poor so that people would overlook the luxury of his palace. Nowadays, as Fabrizio Coscia put it on occasion of an exhibition on "Il presente e la memoria," this building witnesses "the fall of utopia." See "Albergo dei poveri, utopia e tentativo di industralizzazione," *Il Mattino*. 5 Agosto 2000.
[9] *Albergo* 13.

The Parthenopean adventure of the protagonist, a new Orpheus who is told never to turn back, begins within the confines of the inn. He enters the tunnel and the dark smelly alleys of the city, where he meets a beggar "whose skin is all wrinkles, a large woman both dirty and made – up, a memory unable to remain silent." She is a Jewish woman who claims to be the mother of a Senegalese by the name of Momo, a huge man with a tiny brain. The bag lady arguably represents the feminine side of the city, a Naples that is mother, mistress, lover and the listener of all the tales of the city's derelicts:

> They arrive from the sea, from Sicily and Calabria, dressed like figurines, to disembark into chaos. They walk without paying attention. Every now and then a manhole opens up before them, and they fall into one of these holding places.[10]

In this place the woman frees them of their burdens. They arrive, heavy and vexed, they tell what has happened, tell all, without hiding anything, and they leave uplifted, often in a better state. The woman "listens, receives, grinds" and then files their stories in a box. Once they have unburdened themselves of the stories that have poisoned their existence they may forget thanks to a candy-coloured pink liquid that Momo has brought from Africa. The bag lady is the history and memory of a Naples both "dirty and turbulent," with a soul that is "fat, good, and warm." Momo is "one stowaway among the many immigrants cast off at the mercy of the currents, the ghost of a ship that continues to slip away with that little light always lit at the end of a corridor, a hope of emerging and becoming a citizen among other citizens" (*Albergo* 194). The reader learns of events through the tale that Bidoun constructs in letters he will never send, addressed to a fictious woman named Ouarda. Thanks to the strategy of the letter, Bidoun along with Ben Jelloun, offers a magical and merciless portrait not only of Naples, but also of Marrakech, Casablanca, Tangiers, and Morocco in general, so similar to the Parthenopean city that "the need of a poetry of folly and imagination should one day annex Naples to Morocco" (*Albergo* 14). However, since Ben Jelloun became familiar with Naples, after having

---

[10] *Albergo* 31- 32.

been commissioned by the Italian daily *Il Mattino* to write a series of articles on the Italian south, he has been attracted to the city because of his inability to say something about it. As the writer justly observes, to capture the smallest image of Naples one needs to be able to put oneself in many places at once. Therefore he decides to evoke the dream he had of Naples:

> One should write thus of cities where one has never been, of suspicion, the images of the history that hovers over a city, to capture the noise, the sounds, the music that rock its inhabitants, guess what keeps them in that place and not in another, describing the subterranean combinations. The unsuspected interference, the slum dwellings behind the cemeteries. Paint the portrait of the dream because every city has its own particular one. Something that belongs to it, that defines it before it is named. That manifests it, makes it felt and projects it into the intimate universe of every person.[11]

It is within the space of Naples that the story of Bidoun unfolds. The novel is not overtly about immigration, yet one finds themes dear to the author: exile, alienation, and solitude,[12] all of which make this and *Labyrinthe des sentiments* an integral part of the "nomadic texts" that characterize the repertory of Ben Jelloun and other Maghrebian writers such as Leila Sebbar.[13]

As a continuation of previous research,[14] I trace here the special role carried out by the city of Naples in *Albergo dei poveri* and how the Southern writer approaches the theme of individual and collective memory. In Ben Jelloun's pages, for the first time the city has become the difficult space for an inquiry into immigration to a "Naples the lonely that mixes its own solitude with that of all the solitudes of the

---

[11] *Albergo* 14.

[12] Among the most touching novels about solitude by Ben Jelloun there are *Reclusion solitaire* and *La plus haute des solitude* (Paris: Seuil, 1977).

[13] Winfred Woodhull points out in this respect that for Ben Jelloun, as for Abdelkebir Kathibi, "textual nomadism stands in relation to real changes in the writers'geographical location – their movement between France and the Maghreb" see "Exile," *Transfigurations of the Maghreb. Feminism, Decolonization, and Literatures* (Minneapolis: University of Minnesota Press, 1993) 89. The chapter on exile is particularly useful for considering "some of the ways real and symbolic exile and nomadism have figured in postructuralist theories."

[14] See footnote 3.

Mediterranean" as the Neapolitan writer Peppe Lanzetta eloquently describes it.[15] If it is true, as Graziella Parati writes in the Introduction to *Mediterranean Crossroads*,[16] that the common thread linking many of the immigrant writers is "the concept of the dispersion of an identity in space and time," along with, quoting from Bartowsky, "the attempt to trace a mapping of identity through dispersion in place and time," it is equally true that apart from a collection of essays on Southern Italy by Ben Jelloun and the rich repertory of Peppe Lanzetta, particularly his novels *Un Messico napoletano* (1994), *Una vita postdatata. Lampi e tuoni dal Bronx napoletano* (1998) and *Tropico di Napoli*, (2000)[17] it seems that no other works have examined not only the situation of immigrants in Naples, or tied their situation to that of under-privileged locals by means of the subtle thread of solitude. In the writings of the two authors, Naples is portrayed as a space welcoming all that is marginal: a space for the solitudes of those who arrive and can no longer leave, the immigrants, and those who could never leave:

> come quelli che vanno al Lido Costasmeralda che non ha niente della Costa Smeralda, né la Costa né lo smeraldo. Quei dannati, persi e disperati che non ne possono più e che quel nome del Lido che è stato messo apposta, li fannno chiudere gli occhi e sognare, sognare di volare. Senza passare per Olbia, senza Fiumicino, senza check-in, senza valige, solo unte borse da mare e ceste piene di termos e fette di melone.[18]

On the other hand, while Naples constitues itself as the natural setting for Lanzetta's novels, *L'albergo dei poveri* occupies a special

---

[15] Peppe Lanzetta, *Tropico di Napoli* (Milano: I Canguri/ Feltrinelli, 2000) 61.

[16] *Mediterranean crossroads. Migration literature in Italy.* Edited and with an introduction by Graziella Parati (Madison: Fairleigh Dickinson University Press, 1999) 31. Graziella Parati also quotes from Frances Bartowsky, *Travelers, Immigrants, Inmates: Essays in Estrangement* (Minneapolis: Minnesota University Press, 1995) 156.

[17] T. Ben Jelloun, *L'Ange aveugle (*Paris: Seuil, 1992). All of Lanzetta's novels have been published by Universale Economica Feltrinelli except for *Tropico di Napoli,* published by (I Canguri/Feltrinelli, 2000).

[18] Like those who go to the Lido Costasmeralda, which has nothing to do with the Costa Smeralda, neither the coast nor emeralds. Those damned, lost, and desperate ones who can't take it anymore, and that name of the beach made up on purpose, it makes them close their eyes and dream, dream of flying. Without going through Olbia or Fiumicino, no check-in, no luggage, only dirty bags and baskets full of thermoses and melon slices" *Messico Napoletano* 81.

place within Ben Jelloun's repertory, as it is the first novel that he has not set in Morocco or in the world of immigrants in France, where he has lived for the last 30 years. For the first time, the setting for Ben Jelloun's reflections on exile, uprooting, solitude and memory in the novels *L'albergo dei poveri* and *Labyrinthe des sentiments* is the city of Naples, in Southern Italy, and not Paris.

He always keeps himself between "les deux rives," Paris "une langue, un lieu pour écrire, un endroit pour vivre," ("a language, a place to write, a place to live,") and Morocco, "son poéme natal" ("his native poem")[19] as he defines it. Ben Jelloun is not only one of the most prolific North-African writers, among whom we may include Leila Sebbar, Assia Dejbar, and Abdelkebir Khatibi, but also one of the most unusual. By writing in French he has set himself "in an anomalous or 'ex-centric' position'" writes Valérie Orlando in "Being Anomalous," and justly so. Orlando claims that "writing from two perspectives – one French and one Moroccan – Ben Jelloun is forced to the peripheries of both Western and Maghrebian narrative traditions. In order to look into both narrative spheres, Ben Jelloun creates a 'third space' in which to write – a space of mediation. In weaving his narratives in this outside peripheral space, he inscribes the subjectivity of all who are abnormal: those who represent the marginalized, lost, repudiated, weak, handicapped, and different."[20]

It is worth continuing the discourse begun by Orlando, which limits itself to analysing metaphors of marginality in a study of feminine identity in francophone literature, in order to explore how Naples functions as a "third space" following Homi Bhabha's definition, and, to use terms from Deleuze and Guattari's *Thousand Plateaus*, as a "plane or space of enunciation." By "third space" one means an "interstitial place in which difference is distributed so as to allow for no opposition between the One and the Other." In this peculiar space, especially in the novels of immigrations written by immigrants, it is possible at least to problematize, if not to overcome, the notion of alterity: in Naples, the 'other' meets with the other and difference gradually fades until it becomes 'imperceptibility.' "The open, smooth

---

[19] See the book review of T. B. Jelloun, *La nuit de l'erreur*, "Les deux rives de Tahar Ben Jelloun." See the web page of the publishing house, Seuil.
[20] Valérie Orlando, "Being Anomalous," *Nomadic Voices of exile: Feminine identiy in Francophone Literature of the Maghreb* (Athens: Ohio University Press, 1999) 75.

plane of possibilities. The place of the imperceptible marks the end of all difference, duality, and otherness. It is the entity where an entity can go unnoticed, unhampered by gender, deformity, or handicap."[21]

It now remains to be explained what we mean by Deleuze's definition of the "plane of enunciation." Playing with the mythical and the real as in most of Ben Jelloun's works, among which has to be counted his novel *La nuit de l'erreur*, in *L'albergo dei poveri*, as in *L'enfant de sable*, there is a *Halqa*, a circle of storytelling, a place where the ones who live "on the fringes" as Orlando says, can speak out. It seems in fact that *Albergo* in this sense precisely repeats the pattern of *L'enfant de sable*. In this novel there is a woman who is a principal storyteller. She reads Ahmed's manuscript of Zahra, a woman obliged to behave as a man, but suddenly she disappears along with her manuscript. From this moment on, four storytellers, Salem, Amar, Fatuma and the Blind Troubador try to continue the story of Zahra by giving an ending to a tale left incomplete. Each of them represents a minority group, each is a marginalized figure in Moroccan society: Salem is black, Amar is heretic, Fatuma is an old woman who never married nor bore children, and the Troubadour is blind. In *L'albergo dei poveri* each lodger tells his or her life story, and each, once again, represents the cultural 'other', a marginalized figure in Southern Italian society. The woman of the inn is a Jew, Momo is a black Muslim who along with his tribe had come to pick tomatoes at Villa Literno. There are also a family of Gypsies, and some other socially marginalized characters.[22] Moreover, in both novels the stories are told in a marginal space, which in *L'enfant de sable* is the old part of the city, while in *Albergo* it is the inn which represents the old, the 'other' Naples, the old, subterranean, neglected part of the city. However, the similarities end here. What Orlando has demonstrated about *L'enfant de sable* may in fact be valid to a certain point for the lodgers in *Albergo*. It is undeniable that in *L'enfant de sable* "Ben Jelloun creates a metaphor in order to prove a point: to reinscribe the lost voices of the marginalized. They too must

---

[21] Gilles Deleuze and Felix Guattari, *Mille Plateaux* (Paris: Editions de Minuit, 1980) English translation by Brian Massumi, *A Thousand Plateaus* (Minneapolis: University of Minnesota Press, 1987) 76.

[22] For example: Armando is a the crazy boxer, Ilaria is a singer who lost her voice and now is obsessed by her hate for Arabs, blacks and communists; the Romano's family who could not find a house since the earthquake and others.

be given a place of enunciation – a third space – in order to mediate their individual identities."[23]

In *Albergo,* on the other hand, the inn becomes their space of enunciation not only because it is the only place where differences are imperceptible and the lodgers can all express their 'otherness' freely, but also because it is the only place where enunciation of one own's story lightens the burden of memory and guarantees its duration without destroying or erasing it. In fact it will be conserved by the fat old woman who represents the millenary memory of Naples, the devourer of stories (love stories) that she keeps in her great belly. Ben Jelloun's extreme interest in exploring the art of storytelling, as he shows also in *La nuit de l'erreur*[24] provides an answer to Orlando's unresolved doubt about the significance of the four storytellers who offer different versions of Ahmed's story in *L'enfant de sable.*[25] In *La nuit de l'erreur* Dahamne the storyteller goes from place to place to tell the anomalous story of Zina, a woman incapable of love who destroys all the men she encounters. Dahamne, hovering between myth and reality, transforms the story according to his inspiration and audience. In *Albergo,* Ben Jelloun is still experimenting with various ways of telling stories, however here he is more focused on the issue of forgetting. The inn is the eminent space of enunciation. Each time that the story is recalled, it returns to life to never again be forgotten. This is Ben Jelloun's fight against forgetfulness, cultivated by the immigrants like "Larbi the Moroccan who sells Kleenex and lighters, speaks Italian, and cultivates forgetfulness of his country" (*L'Ange aveugle* 105). Ben Jelloun moves from the need to provide the dead with a decent burial in *La remontée des cendres* to the fatal risk of losing individual and historical memory. This is a new aspect of Ben Jelloun's phenomenology of memory, a fear that he reveals in the following interview:

---

[23] Orlando ("Being anomalous" 93) continues: "Ben Jelloun tells his readers that those relegated to the peripheries of a society that is blocked by its own dogmatic rhetoric will never be guaranteed freedom of expression. They have been the bearers of aggression and injustice in a society that has been formed out of imperialism, religious dogma, ancient tradition, and sexual taboo."

[24] A. Ruth and E. Robert have explored this aspect of Ben Jelloun's narrative in "De l'oralité dans le récit benjellounien," *Le Maghreb littéraire*, 1 (1997) 35-53.

[25] Orlando ("Being anomalous" 93) says that "perhaps the most difficult aspect of Ben Jelloun's novel is determining the significance of the four storytellers who finish the story of Ahmed."

I would never have thought thirty years ago that this obsession with the memory that constitutes us, which is millenary memory, could today bring me to these young people from my country, or in any case from my sphere, who are losing their way because they have no culture and no memory behind them. [26]

Kundera[27] proposes a temporary solution to the problem of memory loss related to exile: Only by recalling one's own past can nostalgia be challenged:

For twenty years he thought only about the return but when he went back home, he finally realized that his life, his centre, his treasure was actually outside Ithaca, in those twenty years of wandering about. That treasure now was lost and he would get it back only by narrating.[28]

Kundera also recalls that during his forced sojourn among the Phaeacians, he had meticulously narrated his adventures, but on his return to Ithaca, seeing as he was not a stranger, no - one asked him to tell his story. However, "memory to work properly needs a continuous training: souvenirs run away if they are not evoked continuously in conversation amongs friends. The exiled when they get together, tell each other *ad nauseam* the same stories so that they become unforgettable."[29] Shirin Ramzanali Fazel tells us in *The Exiles*, that during the gatherings of the exiled there is a desire to speak for hours in their own language, a need to remind everyone of different things, even the flavour of foods. They cook traditional dishes. They update each other. They dream of their return....and they ask themselves painfully "How we got here......?" "For us, she says 'these gatherings are a total im-

---

[26] P. Maury, "Tahar Ben Jelloun. Deux cultures, une littérature'. *Magazine littéraire*, 329(1995) 107-11. Ben Jelloun says of immigrants that they are destined to a non-life, "what they are missing most is memory" because they have neither the memory of their country of origin nor that of their country of arrival.

[27] The same theme characterizes Kostantinos Kavafis' poem *Ithaka*. An English version of Kavafis' poems can be found in *http://users.hol.g/~barbanis/Kavafis/ithaca*

[28] *Ignorancia* 40.

[29] *Ignorancia* 39.

mersion into memory; they give us a charge that reawakens our African consciousness.'"[30]

Ben Jelloun portrays Naples as a city where one may exorcise one's past by 'exercising memory.' His dream of Naples thus takes shape:

> I dreamed of Naples with few words and few images, I invented it as one writing a story that begins with an intuition, like one who dresses a beloved woman with simple words, like one who undresses her delicately, sweetly, without her realizing that a hand is busy working over her back in search of the magical opening...[31]

"I dreamed, I invented it," he says of Naples, and yet it is so familiar, even to the most distracted traveller, this "Naples with its *bassifondi* [slum dwellings], its station on a day of wind and rain showers, huge and dirty, like the rest of the city. The sound carried by the wind, the shouts of Gypsy children running after terrified English tourists," but especially the 'piazza,' which is Piazza Garibaldi, although the writer does not explicitly say so, recognizable because it is described as "a piazza of miracles whose colours change with odours that come from afar, African spices mixed with the sweat of men who don't know where to stay, where to be forgotten" (*Albergo* 12).

Like a *Griot* whose function is to conserve and transmit, from one generation to another the historical memory of the various people,[32] I wish to tell the story of these men "who inhabit the station, who do not know where to stay, where to be forgotten,"[33] and whom Ben Jelloun has eloquently described in *L'écrivain publique* as "bodies of nostalgia" or "pilgrims of the past" as Shirin Ramzanali Fazel would call them because memories of their past crowd their mind, follow them like shadow.[34] Ben Jelloun considers a city "a multitude of bodies, me-

---

[30] Shirin Ramzanali Fazel "Far away from Mogadishu" *Mediterranean Crossroads* 156.
[31] *Albergo* 15.
[32] I learn about the *Griots* from "Hamadi's promise" by Alessandro Micheletti and Saidou Moussa Ba, *Mediterranean Crossroads*, 79- 98. About the *Griots* and their function see the note of the translator p. 9.
[33] *Albergo* 12.
[34] T. Ben Jelloun, *L'écrivain publique* (Paris: Seuil, 1983) 125. S. Ramaznali Fazel, "Far away from Mogadishu," *Mediterranean Crossroad* 153.

mories and faces"[35] and so is Naples but the importance of the body rests also in the definition of the 'body of Naples.' Besides recalling the image of Parthenope, the mermaid whose body was dashed by the waves onto the shores of the city, Ben Jelloun believes that Naples is made to deceive the enemy, to make him lose his way, to make him regret having ventured into its entrails, its dark and narrow streets"(*Labyrinthe* 130). [36] Naples is a beggar named Napolita whom he first meet at the train station where she normally lives. She is old, dirty, badly dressed, and carries a bag full of old clothes. Her messy hair make her look as though "she had just woken up from a nightmare or a long period of insomnia. Her eyes drawn, her face haggard, she was waiting for someone."[37] Travellers avoid her. Only unemployed Africans circulate around her, uncertain of what to say or propose to her. This image of the city as the body of a woman and mother bearing her children within her goes back to distant eras and ancient cities such as the Baghdad paradigmatically represented in *La remontée des cendres*.[38] It is also present in the works of Neapolitan writers such as the recent *Nel corpo di Napoli (In the Body of Naples)*.[39]

---

[35] *Labyrinthe* 11.

[36] Concerning faces, Ben Jelloun had already stated that his novels always start with human faces: "I make a poetry that stars with faces, human beings, and earth. And the word 'earth' often returns. Starting with something very concrete, very physical, I can guess what happens behind faces and bodies, but I need them" *Magazine littéraire* 110.

[37] *L'Ange aveugle* (Paris: Seuil, 1992) 189-202 and especially p. 195.

[38] Baghdad no longer has a belly/ she has opened her veins/ for a people that is hungry "Bagdad n'a plus de ventre/ elle a ouvert ses veines/pour un peuple qui a faim" 18. The passage was brought to my attention by Carolina Diglio in her "La memoria dalle ceneri. *La remontée des cendres* di Tahar Ben Jelloun" 98. *Annali Istituto Universitario Orientale di Napoli*, Sezione romanza 35.2 (1993).

[39] Giuseppe Montesano, *Nel corpo di Napoli* (Milano: Mondadori, 1999). Giuseppe Montesano, recently winner of second place in the prestigious literary premio Strega. The novel brings one unmistakably back to *Il ventre di Napoli*, the novel by Matilde Serao, and to the background theme of Ben Jelloun's novels and Peppe Lanzetta's *Messico Napoletano* and *Tropico di Napoli*, because in the body of Naples one meets the 'other' Naples, a city-world, that throws all which it believes to be infected into the caverns of its own cellar. Here into this upside-down universe where everything seems to function thanks to disorder, the protagonists of Montesano's unusual story fall in search of inexhaustible and true energy, the philosopher's stone, the mythological egg that explodes and gives birth. Burying it, they had the caverns dug under the city suck it all down. To the esoteric descent calculated and willed by this group of young people in order to liberate the senses against the selfishness of society, is opposed the chance descent of Bidoun into the inn of the poor inhabited by "bodies of nostalgia."

Another aspect of the city that strongly emerges in *L'albergo dei poveri* finds an equally strong echo in numerous novels of the Neapolitan writer Peppe Lanzetta: solitude. At the centre of his attention there are the "children of a lesser Bronx," from the title of one of his novels, the children of the 'other' Naples, the forgotten one. Those lost, damned souls include Rossa, the daughter of Secondigliano, Barra, Ponticelli, Sangiovanni, Volla, SanPietro, Patierno, Bagnoli,[40] like the protagonist of *Tropico di Napoli*, Carmine, those who listen to the music of "La Famiglia" or "'99 Posse" singing "We are all Hannibal's children," or Willy, the gay hairdresser from Pomigliano d'Arco who listens to Natalie Imbruglia sing of an America that they "see through the binoculars of their imagination" (*Tropico di Napoli* 17).[41] They dream of leaving accompanied by the notes of American songs, but it seems an impossible dream since it appears that Naples also has its Hotel Terminus, where the voyage ends, where the dream ends, where the sea does not reach, where its odours are captured by the stink of the fat belly of Naples. Because Naples has two bellies. The healthy one lies elsewhere (*Albergo* 18). Anna Maria Ortese, who, significantly, is quoted by Ben Jelloun and Peppe Lanzetta, was right: "Il mare non bagna Napoli," at least not the "unhealthy one," the 'other' Naples where the immigrants of Ben Jelloun's novels (but also the Neapolitan of the slums and its outskirts like the protagonists of Lanzetta's *Tropico di Napoli*) live. For immigrants that's Naples:

> Questa è la loro Napoli: Napoli di Domenica lunga da passare spendere consumare, Domenica di siesta, Domenica popolata solo da extracomunitari. Capoverdiani, senegalesi alla villa comunale fatta di birra Peroni già alle tre di pomeriggio, stereo e radio con cassette che diffondono musica africana, gergo stretto e si capiscono tra di loro, seduti sulle panchine, sui muretti, appartati a pomiciare dietro qualche cespuglio o a pisciare guardano il mare e sognano. Sognano,

---

[40] These are towns of the Neapolitan hinterland.
[41] Willy had been in Amsterdam the previous year and would have liked to return because "he could have done what he wanted, but in his sad eyes one could already see that Amsterdam would remain in Amsterdam and he on the privincial Pomigliano highway." (ndr. Pomigliano is a small town of the Neapolitan hinterland). Naples "lost, air that smelled of the old Alfasud [ndr: a car factory]. Nothing around, humidity that in the winter descended on the cars, making them cold even on the inside…" (*Tropico* 17)

quelli dello Zaire, dello Zambia, della Costa d'Avorio e del Pakistan. Sognano, i nuovi abitanti della città, i nuovi invasori, quelli che trovi fuori a qualunque ora del giorno, ma in particolare alle tre della domenica pomeriggio. Sognano e vendono sigarette, sognano e spacciano. Sognano e vendono cinture di finta pelle, accendini, amuleti, collanine, macumbe e finto corallo. Allineati lungo l'ultimo tratto di via Roma, per terra, uno vicino all'altro con le loro mercanzie, si fanno compagnia e si difendono dalla indifferenza della gente, impegnata in altri giri, altre corse, altre passeggiate, altri appuntamenti. Nessuno si chiede se hanno mangiato, se hanno riposato, dove dormono, da dove vengono, quanti sono, se si sono lavati, asciugati, puliti, sistemati, profumati. Nessuno ha tempo, vanno tutti di fretta, uno sguardo distratto per terra verso le formiche nere e via.[42]

For Carmela and Carmine, the protagonist of Lanzetta's *Tropico di Napoli*, Naples is:

> sera di luglio, futuro segnato, lei sigarette da vendere e qualcosa del passato da farsi perdonare e lui casini e *vitaspericolata*, senzasoldi, uno spaghetto rimediato su occhi accesi di *rabbiavitasaponeso-litudine*. *Estatesenzafine* e senza tregua di chi non si muove di casa, di chi non si può allontanare da casa, di chi non può lasciare per impicci obblighi *arrestidomiciliari* e altre sopravvivenze la casa [...]. Scende la sera su quelle due solitudini mentre dai bassi tutt'intorno

---

[42] "This is their Naples: the Naples of a long Sunday, to pass, spend, consume, a Sunday of siestas, a Sunday populated only by immigrants. From Cape Verde or Senegal, on the public common made of Peroni beer already at three in the afternoon, stereos and radios playing African music, a pure jargon they understand, sitting on the benches, the walls, off behind some bushes making out or having a pee, they look at the sea and dream. From Zaire, Zambia, the Ivory Coast or Pakistan, they dream. They dream, the new inhabitants of the city, the new invaders, the ones you can find out at any time of day, but especially at three on a Sunday afternoon. They dream and sell cigarettes, they dream and sell drugs. They dream and sell fake leather belts, lighters, amulets, necklaces, macumbas and fake coral. Lined up along the last stretch of Via Roma, on the ground, one next to the other with their merchandise, they keep each other company and defend themselves against people's indifference, people busy with other affairs, errands, walks, appointments. Nobody asks if they have eaten, or are rested, where they sleep, where they are from, how many they are, if they have washed, dried, cleaned, set themselves up, perfumed. Nobody has time, they are all in a hurry, a distracted look at the ground towards the black ants and off they go" *Messico Napoletano* 57.

arrivano odori di peperoncini e melanzane e pomodorini e basilico e frittate di cipolle, e la paella cos'è?[43]

These are the "odori dell'estate di chi non conosce altro mare che quello che non bagna e non ha mai bagnato Napoli" (*Tropico* 63) and in the background we can hear the song "Partono 'e bastimenti pe'terre assaje luntane" ("The ships leave for far-away lands"). In Lanzetta's novel this song that has accompanied the dreams of so many emigrants ironically expresses the impossible departures of some people from Naples "nelle loro sere che non passsano mai fatte di sanzare e sedie fuori al balcone" ("in their evenings that never end made of mosquitos and chairs outside on the balconies"), from a station too symbolic not to reveal its metaphorical nature in a Naples the lonely that mixes its own solitude with that of all the Mediterranean solitudes.

> E mischia colori, amori, afrori, parlate, sudori, cazzi, fesse, ferite, sangue, sperma, notti, albe, caffè, brandy, anice, rum e limoncello, mischiando Porta Capuana poi col Rettifilo da dove già si vede the railway: from which one feels, one trembles, hopes to leave, to return, and to arrive di abbracciare di scappare di spacciare di vendere di trafficare di contrabbandare di sfruttare di chiavare di sbocchinare.[44]

In an extremely concise passage Lanzetta portrays the city of Naples overcome by solitude and ironically echoes the words of Geno Pampaloni, who instead believes that "in Naples solitude does not

---

[43] "Naples, on a July evening, a marked future, she with cigarettes to sell and something in the past to be forgiven and he with rows and a recklesslife, nomoney, a scraped-up strand of spaghetti with blazing eyes *angerlifesoapsolitude*. A *summerwithoutend*, relentless, of those who never leave the house, who cannot depart, who cannot leave it because of problems obligations housearrests and other household survivals [...]. Evening falls on those two solitudes while from the tenements all around odours of hot pepper and eggplant and tomatoes and basil and onion omelettes arrive, and what's paella?"

[44] "It mixes colours, loves, stench, dialects, sweats, cocks, asses, wounds, blood, sperm, nights, dawns, coffee, brandy, anise, rum, lemon liqueur, mixing Porta Capuana with Rettifilo, from where one already sees the railway: from which one feels, one trembles, hopes to leave, to return, and to arrive to hug to escape to deal to sell to traffic to bootleg to exploit to fuck to suck."

reign.[45] Lanzetta's Naples is the city of those who do not move, here where it seems to be always summer there are no bags to be packed and the days pass losing oneself in the multitude of races: Amazon, Caribbean, tropical. People arrive here as if to heal their wounds and then stay, putting off their departure that seemed announced. It is not by chance that the theme of solitude dominates the novel and is associated with Naples seven times. All are alone in the city hit by the suffocating heat: the girl who makes love to the North African boy because he feels lonelier than she does, the Jamaican who left his native land where everyone else would run to, even the saints are alone in their empty chapels." This *city of love* is lonely, "this port where strange ships arrive, this city to love, to escape from." Here we have the meeting of solitudes: between the people of the slums and the Jamaicans, Romanians and Ugandans. Time here is measured by religious ceremonies. Coinciding with the celebrations, things happen to the poorest, the forgotten. This clearly seems to indicate that even the saints have forgot them. They are all children of this Sant'Anna, who knows, sees, looks, and permits *tuttociò,* all of this. This is how Sant'Anna is seen by those who stay, who never move, who cannot leave.

Naples the lonely and our daily railway are recurring images in the two novels of Ben Jelloun and Lanzetta's. Both the immigrants and the Neapolitans of the 'other' Naples, frequent the station, their new homeland. Lanzetta tells us of the Naples

> di chi deve prendere o lasciare
> Napoli di chi non ha scelta.
> Napoli della Costa d'Avorio, di Capoverde, di Algeri, de Il Cairo, Tunisi, Agadir.
> Napoli del Mediterraneo che affonda il suo sale sulle ferite [...]
> Napoli nostra ferrovia quotidiana.

---

[45]Solitude is a key word; the word 'solo' is repeated 23 times in *Tropico*. See p. 59-60. On Pampaloni's statement that solitude does not live in Naples see Morosini "A Plebeian Nymph in Naples" 60-61.

Partenza di anime erranti senza meta, anime perse, anime sudate, meticce, contrabbandate, anime albanesi scappate da Valona in cerca di un sogno italiano visto alla televisione.[46]

The image of the station is strictly linked to the displacement in time and space experienced by the immigrant who "comes from Africa with bags full of sand and suitcases full of maps and history books, trunks full of stories and fables. They come from the other shore, inside giant bottles tossed into the sea by their ancestors. Their faces are a century older. Their hands are long and heavy. The station is their homeland. Naples is desire and forgetfulness" (*Albergo* 17). In the same manner, the bag of sand indicates the destiny of immigrants who are seen as objects: "nothing is more anonymous than a bag of sand." They are thrown into a place that one cannot call land. In *La réclusion solitaire*, Ben Jelloun's most anguished novel on uprooting and the solitude of the immigrant, the author writes: "there is a territory where they will drop you like a bag of sand." Agnès Hafex-Ergaut points out that "the sand indicates a first dispossession of the self, which has become sand; a first derision, as sand is non-productive. To everyone else, the immigrants are bags of sand." [47] If Bidoun, like the protagonist himself, are people deprived of their identity, without dignity, the "Albergo" is definitely their shelter. Despite the undeniable similarities between *Labyrinthe des sentiments* and *L'albergo dei poveri*, in the latter Ben Jelloun offers solutions to coming to terms with one's own past, as he does in *L'enfant de sable*,[48] its worthy predecessor in this sense. In *Albergo* all of the inn's lodgers tell their life stories and thus fight forgetfulness, because their stories will be remembered forever in the memory of Naples. In the honored tradition of *The Thousand and One Nights* Ben Jelloun proposes a saving of memory through a

---

[46] "Naples of those who must take it or leave it. The Naples of those who have no choice. The Naples of the Ivory Coast, Cape Verde, Algiers, Cairo, Tunis, Agadir. Naples that rubs its salt into wounds […]. Naples, our daily railway. Departure of wandering souls without a goal. Lost souls, sweaty souls, half-breeds, bootlegged souls, Albanian souls who have escaped from Valona in search of an Italian dream seen on television" *(Tropico* 61-62).

[47] Agnès Hafez-Ergaut in "Le déracinement.' Introduction à l'étude de l'œuvre de Tahar Ben Jelloun *Revue Frontenac* 12(1995) 73. The sand returns in Ben Jelloun's novels as a reminder of the land left behind.

[48] Tahar Ben Jelloun, *L'enfant de sable* (Paris: Seuil, 1985).

storytelling that makes the Italian city a worthy sister of Marrakech. In this sense *L'albergo dei poveri* the city of Naples, takes shape as a "third space" and a "plane of enunciation."

All the lodgers of the *regium totius regni pauperum hospitium* have experienced marginality in space, but also in time. As they are only effigies of reality, all of them, even the old woman, have deformed bodies and lives and live in this enormous and grotesque construction, which looks like a Purgatory.[49] The difference from the "rest of the world," with normality, becomes "imperceptible," and it is this that makes the inn the metaphor of the 'other' Naples, the third space, where the perceptibility of difference is minimal, or rather nonexistent. *L'albergo dei poveri* is a refuge for life's castaways and a monument to solitude because to be poor means not to be loved. Here, the old woman reviews the stories of mortal love; love that deforms the body is represented and *pour cause* in the figure of Frida Kahlo,[50] whom Bidoun sees when he leaves the inn. He is disturbed by the huge reproductions of the works of Diego Rivera and Frida Kahlo projected onto the Castel dell'Ovo and the paintings of that woman whose physical pain deformed her body. Diverse and unusual objects with which the old woman surrounds herself reflects diversity, the cultural hybrid, although "imperceptible." Even the guests are 'different.' What they have in common, besides being castaways is their foreignness, their coming from different cultures and having different religions. There is a great rabbi from Anvers, Mufti from Jerusalem, the 400-metre world champion, the tailor Brahim B., the Turkish chief of chiefs, an Australian astronaut, a Russian chess player, an Irish ex-terrorist, an uninhibited singer, perhaps Bishop Tutu, accompanied by Benetton, who wants him to appear in an anti-racism advertisement.

---

[49] Obliged to remain naked, men and women together, The water was tepid, not even hot. There were men who were ashamed and covered their sex with their hands, women destroyed by life lowered their heads. Those bodies exposed in such a manner retained an element of mystery. It was impossible to imagine them as they were before. One would have said that they had always been old. Bent, ill, lifeless, without joy, without hope. [...] Men and women who walked bent over, as if they had committed a crime and found themselves there to expiate their sins. I had no desire to resemble them. They did not look at each other, they must have felt ashamed at being so humiliated, so mistreated by life... over time I learned to know some of those men and women that had taken refuge there out of desperation and solitude" *Albergo* 58.

[50] "The woman from Oaxaca," a painting by Diego Rivera, graces the cover of the Einaudi edition.

The characters that bring meaning to this novel are Momo and Ava, an Arabic-Italian interpreter. Momo represents that "parte della coorte di ombre non invitate alla festa" ("part of the cohort of shadows not invited to the party").[51] Momo is also an overgrown child who believes in a great cavern where all stories are stored: the inn of the poor, which is also a court of miracles. One evening Momo goes to an African party where he meets Malika. From this point on he is no longer himself: he changes after meeting his own people.[52] Like Bidoun and, one would say, even Ben Jelloun, Momo believes that "stories have a shelter, a sort of refuge where they are stored a bit like a cemetary, but able to be brought back when they are retold."[53] Nevertheless, for the tale of memory and necessity of storytelling to begin to make sense, one must consider the decisive meeting with Ava, which constitutes also one of the most moving pages of the novel. The character of Ava represents the collision of the African and Neapolitan souls of the city as they do in the old Jewish woman converted to Islam: Arab, Muslim, African, exotic, as old as the world, as Africa: the African-Italian mamma is Naples, "an unfaithful woman that has children scattered throughout the world.... a mix of many spices."[54] Ava is the offical translator of the congress on Islam that Bidoun is attending. She has seen in the inn of the poor in a dream and she knows it well. We then discover that she is Momo's long-lost sister. It is up to her to open the chest full of skulls shined by a group of children. Each skull is a story, because the inn is like an old library, a museum of stories. Ava pulls out a skull, the only African one. She must caress it until its memory, crossing oceans and continents, arrives and gives her images of darkest Africa. It is no coincidence that out of all the skulls she has

---

[51] For the conditions of North African immigrants in Villa Literno, a suburb of Naples see "La nuit africaine" *Ange aveugle* (Paris: Seuil, 1992) 75-97. This is a document about the shameful physical and psychological conditions in which immigrants find themselves on arriving in Naples.

[52] "It is unbelievable how one needs to congregate around common things. Momo had to re-establish contact with his ancestors. His eyes wandered, he travelled in Africa, walked through his native village, stopped under the tree of words, he was another man, different from the one we see here. The African evening had shaken him, he who always claimed to be a citizen of the world and who had gone on a hunger strike to have his papers put in order. On his temporary residence permit he had written under Profession that "he was a merchant of dreams."

[53] Remembering to fight forgetfulness brings to mind the formula of the Bis, the "Riessere" as elaborated by Gesualdo Bufalino. See my " A Sud ...."

[54] *Albergo* 91.

chosen the African one. Remembering her past she dicovers her true roots. Remembering, and having deposited her story, she also may reappropriate her roots.

The reflections on memory and the need to tell, to fight forgetfulness, central themes in Ben Jelloun's work, are here treated in tones ranging from mythic to the legendary, which is not necessarily picturesque.[55] A daughter of the South, the same one represented in the anthology *Disertori*,[56] the Naples of Ben Jelloun and Lanzetta's novels is not that of the Mediterranean fable foreseeing "an open-armed welcome to the so-called other South of the world, but the non-rhetorical one, xenophobic, as mercilessly represented by Peppe Lanzetta as well, when he speaks ironically of the "new invaders." Thanks to the characters of Momo and Ava and the old woman's vicissitudes, the reader realizes that *Albergo dei poveri* contains more than a picturesque initiation to the city. It is important to distinguish between "picturesque" and the mythic-realistic tone characterizing Ben Jelloun's works. In this novel he celebrates traces of history that "have revealed themselves as essential," and that reveal themselves among people, myths of the city and of his native land, Fez, where the author was born, Tangiers, Casablanca, Morocco, and its people. It is the occasion for Ben Jelloun to describe a Naples so similar to his native Morocco: "this Morocco, as Mohammed Khair-Eddine said, this Morocco that we love and which hurts us, this Morocco that lacks audaciousness and folly, where to live by getting along is a tradition." Ben Jelloun does not miss the occasion to denounce the sad living conditions of his compatriots in southern Italy, but without victimized or sentimental tones.[57]

---

[55] For a different interpretation see Angiola Codacci – Pisanelli, *La Repubblica*, 25.05.1999. For Codacci - Pisanelli "the man is left fascinated by the life of Naples, by chaos, passion, the happy misery of a world in which "lies are necessary, thievery is an art, laughter a will." She adds that "holding together this chaos is an old beggar woman who knows all of Naples' stories, and who gathers around her all the derelicts of the city. The result is a fascinating portrait of the city, but perhaps one that is a little too spicy for the Italian reader: because the story of a magical and miserable Naples has already been told, among others, by Anna Maria Ortese. Today one expects something more concrete and less picturesque from a novel about Bassolino's Naples."

[56] *Disertori* (Torino: Einaudi, 2000) a cura di G. Angeli. See the book review "Il profondo Sud? Una nouvelle vague" by Giordano Teodoldi in the daily newspaper *La Repubblica* 11.23. 2000.

[57] "Enough," he writes, "Enough crying over the fate of the Arabs and Muslims! I don't like it when people cry over the past," is Bidoun's reply when invited to attend a congress

Bidoun is not interested, and neither is Ben Jelloun, in crying over aspects of Morocco that cannot be changed, which he describes and condemns during his sojourn in Naples. Concerning Ben Jelloun's other books, Ergaut remarks that "solitude and physical isolation are expressed in form and in structure: everyone talks, but always to themselves or to a supposed or imagined interlocutor."[58] In *Albergo* thanks to the expedient of a letter to an outsider, Naples also becomes a place from which to observe. Therefore the city is qualified as a space of mediation, "a third space" not only for the lodgers of the inn, but also for Bidoun and Ben Jelloun. It is a privileged space from which he can look at his own country, at his own past. For Bidoun and Ben Jelloun, Naples is indeed desire and forgetfulness. It is an escape to become like Gino in the novel, a pickpocket of time. Thanks to the same strategy of the letter, Naples also becomes the "space of enunciation" for Ben Jelloun and his character Bidoun. The city becomes the discursive space of a partial identification in a frame of time that Homi Bhabha would call "a strange time," where forgetting paradoxically becomes the way to remember:

> It is through the syntax of forgetting – or being obliged to forget 'or forgetting to remember,' that the nation, peopling it anew, imagine the possibility of other contending and liberation forms of cultural identification.[59]

By sending letters to the imaginary Ouarda Ben Jelloun primes "a process of distancing." Graziella Parati finds a similar phenomenon in *Scirscir N'Demna*? ("Let's Go for a Stroll") by the immigrant writer Maria Viarengo. In both cases, as often happens in other immigrant writings " a process of distancing, of multiple unbelonging, defies any attempt at creating a definite sense of the familiar. This process is also grounded in the perception of the separation from the country of

---

on "Islam and the West: Islam, the West, Clash of Cultures, the Golden Age of the Arabs, their Decline, Petroleum, War…"

[58] Agnès Hafez-Ergaut, 'Le déracinement. Introduction à l' étude de l'œuvre de Tahar Ben Jelloun,' *Revue Frontenac* 12 (1995) 88.

[59] Homi K. Bhabha, "DissemiNation: time, narrative, and the margins of the modern nation," *Narration*, ed. H. K. Bhabha (New York: Routledge, 1990), 291- 322. I quote from p. 310-11.

origin."[60] However in Ben Jelloun's case, writing from a literary space that it is not his own does not negotiate distance on the contrary, it emphasizes the distance allowing him to look more closely and with more severity at his Morocco. He needs this leap: "Now I am elsewhere," writes Bidoun. "Let's leave the red earth of Marrakech to stop one rainy day on the edge of the Mediterranean. Yes, I've made the leap…"

But why Naples and not Marrakech? Marrakech is the southern gate of Morocco. "It is a city where the earth is red and the people hospitable, often endowed with a sense of humor. A Mediterranean far from the sea, because there is less mystery, less noise and less blood on the stones." Naples thus becomes the privileged place for telling of Ben Jelloun's Morocco and its people through the story of "a sad man, so sad that he has become the official repository of the great sadness of Marrakech.

It is a sadness that has taken on the colours of the imperial city, red ochre, blood red, brick red, sunset red, poppy red, crimson red, red however red, like a vigil at the end of Ramadan, red like an open wound, like an opaque night, like a river painted by the sun at sunset, like the silence of those who have left us and continue to speak to us leaving signals of red light, like the fire that extinguishes when it has nothing left to burn, red like the words that wear themselves out on the threshold of an old door, just and ruthless words that hurt both during the day and at night, a colour melted into the isolation of silence that sinks into the mute anger of tears, in the wear of material, colour of the stone where time is lost, a trace of iron that has endured harsh trials above the walls that watch over the city without succeeding in preventing sadness from advancing and gnawing at the body and the spirit of the sad man, the man of confused secrets, with the broken gaze who waits…[61]

---

[60] *Mediterranean Crossroads* 31-32.

[61] "Enclosed in their clothing as their minds are closed, attentive to common morals and to social conventions, and who make an effort to remain within the norms, to be a part of that horrible, resigned majority who, when there aren't too many risks involved, allow themselves to criticize the government, to say that corruption has ruined the country and its people, that the king is an intelligent man who has unified the country, but it's the ones around him who are bad. A majority that mumbles a vain and sterile discontent! That says that the Moroccans are good people, but unfortunately the difficulties of daily life have them in a stranglehold, they are afraid of one day finding themselves in need, or

Like Homer's nostalgic traveller Ulysses,[62] Bidoun moves through the Mediterranean and he returns home and feels out of place, a stranger in his native city. Several elements link Bidoun to the other lodgers of the inn and to Homer's Ulysses rather than Joyce's character as the narrator of the book would have us to believe. An antihero, but a hero of daily life like Leopold Bloom, whom he would like to resemble, Bidoun is himself a shadow, an effigy of reality like the rest of the lodgers and like them he only needs a space to tell his story in order to free himself of it: "I need only to free myself of this story, to tell it without cheating, even if I like exaggerating a bit."[63] Kundera is right when he reminds us that "those who, like Ulysses pine away with nostalgia are affected by amnesia. When nostalgia is strong, memory empties itself because nostalgia does not intensify the activity of memory and does not stir up souvenir. Nostalgia is so absorbed by the suffering that needs only its own emotion."[64]

For Ben Jelloun and the narrator of the story, Naples provides the distance needed for understanding. In the city he acquires the necessary distance for observing his own country and "following the labyrinth of sentiments of long and magical sentences and to reveal the heart of the Fez medina with Joycean colours" (*Albergo* 7-8). The meeting with the old woman in the inn, in other words Naples, acts as a catalyst: a capable midwife that helps him to discover the essence of his life, his past, his land. It is no coincidence that on his return to Morocco Bidoun is stopped by an Italian tourist in whom for a moment he recognizes himself, his double.[65] The tourist asks how to get to the dune of stories buried by careless travellers. The sand has buried the tales. In fact the two experiences of voyage and memory go together in the vicissitudes of an immigrant who is, as defined by Alain Touraine, "a traveller

---

of being denounced by the condominium doorman who is a police informer. Ah! The terror of falling into the hands of the police, brutal with the poor, conciliatory with the powerful, that obsession with maintaining order" (*Albergo* 4-6).

[62] One should also take into account Dante's Ulysses who choses the unknown (for which is being condemned) to the 'known:' his land and Penelope.

[63] *Albergo* 12. Also in *L'enfant de sable* one of the storytellers, after having narrated his version of Ahmed's story, says to the audience: "Now I feel better. I feel relieved." This confirms Ben Jelloun's concern to guarantee that the story will continue to be passed on in true oral tradition. Cfr. also Orlando 94.

[64] *Ignorancia* 39.

[65] "Gay, free, fanciful, light, apparently happy, in short he was all that I was not, but I am sure that he was my reincarnation, in another life" *Albergo* 212.

filled with memory." Therefore, this is not a case of telling stories for the simple pleasure of doing so, but for saving lived stories from oblivion, to ensure that the traveller has been relieved of his burden, "the trunks full of fables." They must be told to relieve the traveller (as in the berber's tale of the young girl and the old traveller in Ada Lonni's *Mondi a parte. Gli immigrati fra noi*),[66] not only but they must be expressed and collected as the old woman collected them.

If it is true that in *L' albergo dei poveri*, as in several other novels, Tahar Ben Jelloun becomes the chronicler of the South and Morocco, it is also true that one may also find a profound pessimism in *Albergo* concerning the importance that storytelling assumes in his work: "I need something that enchants me and that takes me away from the sadness in which I live" he has Bidoun say. Fiction recreates an existence not only for Bidoun. Ben Jelloun, the heir to the troubadors of the desert sands, has declared that he loves telling stories because he let him tell of things other than the event:

> The most fundamental literary principle of all time is that of *The Thousand and One Nights*: Tell me a story or I will kill you... We are condemned to tell stories under the threat of disappearing. A society without novelists, creators, or storytellers is a society that is already dead.[67]

In the spirit of the inn, whose history bears witness to stories of segregations and sufferings, deviants to be interned and hidden from the community, Ben Jelloun tells us of the drama of exile, return and the importance of remembering through the power of the verb 'to narrate,' an imperative: "racconta" that Ulysses, when he went back to Ithaca, was hoping in vain to hear. Immigrants arrive in Europe from Morocco with "bags of sand and trunks full of fables," like the writer himself who confesses to have been for long time an itinerant public

---

[66] Cfr. Ada Lonni, *Mondi a parte. Gli immigrati fra noi* (Torino: Paravia Scriptorium, 1999).

[67] The art of storytelling wins boredom as shows also Ben Jelloun's story "Pietro le Fou, Pietro le sage:" When Pierrot le Fou disappearred no newspaper spoke of the matter. "It would seem that Pierrot is now in Marrakech where, in a great public square, storytellers, wise or foolish, ingenuous or malicious, tell stories to pass the time of the people who are bored" *L'Ange aveugle* 110.

writer, somebody who tells fables, stories, fictions.[68] Like Bidoun, who already sees himself on the famous square of the storytellers, Jamaa el Fna, bearded and intent on telling passers-by the mythical story of the old woman, or like Pierrot le Fou whose memory "had learned to search through that which is absent and give it presence," Ben Jelloun has left for the South to collect stories to be told in the public marketplaces. As a storyteller of a Naples of solitude and of a Mediterranean in which are floating trunks of fables, the writer, like one of his character Pietro le Fou, speaks of a South that is perhaps a mistake, a misunderstanding, may be "a useless passion" but he loves it.[69] About solitude of the immigrants "all beings carry it within themselves," says Ben Jelloun who hopes that Italy may not be the country that causes and feeds desolation and it may it remain a welcoming, hospitable and generous country, "which after all means a profoundly Mediterranean country."[70]

On the poetry of returns, "di emigranti e isole, cercando l'invisibile, l'appartenenza,"[71] Kundera's question still remains: "sarebbe concepibile oggi *l'Odissea*? e l'epopea del ritorno appartiene ancora alla nostra epoca?" (Would the Odyssey still be conceivable in our age? And the epic of return, does it still belong to our age?) Maybe the answer can be found in De Chirico's painting, *Il ritorno di Ulisse,* on the cover of the Spanish edition of Kundera's novel showing the Homeric Ulysses rowing in vain in a confortable, closed room.

---

[68] *L'Ecrivain publique,* see footnote 34.
[69] Pierrot le Fou and Ben Jelloun's reflections on the South are in "Pietro le Fou, Pietro le Sage," *L'Ange aveugle* 99-110.
[70] Jelloun, *L' Estrema solitudine* 11-12. For an update on migration/s in Italy, see *International Journal of migration studies. Studi e migrazione, rivista trimestrale del centro studi emigrazione di Roma.*
[71] "Poetry of the returns, of emigrants and islands looking for the invisible: belonging." See the quote from GianMaria Testa and Pier Mario Giovannone's song, "Sono belle le cose," in the epigraph for this article.

The Italian Contribution to Argentine Popular Culture and Theater

María Teresa Sanhueza
WAKE FOREST UNIVERSITY

HISTORICAL BACKGROUND

Argentina opened its doors to European immigration in the second half of the nineteenth century in order to populate and develop the new and empty nation.[1] This Policy of Immigration and Colonization,[2] developed by the elite, would drastically modernize Argentina's provincial society. In his polemical essay, *Facundo*, Domingo Faustino Sarmiento – later president of the nation – denounced the "barbarous" aspects of Argentine rural life and customs contrasting them with "civilized" urban life, fashioned after European manners and values.[3] At the heart of his "*civilización y barbarie*" argument was the accurate perception of two nations, foreign to each other, coexisting in Argentina. One faction included the wealthy, politically powerful, educated, urban elite centered in Buenos Aires, the capital city and port of entry; the other, scattered through the undeveloped interior, comprised a primarily rural, vagrant mass population, subject to local traditional values and norms. Sarmiento echoed Juan Bautista Alberti's famous slogan, *gobernar es poblar* ("to govern is to populate"), and he believed that by encouraging the immigration of Europeans (preferably of the "Nordic races") to Argentina, the desired affinity for "English liberty, French culture, North American and European values" would be

---

[1] Article number 25 of the Argentine Constitution of 1853 points out that:
The Federal Government will promote European immigration. It will not restrict, limit or burden with any kind of taxes, the entry of foreigners who come to work the land, develop industry, and introduce and teach science and art. [Unless otherwise noted, all translations are mine.]

[2] For a detailed description of this policy, implemented by different Argentinean governments, see Castro.

[3] First published in 1845, *Facundo* was fully titled *Civilización y barbarie o Vida de Juan Facundo Quiroga y aspectos físicos, costumbres y hábitos de la República Argentina*. Cf. the English translation by Mary Mann, *Life in the Argentine Republic in the Days of the Tyrants, or Civilization and Barbarism* (New York: Collier, 1961).

"implanted" in the new nation.[4] Immigration was the panacea for progress, and selectivity was the key.

Not all intellectuals agreed with the immigration initiative. José Hernández, author of the Argentine national epic poem, *Martín Fierro*, for example, held with others that to promote immigration without the necessary capital and jobs would only create disorder and backwardness. Just as there was a need to populate the country, he argued, there was an urgency to create agricultural colonies and to provide education and opportunities for the native population. A group of young intellectuals, known in Argentine historiography as cultural nationalists, went beyond this protectionism. They conceived that membership in the nation should be closely associated with ethnicity. To be a part of the national community was a question of descent rather than assent or simple residency. Immigrants who resided in Argentina but belonged to other ethnic groups could never be full-fledged Argentines.[5]

> ...in such diverse publications as the mainstream paper *La Nación* and cultural journals such as *Ideas*, *Nosotros*, *Hebe*, *Sagitario*, *Estudios*, *Renacimiento*, *Verbum*, *Valoraciones*, *Revista argentina de ciencias políticas*, *El monitor de la educación*, and *Revista de filosofía*, contributors warned of the dangers of cosmopolitanism and discussed the need to defend *la raza argentina* from the threat posed by massive European immigration. Fears about the loss of national identity and the idea that Argentines formed a distinctive ethnocultural group threatened by foreign influences were constant and pervasive themes of the cultural debates of the period.[6]

---

[4] Juan Bautista Alberti, *Bases y puntos de partida para la organización política de la República Argentina*. 2nd ed. (Buenos Aires: Eudeba, 1984), 60-62, 67. For more information, see Slatta 186-88.

[5] Cultural nationalists changed their opinion when they realized that the immigrants had to be integrated into the nation for a nation-building project based on the evolution of a putative Argentine race. De Laney says that "while deploring the newcomers as a threat to the collective Argentine race or personality, cultural nationalists and their sympathizers accepted, albeit at times begrudgingly (sic), that immigration was inevitable and believed that the incoming masses should be assimilated or 'Argentinized' as completely as possible" (Screen 2). The emerging *raza argentina*, then, would include, rather than exclude, the immigrant.

[6] De Laney, *Screen* 2.

These points of view were entirely overshadowed by immigration proponents, and census figures tell the outcome of the debate.

Between 1880 and 1900, more than two million immigrants arrived in Argentina, a country with a total population of less than five million before the influx began. Sixty years added four-and-a-half-million Europeans, and by 1914, a thousand immigrants entered the port of Buenos Aires daily. "The intensity and volume of immigration in relation to the resident native population was such," Germani wrote, "that in a non-metaphorical sense one could speak of a substantial renovation of the country's population, particularly in the areas of greater economic, social and political significance."[7]

Sheer numbers might indicate that the nineteenth-century plan had worked were it not for the fact that the greater number of immigrants were manual laborers fleeing depressed areas in Europe and hardly the "Nordic" ideal of Argentine intellectuals. Shaped by an elitist ideology and a racist perspective, they unabashedly expressed disappointment.[8] Instead of the Anglo-Saxon farmers envisioned by Sarmiento, throngs of Italians, who, in his judgment, represented no appreciable improvement over the existing population, occupied the land. The majority of foreigners who settled in Buenos Aires were Spaniards (26%) and Italians (55%). Spaniards had one clear advantage: they spoke the language and could easily adopt local customs. Northern Italians were warmly welcome, above all because their physical

---

[7] Francisco Stach, in "La defensa social y la inmigración," *Boletín Mensual del Museo Social Argentino* 5 (July/Aug. 1916): 55-56, hoped to create a "strong, healthy, physiologically and physically capable, a uniquely Argentine race that possesses its own moral and intellectual force, and unites all that is indispensable for a progressive and hard-working society; and people who love their country, are proud of their past and care for their future, a race that will continue to strive to perfect itself in both a real and ideal sense." He adds that in order to create this race, the Argentine people should oppose "any of the difficulties presented by the influx of inferior races." Included among these races were Africans, Arabs, Jews, and Asians.

Stach proposed a racial classification of the Argentine society of 1916 as follows:
a) Africans and Asians were decidedly "inconvenient" for the country.
b) Spaniards and Italians initially aroused suspicion, but later, due to anarchist activities at the beginning of the twentieth century, in which many Italians were involved, the elite developed a sense that Italians should be denied entry into the country.
c) Jews and "Turks" were "less or completely undesirable."
d) Northern Europeans were the kind of immigrant that the country should aim to attract.

[8] Gino Germani, *Política y sociedad en una época de transición: De la sociedad tradicional a la sociedad de masas* (Buenos Aires: Paidós, 1962), 179.

appearance was similar to the Anglos, but Southern Italians (Sicilians, Neapolitans, and Calabreses) were regarded with caution and, sometimes, with outright xenophobia.

Nevertheless, the ruling class and, ultimately, the nation, capitalized on the new labor force.[9] Most newcomers had abandoned Europe for the New World in hopes of "making their fortune in America" (*hacer la América*), but they performed tasks and endured hardships rejected by, or unknown to, the Argentine elite and considered menial by rural *criollos*.[10] Not all immigrants were poor, however; some proved quite successful, inserting themselves in a position above the unskilled Argentine masses but below the traditional landed elite. They were to be the key element in the configuration of the emerging middle or entrepreneurial class.

Flushed with the belief that money was easy to come by in the New World and a tireless willingness to work, these immigrants would soon transform Buenos Aires from *la gran aldea* (the "big town") to a modern industrialized city. By 1914, Buenos Aires epitomized the phenomenon of unbridled urban growth and the consequent clash of diverse national groups. Problems quickly arose, as the city was not prepared to provide services for those who chose to stay in the capital. The mere presence of so many immigrants, speaking different languages,

---

[9] Jorge Panettieri, in *Inmigración en la Argentina,* indicates that a massive number of foreigners were incorporated into domestic service. Far from finding the promised land that they were seeking, immigrants were trapped on a soil that soon became hell. They couldn't "*hacerse la América*" or live their dreams in this new land. More information on Italian immigration in Argentina can be found in Fernando Devoto and Gianfausto Rosoli, eds., *La inmigración italiana en Argentina* (Buenos Aires: Biblos, 1985), esp. Tulio Halperín Dongui, "La integración de los inmigrantes italianos en la Argentina. Un comentario," 87-93; Diego Armus, "Mirando a los italianos. Algunas imágenes esbozadas por la elite en tiempos de la inmigración masiva," 95-104; and María Rosa Ostuni, "Inmigración política italiana y movimiento obrero argentino," 105-26.

[10] The word *criollo* has been used in diverse ways since the discovery of America. See José Juan Arrom, "Criollo: definiciones y matices de un concepto," *Certidumbre de América* (Madrid: Gredos, 1971), 11-26. The reference here is to the native, though not indigenous, population of Argentina, whose cultural identity was shaped by local history, geography, and demography and to aspects of their customs and traditions. In the Argentine context, *criollo* can be applied to both urban and rural groups, elite and non-elite populations, with varying connotations. Culturally, *criollo* often refers to aspects of *gaucho* or rural life in Argentina and to values drawn from this context to represent native traditions and national culture. For more information on the gauchos and life in the pampas, see Julio Mafud, *Psicología de la viveza criolla: Contribuciones para una interpretación de la realidad social argentina y americana*, 5th. ed. (Buenos Aires: Americalee, 1973), 54-55; and Ricardo Rodríguez Molas, *Historia social del gaucho* (Buenos Aires: Marú, 1968), 48-49.

eating different foods, and engaging in what was thought to be threatening behavior, such as labor organizing, brought large numbers of natives face-to-face with the foreigner, the "other." Working-class immigrants were packed into a shared space – the courtyard or patio of the urban tenement, called the *conventillo*. Here, they faced common struggles, political events, and family issues. Housing conditions and rents were for decades among the most important political issues for the urban working classes of Buenos Aires.

In the countryside, while *gauchos* were drafted away from their land to secure the frontier and hold back Indian raids, industrious Europeans cultivated the plains. A curious and tenuous symbiotic relationship developed, as a result, between the immigrants and the governing elite who profited financially from their labor. Those especially threatened by the new arrivals and ensuing changes were rural and urban *criollo* working men, competing for housing, jobs, women, and social status against an overwhelming, predominantly male, foreign influx. Rural *criollos* were most affected. The once open *pampa* (desert) was scored by barbed-wire fences, and the unstructured life of the *gaucho*, violated by the "invasion" of foreigners, underwent a radical metamorphosis. Clearly, the demographic and cultural character of the *pampa* was irrevocably altered. Rodríguez Molas mentions that "with immigration the *pampa* ceases to be *gauchean* and becomes *gringa*."[11]

> Although the foreigner posed no direct economic threat to the native, he did personify the rapid, bewildering changes that altered forever the nature of *pampean* life. He dug ditches and erected fences that closed off free transit on the open range. He constructed and operated railroads that ended cattle and sheep drives to the *porteño* markets of Liniers and facilitated the spread of urban life and culture across the plains. The *gringo* ran his iron plow over the *pampa*, slicing away rich pasture lands and replanting cereals. He walked rather than rode horseback. The *gaucho* found ample reason to detest, disdain, and fear the *gringo*, and numerous incidents attest to this xenophobia.[12]

---

[11] The word *gringo/a* is used colloquially in Argentina to designate any foreigner who speaks a language other than Spanish. Since at the turn of the century the majority of immigrants were Italian, it especially referred to them.
[12] Slatta 168.

Ironically, *criollo* life was not entirely erased. Newcomers recognized in the idealized *gaucho* a cultural model by which they could penetrate Argentine culture. The foreigners' very antithesis, in other words, now served as their vehicle for cultural integration. They assimilated and imitated *criollo* habits and expressive forms and inevitably affected the actual old-style *gaucho* life of cattle hunts, saloons, and the open *pampa*.

Among the immigrants, Italians, in particular, altered and changed Argentine habits. "They added macaroni, spaghetti, and vermicelli to the national diet; they brought Italian expressions and words into the spoken language; they created lunfardo, a dialect of the slums and underworld of Buenos Aires; and they revolutionized urban architecture," historian James Scobie points out.[13] However, this brief list scans only the most evident manifestations of a far deeper and more dramatic transformation and redefinition of Argentine life brought about by the negotiation of cultural differences at a popular and unofficial level.

The Italians had great influence in labor organizing. They comprised a highly politicized labor force that engendered a new urban proletariat with a distinctive idea of the worker, working conditions, and the value of work. Workers were seen as important members of society whose labor contributed to the development of the country. As a result, they wanted recognition and fair wages to support their families. The working masses were open to the radical ideologies of such political movements as socialism and especially anarchism, brought by Italians. Their focus on the radical transformation of Argentina's social structure and their appeal to dissident elements of the working class would eventually exploit social tensions between the classes to foment open rebellion. Street clashes between workers and the police signaled a new era in the evolution of Argentinean political life.

Argentina's ruling class, both publicly and privately, characterized this labor organizing as foreigners', especially Italians', doing (*cosa de gringos*). They believed that if the new union movement could be destroyed, the native worker's apathy would stifle all vestiges of insur-

---

[13] Scobie 134.

rection.[14] Meanwhile, violence and strikes increased. In 1902, an anarchist assassination attempt against President Julio Roca resulted in the passage of the Law of Residence (*Ley de Residencia*),[15] which allowed the government to declare a state of siege, close down newspapers, and deport within three days any foreigner accused of political misconduct. This law marked a new tendency to limit immigration, but despite all these restraints, the social situation did not improve. Union activity steadily increased until the government implemented harsh repression in 1910, after a firecracker went off in the Colón Theater. Congress passed a new law, related to the Law of Residence. The Law of Social Defense (*Ley de Defensa Social*) or The Sáenz Peña Law, further restricted freedom of the press and the rights of association and gathering. For every attempted strike, the government answered by deporting or imprisoning foreigners. In less than a century, the immigrant had lost the status of nation-builder and became a threat to the national security. The distance between the nineteenth-century vision of the immigrant as a source of democratic values and the early twentieth-century view of the immigrant as an agent of national disturbance was great indeed.

As Maristella Svampa affirms:

> ... the immigrant, the old ally, has become a new enemy; he has gone from potential worker to real danger, and thus he helps to create a new image of the barbaric. It is the step from an illusion (Sarmiento's and Alberti's ideas) to the reality of immigration.[16]

POPULAR MANIFESTATIONS OF ITALIANS

As a result of their increasing number and political involvement both in the country and urban centers, Italians became the target of *criollo* attacks and complaints mediated by traditional verbal art and play. Following the popular spirit of the middle ages, carnivals were lived as collective rituals in public urban spaces. *Criollos* insulted and made fun of Italians in songs. Italians made fun of natives by

---

[14] For more information on the elite and intellectuals' reaction to immigration, see Terán. For the perspective of immigrants, especially Italians, see Cibotti.
[15] Also known as the 4144 Law.
[16] Svampa 81.

masquerading as *gaucho*. The Italians, in particular, formed acting groups called, for example, "Gli acriollati," "Acriolatto,"[17] in which they performed *criollo* roles. Through these masquerades, the foreigners wanted to assimilate, but more importantly, they wanted to do it by impersonating the most typical characters of the *pampa*, the heroes of the *gauchesca* literature, such as Martín Fierro and Juan Moreira.

Buenos Aires common laborers also turned to traditional song and verse forms to accuse Neapolitans (Italians) of being "usurpers," "thieves" overtaking the land and robbing natives of jobs. Afro-Argentines, in particular, suffered the loss of jobs and menial tasks taken over by Italians, as the following complaint voiced at the 1876 carnival attests:

Spanish	Translation
Apolitanos	Neapolitans
usurpadores,	usurpers,
que todo oficio	who every occupation
quitan al pobre.	take from the poor.
Si es que botines	If shoes
sabes hacer,	you know how to make,
¿por qué esta industria	why don't you
no la ejercés?	practice that craft?
Ya no hay negros botelleros	Now there are no more black [bottle carriers
ni tampoco changador	nor errand runners
ni negro que venda fruta	nor blacks fruit vendors
mucho menos pescador.	nor even fishermen.
Porque esos apolitanos	Because those Neapolitans
hasta pasteleros son,	even bakers have become
y ya nos quieren quitar	and now they want to take [from us
el oficio de blanqueador.[18]	the whitewashing trade.

---

[17] Prieto 152.
[18] Enrique H. Puccia, "Breve historia del carnaval porteño," *Cuadernos de Buenos Aires* 46 (1974): 58.

Another carnival song, entitled "El negro Pancho Mafuri," mentions not only the replacement of blacks by Italians, but notes the immigrants' ability and willingness to dissimulate their own foreignness and assimilate native customs by adopting expressive forms:

SPANISH	TRANSLATION
Ya no hay sirvientes	There are no servants
de mi color,	of my color,
porque bachichas	because *bachichas*[19]
toditos son;	they've all become;
dentro de poco,	before long,
¡Jesús, por Dios!	Jesus, by God!
bailarán samba	they'll be dancing samba
en el tambor.[20]	on the drum.

The blacks are complaining, because the Italians have replaced all the old black servants. They are afraid that, within a short period of time, the Italians will even steal what sets them apart from all other Argentines – their dances.

The following "Contrapunto Criollo-Genovés," written by Angelo Villoldo around the turn of the twentieth century illustrates the relationship between *gauchos* and Italians. It offers a good example of a contrapuntal, *payada*-like verse dialogue or challenge, where a native *criollo* and a Genoese Italian contest each other. In spite of their diverse cultural backgrounds and markedly different speech, both singers are "matched" and reconciled by their parallel mastery of this *criollo*, *gaucho*-like artful talk:

Contrapunto Criollo-Genovés
(Criollo-Genoese Counterpoint)

Criollo	*Criollo*
Veo que sos muy compadre	I see that you are very [*compadre*[21]

---

[19] Italian, especially Genovese, "baccicia": Juan Bautista. The pejorative connotation suggests the presence of Piedmontese *bacicia-bacicio*: fool.
[20] Puccia 58.
[21] A unique combination of city *gaucho* and trouble maker.

y te tenés por cantante	and you take yourself to be [a singer
pero aquí vas a salir	but you are going to come [out of this
como rata por tirante.	like a rat out from a dump.

Genovés
Ma decate de suncera
nu venga cun lo ratone

e cantemo cada uno
alguna improvisacione.

Genoese
Cut out the nonsense,
and don't come to me with [mice,

and let's each of us sing
an improvisation.

Criollo
Ya que vos has desafiado

y te gusta improvisar
yo te doy la preferencia

y podés, pues, empezar.

Criollo
Since you've stated the [challenge,

and you like to improvise,
I'll give you preference [then,

and, well, you can start.

Genovés
Sun in bachicha italiana
ma de grande curazón,
e también sum arguentino
cuando llega l'ocasión

Genoese
I am an Italian *bachicha*
but with a big heart,
but I am also Argentine
when the occasion calls for.

Criollo
Oigale al gringo acriollado

aura si te has lucido,

sin querer meter la pata

hasta el muslo la has metido!

Criollo
Listen to the creolized [gringo.

Now you've really outdone [yourself.

By not wanting to stick [your foot in,

you've shoved it up to your [thigh!

Genovés
Ma que pata ne que muslo
pedazo de palandrón,
avisá si per si acaso

Genoese
Never mind feet and thighs,
you bum;
let me know if just by [chance

me has tomado por mancarrón.

Criollo
Pucha el gringo estilador,
ya ni sabe lo que dice.

Y por nada se le sube

la mostaza a las narices.

Genovés
Yo he visto muchos cantores
de bastante inteligencia
ma nu he visto cume vos
un tipo tan sinverguenza.

Criollo
Sos para el canto, ché, gringo,

como para el bofe el gato

tomá una grapa d'Italia
y descansemos un rato.

Genovés
Ma tumemo lo que quieras
tutti insieme in cumpañía
que me queda in tel bolsillo
trenta centavo toavía.[22]

you've taken me for a fool.

Criollo
Gee, that *gringo* is a pain.
He doesn't know what he's [saying,
and the mustard doesn't [even
rise to his nose.

Genoese
I've seen a lot of singers
who are pretty clever,
but I haven't seen
a guy as shameless as you.

Criollo
Hey *gringo*, you're made for [singing
the way cats are made for [hunting,
drink up an Italian grappa
and let's rest for a while.

Genoese
Sure, let's drink anything.
We're all among friends.
I still have thirty cents
left in my pocket.

The contestants move from a defiant, insulting tone to one of festive reconciliation. The Genoese singer is simultaneously challenged and accepted by the *criollo* when he is called a "gringo acriollado" (a *criollo*-like *gringo*), and the Italian accepts both roles when he admits that he can be "un arguentino cuando llega l'ocasión" ("an Argentine when the occasion calls for it"). While the Genoese improviser proves he can stand up to the *criollo* man-of-words, the latter responds in the sixth stanza with surprise and indirect admiration. Similarly, in the

---

[22] Enrique H. Puccia, *El Buenos Aires de Angel G. Villoldo (1860...1919),* Buenos Aires: n.p., 1976, 347-48.

seventh stanza, the Italian compliments his Argentine opponent in an indirect and picaresque manner. The reconciliation at the end of the *payada* underlines the mutual acceptance of the two contestants as they share an Italian brandy (*grappa*) on Argentine soil. By the end of the dialogue, the two contestants are on an equal footing, for in spite of their linguistic differences, they match up in their "native" mastery of a *gaucho*-like performance and *criollo*-like talk.

Anonymous oral verses, however, were not restricted to carnival. They filled the repertoires of street vendors, for example, or anyone wanting to display verbal cleverness with allusions, word plays, and rhymes. They represented genuine renderings by Italians who, even if they had entirely mastered Argentine Spanish, had learned *criollo*-like talk and adapted it for their own expressive needs. After a while, the integration of Italians into Argentine life and their adoption of *criollo* traditions and styles became no longer a matter of jest. The once-humorous and unlikely invention of an Italianized *gaucho* or a "gauchified" Italian had become a reality by the early part of the century.

THE REPRESENTATION OF ITALIANS ON THE ARGENTINEAN STAGE

Italian immigration influenced the development of the national theater. Among common folks, the circus was very popular entertainment. The first *criollo* drama to be presented in the circus ring, *Juan Moreira*, premiered on July 2nd, 1884, as a pantomime. *Juan Moreira* became best known for the characters' impersonation of Italians and its treatment of Italian/*criollo* tensions, mixtures, and collisions. According to local tales, the *cocoliche* character was born when one of the actors broke the theatricalized *gaucho* frame of the play to engage in an improvised verbal exchange with a Calabrese hired hand from the circus crew. The broken speech of the Italian day-laborer, named Antonio Cocoliche, caught the audience by surprise, causing great laughter and instant success, repeated in subsequent performances. Shortly thereafter, Celestino Petray, an actor recently returned from Patagonia, who had temporarily joined the traveling theater company, further improvised on the incident in a most outrageous manner.[23] The scripted character

---

[23] The incident is related by the famous Argentinean actor, José Podestá:
  Without prior warning, [Petray] secured himself a skinny, useless horse not fit for work nor worth its hide and mounted on his Rocinante. Dressed in an

named Francisco, until then impersonated by Petray and later played by actual foreigners with an accent, became known as "Cocoliche" and continued to play a part for two years after *Juan Moreira's* debut.[24]

Cocoliche became the name of not only the comic personage in *Juan Moreira* and a stock character by that name soon common in popular theater, but of any *cocoliche*-like impersonations on or off the stage, in or outside the circus ring. *Cocoliche* also referred to the "mixed" Italo-Argentine speech of Italian immigrants and to a parodic version invented by *criollos* for the stage. It was applied in a generic fashion to all forms of broken, or hybrid speech. In everyday speech, *cocoliche* was employed as a pejorative adjective to describe ways of dressing, interior decoration, or other aspects of daily life considered in bad taste.[25]

---

outrageous fashion, he presented himself at the countryside feast scene of "Moreira," imitating the way in which Cocoliche and his brothers spoke.

When Jeronimo saw Celestino with that horse and talking that way, he let out an Indian-like howl and said: 'Hello, Cocoliche, my friend! How's it going? Why the special get-up?'

To which Petray responded [in a broken, Italo-Argentine speech]: 'Vengue de la Patagoña co este parejiere macanuto, amique!' ('I come from Patagonia with this swell appearance, my friend!')

It goes without saying that the remark precipitated extended laughter.

And when asked his name, [Petray] answered proudly and with a coquettish strut: 'Ma quiame Franchisque Cocoliche, e songo cregollo gasta lo guese de la taba e la canilla de lo caracuse, amique, afficate la parada...('My name is Francisque Cocoliche and I'm criollo to the marrow of my calf bone, my friend, check me out...') (62-63).

[24] "Who was to know from that improvised episode that a new term would emerge for the popular lexicon!" (Podestá 63).

[25] The circumstances under which *cocoliche* emerged at first suggest that it might have been a contact language, reduced in its grammar and usage, and formed from a mixture of two languages. Then we can say that *cocoliche* is an open system in constant flux, whose manifestations could range from a way of speaking that closely resembled any number of Italian dialects to the speech of Buenos Aires Italians. This perspective on *cocoliche* explains the existence of countless individual versions of this Italo-Argentine speech, all classified under the rubric of *cocoliche*. Meo Zilio suggests that speakers of *cocoliche* do not distinguish their speech from Argentine Spanish or Italian and that they differentiate between "speaking Italian" and "speaking Spanish" only by their intention: "The only distinctive criterion ends up being the speaker's intention to express himself in one language or the other, depending on whether he speaks with Italians or natives of the Río de la Plata area" ("El 'cocoliche' rioplatense," *Boletín de Filología* 16:62). For more information on *cocoliche*, see José Gobello, *Diccionario Lunfardo* (Buenos Aires: A. Peña Lillo, 1976), 48-49; María Teresa Sanhueza, "La voz de los inmigrantes en *Mustafá* de Armando Discépolo," *Acta Literaria* 22 (1997): 45-58; and Beatriz Lavandera, "*Cocoliche*," *Diccionario de ciencias sociales* (Madrid: UNESCO, 1974), 429.

Cocoliche permeated various dimensions of everyday life and vernacular culture, becoming a central metaphor and a central agent for the creolization of Italian Argentines. Its manifestations expressed both symbolically and concretely the awkward but inevitable mixture of *criollo* and foreign elements in Argentina at the time and characterized, through the pejorative use of the word, the view of outsiders by nationals. *Cocoliche* and *cocoliche*-like expressions, however, were not merely the manifestation or result of a cultural "mixture." The phenomenon as a whole represented and underlined a paradox: *Cocoliche* was neither *gaucho* nor Italian, while at the same time he was both. As the "*gaucho*," he mocked and played with the immigrant's tongue and behavior, and as the "Italian" he celebrated Argentine culture and tradition, leaving foreigners no alternative but to want to become "native." In this manner, *Cocoliche's* double identity allowed not only for the survival but also the control of both cultural "faces." His image functioned both as a disguise for integration (assimilation) and a masque for dissent (dissimulation).

ITALIAN INFLUENCE ON THEATER

Gladys Onega affirms that "theater reflected the social impact of immigration through all its genres: the rural *drama*, showed the ethnocultural rivalry between *criollos* and Italians and the merger of both by love or by the common struggle against the landowner; the *drama gaucho* presented the immigrant as a recipient of government nepotism; the *obra de tesis* exposed the helplessness of the immigrants at the hands of the Law; the *sainete*, showed the diverse immigrant population living in *conventillos*, characterizing them as comic stereotypes or exploited workers."[26]

THE ITALIAN INFLUENCE ON COMEDY: *CRIOLLOS* VS ITALIANS

In *Las de enfrente* (1909), Federico Mertens shows *criollos* and Italians in clear conflict. The *criolla* Dorotea is the wife of an Italian immigrant, Esteban. Wanting to succeed in life and gain social status, Dorotea and their daughters decide to deny vigorously Esteban's Italian origins and his job as a storekeeper. Esteban does everything he can to stop the women and change their minds. Untiringly, Dorotea

---

[26] Onega 7.

tries to copy all the manners and attitudes of her female neighbors in order to gain prestige. She also develops all kinds of intrigues, like wanting to marry her daughter to one of Esteban's employees, another Italian, just to beat ("*ganarle la mano*") one of her across-the-street neighbors ("*las d'enfrente*") who is also about to get to the altar. In the end, when the neighbor breaks her engagement, daughter Elena also breaks up with Genaro – the Italian. In a heart-wrenching conversation with Elena, Genaro exposes that he has known the truth since the beginning but went along because he was madly in love with her. He lashes out at her shallowness:

> ¡E shí! ¡So gringo pero no so iñorante come ostedes me creen! ¿Se piensa que no comprendí aquer día, aquer domingos, cuando don Esteban bendicos a las d'infrentes, lo que queriba decir, lo que se había dichos adentro de él, adentro de so cuerpos? Cumprendí, sí, cumprendí que se me achetaba per imitar a ellas... cumprendí, sí, cumprendí bien, ma peró me callé la bocas, porque yo la queribas a osté de verdá y no pensaba que iba a pasar esto que pasas; que iba a romper con il novio la d'infrentes, come me acaban de decir recién, e qué – ¡claro! – no casándose ellas, el eterno figurín de ostedes, osté tiene tiempo de esperar e de afilar co otros mecor que éste gringo ordinario a las vestimentas, má quien sabe si no es más fino que otros, dentro de l'almas! (*Pausa.*) Yo me callé la bocas aquer día, perque la queribas demasiou a osté, e poco se me importaba que osté no me queriese ne in chiquitito así. ¡Mi amor era suficientemente grande, per sostituir al que le fartara a ese corazón de trapo, que, como de trapo, sólo sabe mirar er traque der marido e nada más!

> [Yes! I am a *gringo* but I am not ignorant as you think! Do you think I did not understand that day, that Sunday, when don Esteban almost told the women across the street what he wanted to say, what he had told himself, inside of himself? I understood, yes, understood that I was accepted because you wanted to imitate them... I understood, yes, understood well, but I shut my mouth; because I really loved you, and I did not think this would happen; that she was going to break up with her fiancé. Of course, if she is not getting married, you are not either. Now you have time to wait and date others better than this *gringo* who wears ordinary clothing. But who knows – maybe he is classier in his soul than

others! (*Pause.*) I shut my mouth that day, because I loved you too much, and I care little about the fact that you did not love me a bit. My love was big enough, enough to substitute the one that your cold heart did not have. That cold heart that only pays attention to the clothing that her future husband wears and nothing else!][27]

The Italians start out as caricatures. They are comic stereotypes that provide local color but develop deep characters; they are more dignified than the *criollos*. Mertens makes fun of both Italians and *criollos*, but in the end, he elevates the Italians over the *criollos*, who remain comic and ridiculous throughout the play.

In *Un porteño* (1926) by Vicente Retta and Julio Viale Paz, Julio Taccini wants to marry Cora, the daughter of don Goyo, who opposes the union because Julio is Italian. The *criollo*/Italian polarity is clearly set out in the characters of don Goyo, an old-time Argentine, a *porteño*, and the Italian Julio Taccini, an entrepreneur. This way, Retta and Viale use the Italian character to dramatize the opposition among the main characters.

> DON GOYO. ...Te parece bonito añadir a nuestro apellido el de Taccini, que suena a hojalata y que parece anunciar que nuestro abolengo y nuestras tradiciones han ido a parar al mismo tacho?
>
> [... Do you think it is nice to add the Taccini last name to ours? That last name sounds like tin plate, and it seems to announce that our ancestry and traditions have gone to the garbage.][28]

Don Goyo repeats that he would have preferred a *criollo* as a son-in-law, especially because "los apellidos finalizados en 'inis' huelen a inmigración" ["last names that end in 'ini's' smell like immigration"].[29]

But the circumstances here are little different. Don Goyo's family is in decline; their only asset is their last name. Julio is successful, one of those immigrants who have been able to "make their wealth in

---

[27] In Federico Mertens, *Las de enfrente*. Bambalinas, A. 1.2, (1918): 15-53, 50.
[28] In Vicente Retta and Julio Viale Paz, *Un porteño*. Bambalinas, A. 9, N. 427: 6-38, 9.
[29] Retta and Viale 9.

America" (*hacerse la América*). He has many exemplary features: he is a professional driver and a liberal man of action. The play has a happy ending: love succeeds, and the young couple joins the last name of the old family to the economic power of the enterprising *gringo*. Don Goyo reluctantly accepts "que se haya colado en la familia, con el auxilio de todos... Un gringo!" [that a gringo had slipped into the family with every body's help].[30]

The Italian character becomes a symbol of the new times, a representation of a new concept of status, a model of a new Argentine race that will be based on work and social mobility instead of old names.

The same topic is exposed in *Yo quiero ir a Mar del Plata* (1931) by Alberto Novión. Victorio and Filomena are married Italian immigrants who are trying to conquer a place in society, not just for themselves, but also to make their children happy. Fernando, their son, wants to marry Nena, the daughter of don Melitón, a *criollo* who is very proud to be an Argentinean. The love of the young couple and their desire to get married creates a series of confrontations between the parents. The contrast between the *cocoliche* of Filomena and Victor and the exaggerated creolism of don Melitón produces humor but does not ridicule the Italians. They defend their "Italianism" before don Melitón's flippant exhibition of creolism. The dialogue shows a tension that is resolved with the victory of the Italians. The happy ending – setting a date for the wedding with both families' blessing – promises a redefined Argentine generation forged from both traditions. The vision evoked is a prosperous future shared by *criollos* and *gringos*.

ROBERTO PAYRÓ AND ARMANDO DISCÉPOLO

Roberto Payró and Armando Discépolo,[31] in *Marco Severi* (1905) and *La fragua* (1912), staged the effect that the Sáenz Peña Law had on

---

[30] Retta and Viale, 38.

[31] Armando Discépolo is the Argentinean playwright who most accurately portrays the Italians and their daily struggles. Some of Discépolo's plays inaugurated the *criollo* grotesque (*grotesco criollo*) and opened a new discourse on the problems faced by immigrants – Italians especially – when they arrived in Argentina. Italians are not just stereotypes who make the public laugh – the vision presented in the *sainete* – but individuals lured to Argentina with promises of land and high wages who found a hostile, unfamiliar place. For a depiction of Italian immigrants in the *sainete*, Discépolo's *grotesco criollo*, and other forms of theater not covered in this article, see my forthcoming article, "Italian Immigrants in Argentina: Some Representations on Stage" in *Italian Americana*.

the Italian community. This law was especially harmful to Italians who were most involved with social struggle and the ideas of anarchism and socialism.[32] Both playwrights show Italians as active participants in socio-political life; their protagonists are also responsible for introducing anarchism into the country.

Of all the plays in which Roberto Payró wrote about immigration, *Marco Severi* is the best known. When first staged in 1905, the piece was extremely popular, because it reflected a concrete problem with which the audience could easily identify. Luis Vernengo is a grateful Italian who owes his good luck to the new land. Security, peace, work, and a family are the gains of his move to Argentina. He owns a printing business but tries to help his workers. The police are suspicious that Luis might be an anarchist, disseminating propaganda. Benito, a police informant, discovers that Luis Vernengo is the alias of Marco Severi, a fugitive of justice in Italy for fraud. Under the Argentinean Law of Extradition, he must be sent back to his native country. Luis (Marco) pleads with the judge:

> ¡Oh! ¡En Italia! ¡Ah, señor juez! Ustedes que llaman al extranjero para que comparta su trabajo y sus beneficios; ustedes que reciben tan amistosa, tan generosamente; ustedes que al cabo de un corto tiempo lo consideran como miembro de su gran familia, ¿por qué, por qué tienen esta ley implacable que no perdona al que ha merecido perdón, y que no sólo lo castiga a él, sino que maltrata y maldice cuanto tiene alrededor, hundiendo a los suyos en la miseria y en la vergüenza, dispersando al viento cuanto su esfuerzo creó, prolongando la inicua pena hasta en sus mismos hijos... ¡Oh! ¡Vea señor juez! ¡Le juro que desde que pisé este país, desde que empecé a trabajar con fruto, desde que formé un hogar que creía bendito, fui, otro hombre. ¡Marco Severi quedó en Italia con su espantosa pesadilla de un minuto! ¡Luis Vernengo es un hombre útil y honrado! ¡Pero se mata a Luis Vernengo para hacer resucitar en cambio al delincuente Marco Severi! ¡Se destruye lo que ha hecho Luis Vernengo, su hogar, su obra, su porvenir, para que resurja la falta no cometida por Marco Severi!

---

[32] Anarchists and socialists opened a new social space for the working force in Argentina. Not only did they organize themselves as an important social agent but they also developed a new political and cultural identity. For more information on anarchism in Argentina, see Suriano. For socialism, see Adelman.

> [Oh! In Italy! Ah, your Honor! You called on the foreigner to come share your work and your benefits; you welcome us amiably and generously; and after a short time you consider us as a part of your family; why, why do you have such relentless law that does not forgive those who deserve to be forgiven? That law that not only punishes him, but also harms and damns everything around him, plunging his family into misery and shame, dispersing into thin air all that he worked to create, prolonging the iniquitous sadness in his children... Oh! See, your Honor! I swear to you that since I arrived in this country, since I started working, since I established a household that is sacred to me, I've changed. Marco Severi and his one-minute terrible nightmare stayed in Italy! Luis Vernengo is a useful and honest man! But you want to kill Luis Vernengo in order to resuscitate instead Marco Severi, the delinquent! You want to destroy what Luis Vernengo has done, his home, his work, his future in order to bring to the surface the fault that Marco Severi did not commit!][33]

He explains to the judge that circumstances drove him to commit the felony. By arriving in this new land, Luis has reformed himself. He is a changed man. All his good characteristics are confirmed by the man who turned him in. This way, Payró dissipates all doubts that the audience could have about Vernengo. When the Judge asks Benito if Luis is an anarchist, he responds, "Lo que es, es un alma de Dios ["what he is, is a good soul"]."[34] Then he adds,

> Ya le dije, señor Juez, que era un alma de Dios, bueno como el pan y hasta medio tilingo... No se mete en nada. Siempre está con la mujer y el chiquilín, como un bobeta. Pero dice que quiere que todos los de la imprenta sean felices y se hagan ricos junto con él. ¡Mire que otario!
> [I already told you, your Honor. He is a good soul. Good as bread and even a little bit silly... He minds his own business. He is always with his wife and kid, like a fool. But he says that he wants all the workers to be happy and become rich with him. See, what a big fool he is!][35]

---

[33] In Roberto Payró, *Teatro Completo* (Buenos Aires: Hachette, 1956), 176-77.
[34] Payró, 175.
[35] Payró 175.

Vernengo wants his workers to share the wealth with him. He is the typical anarchist who wants to promote social rights and obtain benefits for the human race in an environment of work and respect.

The play is an *obra de tesis* that shows opposition to the Sáenz Peña Law, but it has a happy ending. Luis Vernengo (Marco Severi) is pardoned by the Italian government after authorities receive the excellent report of the Argentinean judge. The last line of the play confirms the critique: "¡Hay que enmendar esa ley!" ["We have to change that law!"].[36]

In *La fragua*, Armando Discépolo uses the explicit exposition of anarchist-socialist ideas to convey its overall humanitarian message through an Italian character. Lorenzo Ferrari, or Renzo, an Italian immigrant and working-class leader who fights social injustice, is presented as a social martyr. As the play develops, he is forced into exile from Argentina due to his deep involvement in the union as a strike organizer. Renzo presents an idealized image because he fights for his ideas in a society that does not comprehend him. His strongly moralistic anarchist theories refute the view of the working class as second-class and portray the worker as the underdog in the conflict between oppressors and oppressed.

Renzo thinks that society and nature must be governed by solidarity, something unknown to the workers. By fighting against the company owners, Renzo becomes a model of behavior for all readers and theatergoers who are in the same predicament.

> RENZO. Señores: ¡El obrero está mal! Esto no es novedad, porque siempre ha sido así, como tampoco es nuevo que el que soporta una vida obligada y no tiene ninguna expansión, es más fácil que se haga perverso que noble. . . ¡pero el obrero está mal y lo saben!
> [Gentlemen: The worker is in bad shape! This is nothing new, because it has always been that way; it is not new either that people who put up with a harsh life might easily turn depraved rather than noble... but the worker is in bad shape; and you know it!][37]

---

[36] Payró 199.
[37] In Armando Discépolo, *Obra Dramática* (Buenos Aires: Eudeba, 1987), 224.

The dominant classes stereotype the oligarchy's point of view. As Renzo can be seen as a role model for the workers, Gustavo Froivard, Sr. – the factory owner – symbolizes the *true* antagonist: the country's political and economic system. Descriptions of Froivard in the text are filled with negative connotations that present him as cold-hearted, insensitive, and egotistical. He shares the government's attitude toward the working class and the Italians involved in the union movement.

After the strike ends, Renzo is deported, explicitly depicting the Law of Residence as an injustice. The law is foreshadowed as early as the first act of *La fragua*, when Renzo's sister Santa tells Renzo, "No eres de esta tierra y la ley es dura con el extranjero. Vos mismo me lo has dicho: ridícula, infame" ["You were not born in this land and the law is cruel to the foreigner. You have said so yourself: ridiculous, despicable (law)"].[38] The injustice of the deportation is magnified by its effect on Renzo's family. Everything is chaotic while he is away. When he finally returns, he discovers that his wife Carlota has been having an affair with his friend Santiago, his daughter is not his, and his sister has become the lover of the factory owner's son.

At the end of the play, a disenchanted Renzo walks out with his young son saying, "El lo dirá cuando tenga conciencia. Será mi legado" ["He will speak when he realizes what has happened. He will be my legacy"].[39] The boy's name – Avvenire – is related to the naturalist theme of a burden that passes from one generation to another. In Italian, *avvenire* means future, and, within the logic of the play, the name alludes to the universal meaning of Renzo's struggle, especially when he states, "mi famila es la familia humana" ["my family is the human race"].[40] The child thus embodies the utopian dream articulated in *La fragua*: even though Renzo has failed, his defeat is not complete, for he can continue fighting by proclaiming, "¡Hay que cambiar la sociedad!" ["We ought to change our society!"],[41] and making it possible through Avvenire.

Marco Severi and *La fragua* portray Italians as positive role models through the characters of Renzo – the victim who defends his principles against adversity – and Luis Vernango – the reformed delin-

---

[38] Discépolo 190-91.
[39] Discépolo 243.
[40] Discépolo 240.
[41] Discépolo 193.

quent who becomes an asset to society. The characters expose social contradictions. By presenting Italian characters as a positive symbol of the immigrant experience, men who are capable of exemplary political actions, Discépolo and Payró add power to the plays' humanitarian message. Their comments also include brutal critiques of the Laws of Residence and Social Defense.

CONCLUSION

Argentine immigration policy went through several stages, and so did the role and status of the immigrant. All these phases were documented in the popular culture and the arts, especially the theater, during its most prolific period: the beginning of the twentieth century.

The characters of Argentinean theater modeled after Italian immigrants reveal a certain irony in Argentina's immigration policies. The elite did not get the kind of immigrant that it wanted, but Italian values and customs, words, expressions, gestures, foods, musical influences, etc., became as much a part of the country as did the expressive forms, styles, habits, and redefined traditions of *gaucho* and *criollo* life. As a result, a new society anchored in both traditions emerged but increasingly asserted its "Argentinism." Nineteenth-century efforts to Europeanize the nation failed, ironically yielding a multifaceted new *criollismo* that embraced native and foreign traditions, rather than a single-vision country with imposed foreign standards.

The Argentinean theater at the beginning of the century is not only a historic record of the country's evolution; it also allows the immigrants to denounce their reality on stage as well as to show their contributions to the new land. The plays made the Italian immigrants "visible" to the rest of society. They showed that the foreigner, "the other," was a human being and created a new understanding of the immigrant condition.

The theater aesthetically organized on stage off-stage events, real social issues in diverse ways: comic, serious, and tragic. Playwrights showed different images of Italians. Mertens, Retta and Viale Paz, and Novión presented, in a simple and humorous way, the conflicts between Italians and natives, but resolved the problems in a harmonious manner. With the resolution of this *criollo*/Italian polarity, the comedy predicted the future of contemporary Argentina, because, today, most Argentines have Italian ancestors. Roberto Payró and Armando Discépolo chose to present the Italians as victims of the system's injustices, a different view than the official version offered by the government. This serious presentation of the Italians' plight as a result of the bad law separates Payró and Discépolo's dramas from the other comedies.

WORKS CITED

Adelman, Jeremy. "El partido socialista argentino." *Nueva Historia Argentina. El progreso, la modernización y sus límites (1880-1916)*. Vol. 5. Buenos Aires: Sudamericana, 2000. 261-90.

Armus, Diego. "Mirando a los italianos. Algunas imágenes esbozadas por la elite en tiempos de la inmigración masiva." *La inmigración italiana en Argentina*. Buenos Aires: Biblos, 1985. 95-104.

Casadevall, Domingo. *Buenos Aires: arrabal- sainete- tango*. Buenos Aires: Fabril, 1968.

Castro, Donald. *The Development and Politics of Argentine Immigration Policy 1852-1914. To Govern is to Populate*. San Francisco: Mellen, 1991.

Cibotti, Ema. "Del habitante al ciudadano: La condición del inmigrante." *Nueva Historia Argentina. El progreso, la modernización y sus límites (1880-191)*. Vol. 5. Buenos Aires: Sudamericana, 2000. 365-408.

DeLaney, Jeane. "National Identity, Nationhood and Immigration in Argentina: 1810-1930." *Stanford Electronic Humanities Review* 5.2 (1997): 30 screens.

Germani, Gino. *Política y sociedad en una época de transición: De la sociedad tradicional a la sociedad de masas*. Buenos Aires: Paidós, 1962.

Gobello, José. *Nuevo Diccionario Lunfardo*. Buenos Aires: Corregidor, 1994.

Guy, Donna. *Sex and Danger in Buenos Aires. Prostitution, Family and Nation in Argentina*. Lincoln: U of Nebraska P, 1991.

Halperín Dongui, Tulio. "La integración de los inmigrantes italianos en la Argentina. Un comentario." *La inmigración italiana en Argentina*. Buenos Aires: Biblos, 1985. 87-93.

Liernur, Jorge Francisco. "La construcción del país urbano." *Nueva Historia Argentina. El progreso, la modernización y sus límites (1880-1916)*. Vol. 5. Buenos Aires: Sudamericana, 2000. 409-63.

Lobato, Mirta Zaida. "Los trabajadores en la era del 'progreso'." *Nueva Historia Argentina. El progreso, la modernización y sus límites (1880-1916)*. Vol. 5. Buenos Aires: Sudamericana, 2000. 465-506.

Malatesta, Enrico. *Anarquismo y anarquía*. Buenos Aires: Tupac, 1988.
Mancuso, Hugo, and Armando Minguzzi. *Entre el fuego y la rosa. Pensamiento social italiano en Argentina: Utopías anarquistas y programas socialistas (1870-1920)*. Buenos Aires: Biblioteca Nacional y Página/12, 1999.
Onega, Gladys. *La inmigración en la literatura argentina (1880-1910)*. Santa Fe: Universidad Nacional del Litoral, 1965.
Ostuni, María Rosa. "Inmigración política italiana y movimiento obrero argentino." *La inmigración italiana en Argentina*. Buenos Aires: Biblos, 1985. 105-26.
Panettieri, Jorge. *Inmigración en la Argentina*. Buenos Aires: Macchi, 1970.
Podestá, José. *Medio siglo de farándula*. Córdoba: Río de la Plata, 1930.
Portantiero, Juan Carlos. *Realismo y realidad en la narrativa argentina*. Buenos Aires: Procyon, 1961.
Prieto, Adolfo. *El discurso criollista en la formación de la Argentina moderna*. Buenos Aires: Sudamericana, 1988.
Romero, José Luis. "Los de arriba, los de abajo, los del medio." *Teatro* 8.35 (June 1988): 8-14.
___. "Las dos leyendas de la inmigración." *Teatro* 6.25 (May 1986): 8-17.
___. *Las ideas políticas en Argentina*. México: Fondo de Cultura Económica, 1946.
Sanhueza, Ma. Teresa. "Italian Immigrants in Argentina: Some Representations on Stage." *Italian Americana*. Forthcoming.
Scobie, James. *Argentina: A City and a Nation*. 2nd ed. New York: Oxford UP, 1971.
Slatta, Richard W. *Gauchos and the Vanishing Frontier*. Lincoln: U of Nebraska P, 1983.
Suriano, Juan. "El anarquismo." In *Nueva Historia Argentina. El progreso, la modernización y sus límites (1880-1916)*. Vol. 5. Buenos Aires: Sudamericana, 2000. 291-325.
Svampa, Maristella. *El dilema argentino: Civilización o Barbarie. De Sarmiento al revisionismo peronista*. Buenos Aires: El Cielo por Asalto, 1994.
Terán, Oscar. "El pensamiento finisecular (1880-1916)." *Nueva Historia Argentina. El progreso, la modernización y sus límites (1880-1916)*. Vol. 5. Buenos Aires: Sudamericana, 2000. 327-63.
Vázquez-Rial, Horacio. *Buenos Aires 1880-1930. La capital de un imperio imaginario*. Madrid: Alianza, 1996.

Giorgio Vasari's *The Ages of Life*

Liana De Girolami Cheney
UNIVERSITY OF MASSACHUSETTS LOWELL

"Lo cielo i vostri movimenti inizia."
("The stars initiate your movements")
Dante's *Purgatorio,* XVI, 73

In *Emblematum libellus cum commentarii,* Andrea Alciato refers to the universe as a forest of symbols, that is to say, "Things that are visible are the mirror of those things which are invisible and all the world objects have a signification."[1] Alciato's theory of the emblem conveys a Neoplatonic view of the meaning of an idea or conceit (*concetto*), which is eloquently explained by Marsilio Ficino in *De vita ceolitus comparanda.*[2] Ficino discusses the use and the magic potency of images by deliberating on the virtue of imagery, what power pertains to the figure in the sky and on earth, which of the heavenly configurations were impressed on images by the ancients, and how the images were employed in antiquity.[3]

Vasari's knowledge of Neoplatonism and interest in emblems are evident in the program decoration for the rooms in his home at Arezzo, in particular, the depiction of the *Four Seasons* or *Ages of Life* of 1548, in the ceiling (*palco*) of the Chamber of Fortune (Figs. 1-2), which is the subject to be examined in this essay.

Vasari's familiarity with emblems derives, as he recounts in his autobiography, from his education in the classics with Pollastra, his tutoring with Piero Valeriano during his formative years, and his

---

[1] Andrea Alciato, *Emblematum libellus cum commentarii* (Lyon, 1546), Introduction. See also, Andrea Alciato, *Emblematum libellus* (Basel, 1529), Italian ed. and trans. by Guilliame Roville as *Diverse impresse accommodate a diverse moralita con versi che i loro significati dichiarono tratte da gli Emblemi dell' Alciato* (Lyon, 1549), and Peter M. Daly, ed. *Andreas Alciatus' Index Emblematicum* (Toronto: U of Toronto P, 1985), 2 vols.

[2] Florence, 1489, reprinted as *Opera Omnia* (Basileae, 1576).

[3] E. Gombrich, *Symbolic Images* (London: Phaidon, 1972), 172, and André Chastel, *Marsile Ficin et L'Art* (Geneva: Droz, 1996), 81-89.

contact with the emblematist Andrea Alciato in Bologna.[4] Moreover, Vasari acquires his knowledge of iconography and emblems through his study of the works of Annibale Caro, a humanist in the Roman court of the Farnese family.[5] In the *Vite*, Vasari praises Annibale Caro, poet and translator of classical literature and secretary to Cardinal Farnese, for his *invenzioni* "cappriciose, ingeniose e lodevoli molto (inventions that contain whimsicality, ingeniousness and are highly praised)."[6] Caro, in turn, considers Alciato's and Cartari's books to be iconographical manuals and praises them for their significance.[7] Furthermore, Paolo Giovio's humanist writings, such as *Gli Elogi* and *Dialoghi*, provides a literary program for Vasari's Roman decorative

---

[4] Vasari was particularly familiar with such emblematic books as Horapollo's *Hierogliphica* (Venice, 1505), Piero Valeriano's *Hieroglyphica* (Venice, 1521), Vincenzo Cartari's *Imagine delli Dei de gl'Antichi* (Venice, 1550), and Andrea Alciato's *Emblematum libellus cum commentariis* (Lyon, 1531, 1536 and 1542 editions). Correspondingly with the knowledge of Alciato's *Emblemata* familiarity with Valeriano's *Hieroglyphica*, Vasari would have assimilated their concepts and learned about the *Greek Anthology*. This book was first published in Florence in 1494 by Franciscus de Alopa. In 1522, Alciato translated it into Latin. According to the scholarly writings of Peter Daly and Daniel Russell, the *Greek Anthology* was a series of epigrams or hieroglyphs with a moral message, composed by different poets concerned with Greek legends and history. Daniel Russell, "Alciati's Emblems in Renaissance France," *Renaissance Quarterly* 34 (1981): 534-54. In a powerful statement, Russell defines the importance of Alciato's emblem book in Cinquecento art and literature "[it] served as a manual to train readers in a particular approach to artistic artifacts. It taught them to participate actively in the moralizing of visual arts..."

[4] Daniel Russell, "Emblems and Hieroglyphics: Some Observations on the Beginnings and the Nature of Emblematic Forms," *Emblematica* 2 (1986), 227-40. For Russell, Renaissance humanists employed hieroglyphics as a vehicle for "redefining the symbolic process with the context of Neoplatonic thought." See Alison Saunders, *The Sixteenth Century French Emblem Book. A Decorative and Useful Genre* (Geneva, 1988), Richard H. Wilkinson, *Symbol and Magic in Spiritual Art* (London: Thames and Hudson, 1994), 16-26, and Wallis Budge, *Magia egizie* (Rome: Newton, 1980), 14-27.

[5] Clare Robertson, "Annibale Caro as Iconographer Sources and Method," *Journal of the Warburg and Courtauld Institutes* 45 (1982): 160-81.

[6] Giorgio Vasari, *Le Vite dei piu eccellenti pittori, scultori, et architettori*, 1550 and 1568, ed. Gaetano Milanesi (Florence: Sansoni, 1970-74), 115-29. All succeeding references to this text will be noted as Vasari-Milanesi. See Annibale Caro, *Lettere Familiari*, ed. A. Greco (Florence, 1957).

[7] In *Survival of the Pagan Gods*, Seznec points out how Cartari was read and used by Annibale Caro and Giorgio Vasari (Paris, 1980, 2nd ed.), 256-62. See Arthur Henkel and Albrecht Schone, *Emblemata: Hanbuch zur Sinnibildkunst des XVI. und XVII. Jahrhunderts* (Stuttgart, 1967) and Mario Praz, *Studies in Seventeenth Century Imagery*, 2nd ed. (Rome, 1964).

cycles.[8] Thus, Vasari's manner of composing images for a program as a compendium of visual iconography parallels and derives from literary practices and conceits of Alciato, Cartari, Giovio and Valeriano.

Vasari's familiarity with the language and imagery of the allegoric, emblematic, hieroglyphic and visual traditions prompts him to create a new vocabulary in art – an encyclopedia of images and symbols. This visual dictionary demonstrates his assimilation of the emblematic tradition in Italian paintings of the sixteenth century, as depicted in his decorative cycles of his Aretine house, in particular in the portrayal of the *Seasons*. Thus, Vasari's encyclopedic artistic and iconographical approach to the assimilation of the emblematic tradition makes him a forerunner of the Roman iconographer, Cesare Ripa, who published in Rome his first emblematic book under the title of *Iconologia,* printed in 1598, and with illustrations in 1603.

From 1542 to 1550, Vasari designed and painted the walls and ceiling of four rooms in his Aretine house – Chambers of Fame, Apollo, Abraham and Fortune. The iconographical program for each room is complex, particularly Vasari's studio or *Chamber of Fortune*. This studio illustrates the most elaborate program of the Casa Vasari. In his autobiography, Vasari jocularly describes his paintings:

> I did… thirteen large pictures, containing the gods of heaven, the four seasons, in the corners nudes, and regarding a large picture in the middle, containing life-size paintings of Virtue and Envy under her feet and gripping Fortune by the hair, while she beats both. A circumstance that gave great pleasure at the time is that in going round the room Fortune at one place seems above Envy and Virtue, and at another Virtue is above Envy and Fortune, as is often the case in reality.[9]

The Seasons or *Ages of Life* are represented in the *Chamber of Fortune*, the only room in the house that has painted ceiling and walls (Figs. 3-4). The walls are visually divided with an upper zone contain-

---

[8] Julian Kliemann, "Il pensiero di Paolo Giovio nelle pitture eseguite sulle sue 'invenzioni'," *Atti del Convegno su Paolo Giovio: Il Rinascimento e la memoria* (Como: Presso la Società a Villa Gallia, 1985), 197-223.

[9] Vasari-Milanesi, Vol. 7. See Leslie Thomson, ed., *Fortune* (Seattle: U of Washington P, 2000), 31-43 and 81-87.

ing personifications of goodness and natural landscapes and a lower zone with classical stories. The ceiling consists of recessed and projected areas. The recessed section in the ceiling contains images of the planets accompanied by their correlated astrological signs. The projected area of the ceiling or *palco* includes the personifications of Fortune, Virtue and Envy or the conceit of *Occasio pars temporis,* signifying one's missing a chance in life as a result of the interference of Time, or conversely, one's good fortune made possible when there is a reconciliation between Chance or Opportunity and Time. This latter result ultimately depends on Chance following the path of Time.[10]

The *palco* scene reveals Vasari's assimilation of the cosmic philosophy of the seasons in Neoplatonism, his use of emblematic sources for the representations of natural phenomena and his symbolic depiction on the artistic life. By depicting in the *palco* the *Ages of Life* with their connections to the planetary gods and the zodiacal signs, Vasari examines the stylistic and iconographical traditions in Italian Renaissance art. For example, his Mannerist style reflects the stylistic convention of decorative cycle for representing cosmological and astrological imagery. The historical tradition provides him with the appropriation of classical art in decorative cycles. In addition, Vasari's iconographical legacy, embedded in ancient tradition, reveals the symbolism and implications of the celestial planets on the individual's life in the decorative cycles.

In *The Survival of the Pagan Gods,* Jean Seznec elucidates the astrological scheme by explaining the relation between the Renaissance Neoplatonic philosophy and Renaissance cosmological theory. Inherited in the Renaissance is an assimilation of the classical and medieval traditions of believing that "everything in the heavens resembles everything which exists below, and everything below resembles

---

[10] In a brilliant essay, R. Wittkower traced the origin and development of the iconography of Fortune and Virtue. He discusses how during Roman times Cicero was the first writer to differentiate clearly between the concepts of Time (Kronos) and Chance (Occasio) and how this differentiation had positive and negative implications. See R. Wittkower, "Chance, Time and Virtue," *Journal of the Warburg and Courtauld Institutes,* Vol. 1 (1937-1938), 313-21, and Erwin Panofsky, *The Iconography of Correggio's Camera di San Paolo* (London, 1961), 225. "The fickleness of Fortune was sometimes contrasted with the personification of Virtue with the explanation: *Sedes Fortunae Rotunda; Sedes Virtutis Quadrata."*

everything in the heavens."[11] This statement, which reflects the Hermetic doctrine expounded by Hermes Trismegistus, is reinterpreted in Renaissance philosophy as "everything lead back to the stars and their influence is everywhere exerted,"[12] that is, the Neoplatonic theory of macrocosm and microcosm. Astrological manuscripts of the fifteenth and sixteenth centuries, for example, clearly illustrate the humanist interpretation of how the individual represents a microcosm, as in *The Individual in the Universe* (Fig. 5), of how the individual is part of the celestial forces, as in *The Individual and the Heavens* (Fig. 6), or how the individual may also represent a macrocosm by encompassing the celestial and terrestrial aspects and forces in the human body, as in *The Zodiacal or Astral Individual* from a German manuscript of the fourteenth century (Fig. 7).

Furthermore, Seznec observes that "since antiquity, a system of concordance in which planets and zodiacal signs served as the basis of classification for the elements, seasons, and humors or temperaments" was established.[13] For this cosmological system, the Renaissance individual is viewed as a summary of the world but depending on the universal cosmic forces (theological, geographical, mineralogical and medical), that is, the individual is a microcosm in a macrocosm, as exemplified in Seznec's cosmological chart.[14]

For Renaissance humanists, the universe or cosmos is ruled by seven astrological planets or planetary gods. Each planetary god represents a planet and is honored to rule the universe for one day out of seven, thus creating the system of the seven days of the week. In addition, the seven planetary gods travel through regions or *houses* occupied by the twelve signs of the zodiac. According to this scheme, Apollo *(Sol)* rules the house of Leo with its corresponding attribute, the Lion. Diana *(Luna)* rules the house of the Cancer with the Crab. Mercury rules the houses of the Gemini with the Twins, and Virgo with the Virgin. Venus rules the houses of Taurus with the Bull, and Libra with the Scales. Mars rules the houses of Aries with the Ram,

---

[11] Seznec, *Survival of the Pagan Gods,* 49.

[12] Ibid.

[13] Ibid.

[14] Ibid. See also James Wasserman, *Art and Symbols: Images of Power and Wisdom* (Rochester, VT: Destiny, 1993), 9-22; and Solange de Maille Nesle, *Astrology: History, Symbols and Signs* (Rochester, VT: Inner Traditions International, 1985), 6-33.

and Scorpio with the Scorpion. Jupiter rules the houses of Pisces with the Fish, and Sagittarius with the Centaur. Saturn rules the houses of Aquarius with the Water-bearer, and Capricorn with the Goat. In the *Chamber of Fortune's* ceiling, Vasari associates the imagery of the seasons with the philosophical and pseudo-scientific studies of humanists.

The Renaissance Neoplatonic philosopher, Marsilio Ficino, sustains his cosmological theory on the writings of classical philosophers, such as Pythagoras, Empedocles and Aristotle. Most of all, Ficino is influenced by Plato's theory of the four elements – air, fire, earth, and water – as astrological symbols in relation to nature and her task of creation or destruction by means of these elements (*Timaeus*, 56ff). As a result of this astrological connection, the natural elements of air, fire, earth and water become associated with planets and zodiac signs. For example, the element of air with Jupiter, the planet, and Gemini, Libra and Aquarius, the zodiac signs. Fire connects with Mars, and Aries, Leo and Sagittarius. Earth associates with Venus, and Taurus, Virgo and Capricorn. And, water connects with the Moon (*Luna*), and Cancer, Scorpio and Pisces.

In addition to the celestial connection of the elements, ancient philosophers further explain the natural articulation that each of these elements rises from a combination of two primary natural principles. For example, water derives from the cold and moist principles, while air from damp and hot. Fire evolves from hot and dry, while earth from dry and cold. This identification is conceived as developing and proceeding in a cycle that begins with the first element, such as water, and ends with the last element, earth, having passed through the intermediate stages of air and fire.

Furthermore, the four natural elements correspond to, and affect accordingly, other natural phenomena, both in time and space, creating a fourfold order of nature, for example, water and air modify the qualities of the atmosphere (hot-moist, hot-dry, cold-dry and cold-moist). Water influences the conditions of the atmosphere (liquid, gaseous, dense and solid) and air changes the forces of nature, such as the winds (south, east, north and west). These natural phenomena also incorporate the organs of the human body (heart, liver, spleen, and brain), which in turn modify the individual sensations (taste buds of sweet, bitter, acid and salty) or affect the humors (blood, yellow-bile, black-bile and phlegm). These humors correspond to the psychic of the individual. The temperament of sanguine, for example, is associated with the blood humor, choleric with yellow-bile, melancholic with black-bile, and phlegmatic with phlegm. The sixteenth-century engraving from L. Thurneysser's *Quinta essentia* of 1574 (Fig. 8) illustrates the Greek concept of the four humors with their natural and celestial correlation to the human body. Illustrated medical books show how physicians, in their treatments, adjust and connect the imbalance of body fluids with the humors and their astrological and seasonal influences (Fig. 9). For example, the illuminated page of *Four Humors* in *Guidebook of the Barber-Surgeons of York* (Fig. 10), an English manuscript of the fifteenth century in the British Museum Library, reveals the importance of the humors as well as their corresponding relation to types to a individual role and tasks in society.

Traditionally, most astrological representations of the planets and signs of the zodiac are anthropomorphic or zoomorphic conceptions. These zodiacal signs affect the particular mode, virtue, and tendency of a ruling planet and its relationship to the other planets. Since these planetary gods are anthropomorphic, their tendencies, behaviors and characters influence the present and future conditions of the individual.

Furthermore, the planets and the astrological signs were viewed as interconnected with the various cycles of nature as the seasons (spring, summer, autumn and winter). The evolution of the four seasons, transformed into budding, flowering, fruiting and decaying, was also paired with the four elements and their natural phenomena as seen in the emblematic tradition of Anulus Barptolomäus' *Picta Poesis* (Lyon, 1552). For example, in a wheel format, Barptolomäus' emblem *Aeterna Hominum Natura* (Fig. 11) depicts the transformation of the fours seasons, while Andrea Alciato's Emblem 101 (Fig. 12), *The Four Seasons of the Year* ("*In quatour anni tempora*"), classifies seasonal birds with their respective chants, representing nature, time and the season.

During the Renaissance, humanists continued to absorb and revive the classical tradition of representing or connecting the seasons with planets, zodiacal sings and pagan divinities. Spring, for example, was sacred to Venus or Mercury, summer to Apollo or Ceres, autumn to Bacchus, and winter to Saturn. In *Allegories of the Virtues and Vices in Medieval Art,* Adolf Katzenellenbogen explains how in antiquity the pictorial representations of the elements of nature allude to the importance of the governing laws in nature, as in *Bacchus Surrounded by the Four Seasons as Planets* at the Algiers Museum (Fig. 13). This Roman mosaic decoration is one of the oldest depictions of this theme.[15]

The alternation of the seasons, like the phases of the Moon, punctuates the rhythm of life and the stages in the cycle of development (birth, growth, maturity and decline). In turn, the cycle relates to the states in human life or Ages of Life (childhood, adolescence, maturity and old age). For example, in Joannes Sambucus' emblem *Partes Hominis* in *Emblemata* of 1564 (Fig. 14), the individual represents a microcosm controlled by the natural phenomena of the seasons and the celestial signs of the zodiac.

Elizabeth Sears in *The Ages of Man: A Medieval Interpretation of the Life Cycle,* and John Burrows in *The Ages of Man*, explain how the Pythagorean tetrad concept of the ages of life became associated with the seasons during the Renaissance. These scholars also discuss the expansion of the cycle of life, from four to six or seven life cycles, as the result of the impact of Arabic science and medicine in the Middle Ages. As in antiquity, the Middle Ages and the Renaissance, the cycle of life is associated with human behavior as well as with their societies and cultures, as depicted in Guariento's *Seven Cycles* or *Ages of Life* of 1330s, in the choir of the Church of the Eremitani in Padova. In this decorative scheme, each age creates a cycle ruled by a planet. In a triptych format, the planet resides in the center while framed by two figures engaged in an activity pertaining to their cycle of life, for example, *Venus and the Third Age of Life* and *Saturn and the Seventh Age of Life*.

In the ceiling of the *Chamber of Fortune*, Vasari combines the Pythagorean tetrad representing of the seasons with only the four *Ages of Life* (childhood, adolescent, adulthood and old age, see Figs. 3-4). These paintings reveal Vasari's awareness of the Neoplatonic theory of microcosm and macrocosm, designed as a wheel of life – an archetype of the universe – and the Renaissance's conventions and notions of the cosmological relations in the universe. Thus, in the ceiling, Vasari's

---

[15] Adolf Katzenellenbogen, *Allegories of the Virtues and Vices in Medieval Art*, (New York: Norton, 1964), 28.

astrological placement of the stars (seven planetary gods with their zodiacal signs), the generating forces of the spheres (seasons and humors of the individual), the power of the stars and their control over the destiny of humanity, relate to the movements of the heavenly bodies as well as to the cyclic and seasonal transformations. This cosmic impact has the power to directly influence the course of events on earth and all human activities, from affairs of the state to their bodily health.

For Vasari, then, these cosmological associations portray the control of the stars on Nature and Art. However, Vasari emphasizes the difference between these two realms – the realm of nature and the realm of art. The realm of nature is one of realism with nature, while the other is of idealism with art. The realm of art is artificial, selective and superior to nature, whereas the realm of nature is actual, general and real. The artist experiences nature, but creates art, as Vasari's *Ages of Life* reveal his artistic sagacity.

The quaternary division of the year as seasons – spring, summer, autumn and winter – representing the recurring cycle of the ages are depicted in different ways in art. Most of the time, these personifications are portrayed as children or female figures, as seen in Vasari's later depiction of the four seasons in the Sala of Opi of 1560 in the Palazzo Vecchio (Fig. 15). For example, Spring is depicted as a lamb, a child or a woman bearing a garland of flowers, accompanied by the zodiacal signs of Aries, Taurus and Gemini. Summer is represented by a dragon spitting fire, or a child or a woman carrying a garland of corn or a sheaf of corn, accompanied by the zodiacal signs of Cancer, Leo and Virgo. Autumn is portrayed by a hare, a child or a woman carrying vine-leaves or bunches of grapes, or a Horn of Plenty brimming with fruit, guided by the zodiacal signs of Libra, Scorpio and Sagittarius. And Winter is depicted by a salamander, a child wrapped in a cloak beside a fire, or an old man holding a sickle or a leafless tree, and accompanied by the zodiacal signs of Capricorn, Aquarius and Pisces.

In the Chamber of Fortune, however, Vasari deviates from the depiction of the *Seasons* in the Sala of Opi and the Renaissance tradition. Because he represents the seasons as a cyclic transformation connected with the progression of life. Nude-male figures personify the seasons and the ages of life. For example, Spring is represented by a sleepy-child embracing a garland copiously decorated with spring flowers. This personification symbolizes Childhood. Summer is depicted by Youth, a daring young-man carrying a garland filled with fruits and vegetables. Autumn as Maturity is portrayed as an adult man looking back while sustaining a garland of vines and grapes. And Winter as Old Age is symbolized by a pensive, aging man resting on a garland with a few wintry vegetables and roots – onions, carrots and turnips. In the representation of the *Ages of Life*, Vasari parallels the fertilization of nature or the realm of nature with the cultivation of the individual. For Vasari, the physical development of an individual is similar to the training and learning experiences of an artist.

Although Vasari borrows from the traditional imagery of the Renaissance, he ultimately seeks emblematic sources for the pictorial innovations. His eclectic intellect is evident in the assimilation and application of Alciato's emblematic imagery and meaning in his paintings. Visually, Vasari does not quote Alciato, but is inspired by the emblematist didactic concepts. For example, from the Alciato's Emblem 101 (Fig. 12), on *The Four Seasons of the Year* ("*In quatour anni tempora*"), Vasari appropriates the meaning of the emblem for the personification of the four seasons (spring, summer, autumn and winter) as Alciato has classified them. But in his emblem, Alciato uses the seasonal birds with their respective chants to represent nature, time and the season, symbolizing the transformation of nature. While in his paintings, Vasari employs the representation of the human form, alluding to the same symbolism of the cycles of nature as Alciato. Furthermore, Vasari's personification of Autumn (Maturity) with a garland filled with grape-vines correspond to Alciato's conceit of a tree wrapped with grape-vines as a symbol for Autumn.

From another Alciato's Emblem 100, *In iuventam* ("On Youth," Fig. 16), Vasari draws the notion of two stages of life in relation to the seasons – Childhood symbolized by Bacchus as the god of Spring, and Adolescence with Apollo as the god of Summer. In Alciato's emblem, the *pictura* of Bacchus crowned with and holding grapes is facing Apollo holding a *lira da braccio.* Both gods stand in a funerary slab, alluding to a *memento mori* – the brevity of youth. In the emblem, Alciato's epigram elucidates and inspires Vasari's portrayal of Childhood and Youth. For example, the epigram describes the motto of "old age may approach with lagging step,"[16] by stating that both Bacchus and Apollo praise the flourishing of youth and pray for its continuation through life with the assistance of their gifts, wine provided by Bacchus and health from Apollo.

Another Vasarian appropriation from Alciato's emblematic corpus is less evident, but still philosophically significant, as the painter connects the forces of nature with the aspirations of art. In Emblem 99, *Ars naturam adviunas* ("Art Helping Nature," Fig. 17), Alciato's *pictura* depicts Mercury with a helmet and a caduceus, sitting on a cube shaped pedestal. In front of him, Fortuna precariously stands on a sphere while holding a windblown sail. The emblem's epigram reads "Art (Mercury) is made to counter the power of nature (Fortune); but when Fortune is bad, it often requires the help of art; therefore, eager youths learn the good arts which have within themselves the advantages of an assured fate."[17]

Vasari interprets Alciato's moral implication in the corners of the *palco* by depicting four *Ignudi* (nude males), symbolizing the ages of life (Figs. 3-4). Each embraces a garland with seasonal vegetation. By linking them together with the festoon, Vasari illusionistically creates a circle within a square shape – the square form is made by the placement of the Ignudi-seasons in the corners of the *palco* and the circle is composed by the implied rotation of the garland motif held by the Ignudi. Thus, Vasari alludes to the stability of nature (square) and to the rotation of its changes (circle). In the *Age of Life* paintings, Vasari also symbolically parallels the circular motion of the seasons to the rotation of the vicissitudes of Fortune.

Moreover, Vasari's jocular teasing of the viewer by rotating the *palco*'s design creates an association with an implied annular movement of seasons (Figs. 1-2). For example, Virtue is above Fortune and Envy, figures that face the seasons of spring and summer or the ages of life of Childhood and Adolescence (Youth). But as the viewer walks around the room, Fortune is above Virtue and Envy, who are facing Autumn and Winter or Maturity and Old Age. In reference to this interpretation, Vasari connects the beginning of the seasons with the early stages of life, as Fortune's vicissitudes guide the incipient life of

---

[16] Alciato, *Emblematum libellus cum commentarii* (Lyon, 1546).
[17] Ibid.

a young artist (Fig. 3). But in subsequent stages of life or seasons, the individual matures through life experiences, learning to control the whimsicality of Fortune and wishing for Virtue to govern and guide his artistic life (Fig. 4).

In the ceiling of the Chamber of Fortune, Vasari places the personification of the *Season*s or *Ages of Life* in a square or cubical space, and the personification of Fortune in an octagonal or circular space, recalling Alciato's emblem (Figs. 2 and 17). Vasari derives several meanings from the relation to Alciato's image, for example, the parallelism between the *locus* of Alciato's Mercury on a cube and Vasari's seasons placed in a square, and Alciato's figure of Fortune resting on a sphere and Vasari's Fortune residing in a circular area. Another Vasarian appropriation of Alciato's didactic principle is related to moral behavior, for example, human endeavors are guided by the planetary gods who control the seasons, months, days and hours from childhood to old age. Fortune, considered by the humanists as a cosmic force of mutability, in turn, may interfere in a positive or negative manner in the human life cycle. If the inference is negative, an individual or artist, such as Vasari, must recall the insightful direction of stable-Mercury, a planetary symbol of knowledge and cosmic force of constancy, by relying on learning and the study of the arts, thus, overcoming unstable Fortune. Vasari's imagery illustrates that he has abided with Alciato's dictum, as his rigorous artistic training has provided him with a flourishing artistic career and accomplishments.

The Renaissance cyclical evolution connected with the Neoplatonic theory of microcosm and macrocosm proclaims the myth of the eternal homecoming. This philosophy alludes to a cyclic alternation and perpetual rebirth, as expounded in Vasari's theory of art, reflected in the *Lives of the Artists* and in the *palco*'s iconographical scheme. Consequently, in depicting the *Four Seasons* or *Ages of Life,* Vasari affirms the ancient and Renaissance conventions on the seasons' symbolism of orderliness, correctness and model behavior – in other words, Nature does not err and Art reveals its victory.

ILLUSTRATIONS

Fig. 1. Giorgio Vasari, Ceiling of the Chamber of Fortune, 1548.
   Arezzo, Casa Vasari
   Photo credit: author

Fig. 2. Giorgio Vasari, *Palco with the Ages of Life*, 1548. Arezzo, Casa Vasari, Chamber of Fortune
Photo credit: author

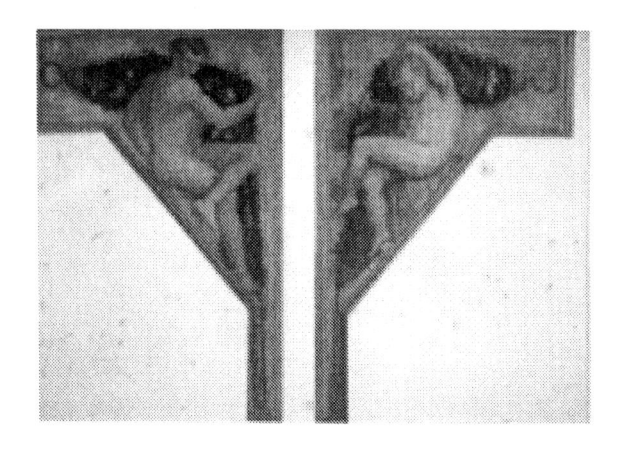

Fig. 3. Giorgio Vasari, *Ages of Life* (detail), 1548.
On the Left: *Youth (Adolescence)* or *Summer*
On the Right: *Childhood* or *Spring*
Arezzo, Casa Vasari, Chamber of Fortune
Photo credit: author

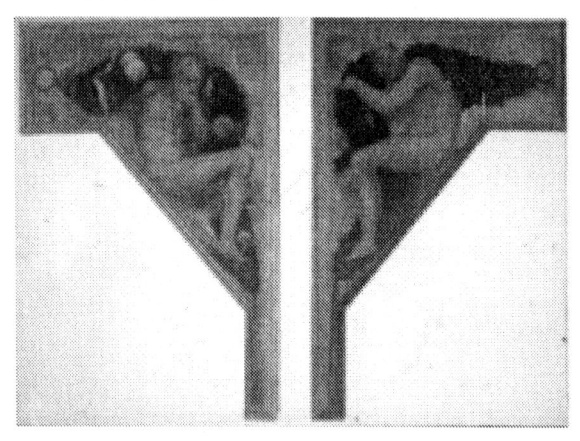

Fig. 4. Giorgio Vasari, *Ages of Life* (detail), 1548
On the Left: *Old Age* or *Winter*
On the Right: *Adulthood (Maturity)* or *Autumn*
Arezzo, Casa Vasari, Chamber of Fortune
Photo credit: author

Fig. 5. *The Individual in the Universe* from an Latin 15th century illuminated manuscript. London, British Museum
Photo credit: British Museum Library

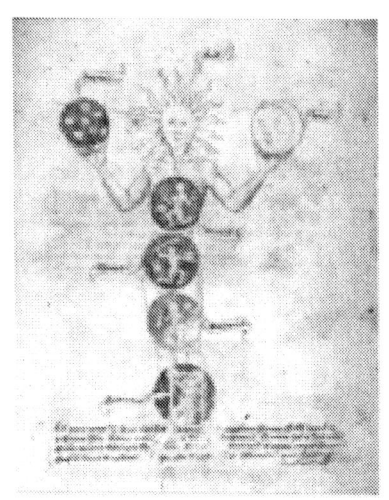

Fig. 6. *The Individual and the Heavens* from a Latin 15th century illuminated manuscript. London, British Museum
Photo credit: British Museum Library

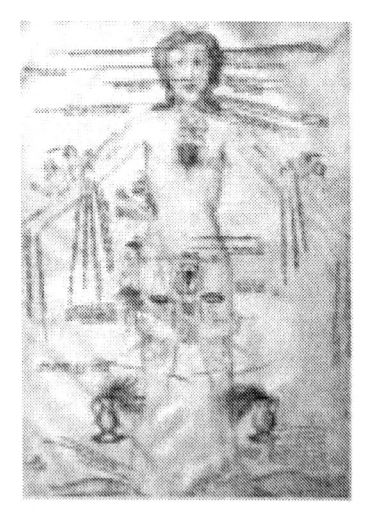

Fig. 7. *Medical Zodiac or Astral Diagram* from a Hebrew 15th century illuminated manuscript, MS 1181, folio 264 verso.
Florence, Biblioteca Nazionale Centrale
Photo credit: Author

Fig. 8. L. Thurneysser, *Quinta essentia*, 1574.
London, British Museum
Photo credit: British Museum Library

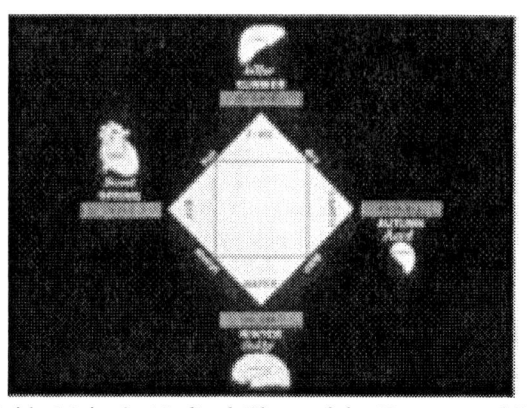

Fig. 9. Guido Maino's *Medical Chart of the Humors and Seasons*
Photo credit: Courtesy of Guido Maino, MD

Fig. 10. *Four Humors* in *Guidebook of the Barber-Surgeons of York*, 15th century. London, British Museum
Photo credit: British Museum Library

Fig. 11. Anulus Barptolomäus, Emblem, *Aeterna Hominum Natura*
In Anulus Barptolomäus' *Picta Poesis*. Lyon, 1552.
Photo credit: author

Fig. 12. Andrea Alciato, Emblem 101, *In quatour anni tempora* ("The Four Seasons of the Year") in Emblematum. Lyon, 1546
   Photo credit: author

Fig. 13. *Bacchus Surrounded by the Four Seasons as Planets*, Roman mosaic of 2nd to 3rd century. Algiers, Museum of Art
   Photo credit: author

Fig. 14. Joannes Sambucus, Emblem, *Partes Hominis*
In *Emblemata*, Lyon, 1564.
Photo credit: author

Fig. 15. Giorgio Vasari, *Spring*, (detail of ceiling), 1560.
Florence, Palazzo Vecchio, Sala di Opi
Photo credit: author

Fig. 16. Andrea Alciato, Emblem 100, *In iuventam* ("On Youth")
In *Emblematum.* Lyon, 1546.
Photo credit: Author

Fig. 17. Andrea Alciato, Emblem 99, *Ars naturam adviunas*
("Art Helping Nature") in *Emblematum…* Lyon, 1546.
Photo credit: Author

Ancient History?
Sicilians in Gianni Amelio's *Lamerica*

Marisa Labozzetta
UNIVERSITY OF MASSACHUSETTS, AMHERST

In his 1994 neorealistic film, *Lamerica,* Gianni Amelio presents a tale of moral conflict on the part of his Sicilian character, Gino, by means of a journey which leads to Gino's atonement and the reshaping of his soul. Though Gino is humbled in the end as a result of his trials, to what extent, if any, is he – the contemporary Italian prototype – aware of the parallel Amelio is drawing between the Albanians and the Sicilians of Gino's ancestry? Moreover, what is the statement Amelio is making about modern-day Italians?

The mirror images of time and place are immediately established at the onset of the film with the use of newsreels depicting the short but significant history of the political union of Italy and Albania in the spring of 1939. In the Porto Durazzo, triumphant cheers from orderly marching Albanians, who show their gratitude to disembarking Fascist officials for the prosperity that Il Duce has brought to the Albanian people, metamorphosize into chants of anarchic Albanians attempting to cross barricading bunkers in the year 1991. "Italy, Italy. You are the world," they cry in desperation. The implicit connection has been made between present-day Albania and postwar Italy: both nations were physically, spiritually, and financially devastated, as well as reeling from the sociopolitical effects of dictatorship. Many Italians left their homeland; one in eight Albanians left.[1]

Italian businessman Fiore and his young apprentice Gino arrive at the chaotic port. The two carpetbaggers have come with the intent of setting up a bogus shoe factory, Alba Calzature, which will be subsidized by grants from the Italian government. Fiore and Gino's father have already pulled off this scam in Nigeria, where they pretend to produce televisions. But in order for the scam to work, Fiore and Gino must find a figurehead chairman – an obscure Albanian without relations, only literate enough to sign his or her name to fraudulent papers. The uneducated and peasant Albanians are likened to children by the

---

[1] Bert Cardullo, "Lands of the Free," *The Hudson Review* 49 (Winter 1997): 637-44.

condescending Fiore, who tells the cocky Gino, "If an Italian told them that the sea was made of wine, they'd go and drink it" – a notion of superiority versus inferiority not only held by Fascists towards the prewar starving Albanians, but by certain Americans towards the large immigrant population of southern Italians several decades earlier. Thus, Amelio extends the connection to encompass the mass emigration of Italians at the turn of the twentieth century.

Fiore and Gino are led by their Italian-speaking guide to a crumbling, squalid prison that more resembles an insane asylum. In an eerie scene, time and protagonist are once again transformed. A frightened Fiore becomes a reincarnated and helpless Italian fascist, who is converged upon by a multiplying mob of prisoners akin to a rioting Italian populace; or perhaps he is a despised Bourbon ruler being attacked by starving Sicilian peasants. This metaphor crystallizes with the introduction of Spiro Tozai, a man in his seventies, who has been imprisoned for fifty years because of his democratic ideology, and for whom time has stood still. Spiro believes that he is twenty years old and, therefore, being so out of touch with reality, appears to be a suitable chairman for Fiore and Gino's dummy corporation. Spiro is cleaned up, given new clothes and shoes, and left at an orphanage where he is to reside under the care of nuns. However, when a corrupt state commissioner requests to meet with Spiro in Tirana, in conjunction with the impending con, Gino and Fiore learn that Spiro has disappeared. An irate Gino is sent to retrieve him.

Spiro has boarded a train on which the passengers, seen through Spiro's eyes, not only bear an uncanny resemblance to postwar Italians, but also to Italians a decade or two earlier. Amelio has said, "the Albanians of today seemed like my father's Italy – the faces, the clothes, the manners, above all, the hunger."[2] That is to say, they are the Italians of the *mezzogiorno* on the tails of the great wave of migration, with regards to their outmoded dress and blank expressions; they too are people in a land that time has forgotten.

After Spiro gets off the train and is attacked and nearly killed by a band of little rogues, Fiore and Gino rediscover him in a hospital, where his true identity has been uncovered by an Italian-speaking nurse. Spiro Tozai is actually Michele Talarico, one of the Italians

---

[2]Michael J. Agovino, "Lamerica," *Migration World Magazine* 24.3 (May-June 1996): 49.

caught in Albania after World War II, who might have created false papers to avoid imprisonment or execution. The duality of time is now further complicated with that of identity.

Fiore returns to Italy and Gino is left to pursue a once again fleeing Michele. It is here that Gino's real journey begins: "the younger crook undergoes a Dante-esque descent into the Albanian whirlpool, and the old man becomes a surprising Virgil."[3] Gino – sporting his shiny leather shoes, jeans jacket, and sunglasses – is continually besieged by imploring Albanians who refer to him as "Italian," in scenes reminiscent of southern Italians who once appealed to World War II Americans GI's as "Joe" or simply "*Americano.*" Furthermore, when Gino's jeep is stripped of its tires and the policeman he had left to watch it is nowhere to be found, the sentiments of bigoted American politicians at the turn of the century are echoed by Gino who cries, "Fucking Albanians, peasants, wretches." Wherever Gino goes, he finds himself in the midst of corruption, chaos, and ineffective and brutal authority. His money is useless since there is practically nothing to buy. And throughout, the arrogant Gino – so far removed from the history of his own country and solely interested in his personal prosperity – finds the Albanian people and their pathetic plight despicable, as he boasts that he and Michele are Italians and therefore above them. While Gino's alter ego Michele, on the other hand, is the voice of experience and compassion, murmuring, "poor people, poor people."

It is not until Gino and Michele are waiting for a truck that will take them to Tirana, that the two truly become mirror identities of one another; for it is then that Michele confesses to Gino that he not only is a defector of the Italian fascist army but, like Gino, he is Sicilian. Time continues to overlap as Michele thinks that the graffiti he sees reads: "Duce: Mussolini," and that he is in Italy with only three or four years having passed since the war. Gino remains unmoved and cruelly reminds Michele of his true time and place, going as far as to say that Michele has no baby son as he claims and that his wife is probably dead by now. Yet, Gino fails to break the indomitable spirit of his alter ego. It is at this very point that Gino appears to undergo an epiphany of sorts and demonstrates sympathy towards the old man while he pretends, for the first time, that they are indeed in Italy and that the truck

---

[3]Donald Lyons, "New York," *Film Comment* 31 (Nov/Dec 1995): 76-77.

they await will take them to Reggio Calabria, where they will board a boat back to Sicily. From this moment on, the intertwined identities of Michele and Gino intensify as does the exchange of time and place. But Gino's epiphany has not really come, because the consideration he demonstrates is towards Michele, not the Albanians, and is motivated by his self-interest.

The following scene on the truck bursting with young Albanian men recalls a scene used in the Ellis Island Immigration Museum Film, *Island of Hope Island of Tears*, when a Jewish immigrant tells of his fleeing an oppressed life in Russia at the turn of the century and of his determination to never again return. One of the men on the Albanian truck tells Gino that, in Italy, he will marry an Italian girl and never speak Albanian to his children so that they will forget that their father was Albanian. These words call to mind those uttered by Pietro Di Donato's Annunziata of the same era, who, in *Christ in Concrete*, dreamed for her children's assimilation saying, "My children will dance for me someday…and in the American style" (33). America – once land of opportunity to the Sicilian peasants, with its roads paved with gold – now becomes an Italy where the Albanian men beg to know if roads only for cars that go very fast really exist. America – home to multitudes of diverse immigrants – now becomes an Italy where, as Gino tells the men, there are so many Moroccans, Poles, and black people that they will be lucky to find work as dishwashers. America – where Italians once dug ditches – now becomes an Italy where the Albanian men say that they will be better off washing dishes than starving in Albania. And while Gino continues to be barraged by the men in search of bread and work, Michele engages in conversation with an exhausted Albanian boy (whom he believes to be a fellow Italian) about America (the place for which he thinks they are headed). Here, Amelio cannot make clearer the generation of immigrants to which he is referring when Michele tells the boy that his relatives had left "before the war" and gone to Patterson, New Jersey, and New York, worked and earned money, and even built houses. *"La giù è un altra cosa,"* Michele says with longing, but the words fall on deaf ears as the boy dies.

Gino continues to display nothing but annoyance towards the Albanians; nevertheless, he is in good spirits with Michele, sharing with him a small piece of cheese someone has given Gino and humoring Michele in conversation. However, when Gino learns (from a phone call made to Fiore) that the shoe-factory deal is off, he abandons Michele by paying off a flophouse owner to keep him. Gino also lies to Michele, promising that the proprietor will take him to Sicily. Michele insists that Gino needs him; Gino responds that he needs no one. Gino has learned nothing. It is not until Gino is imprisoned for having had dealings with the corrupt official and his freedom is threatened with indefinite time in a horrid Albanian jail unless he leaves the country at once, that Gino truly undergoes a change. He is released without a passport and becomes like many of the *turn-of-the-century* Italian immigrants – like all Albanians – without papers.

As a dejected Gino waits at the port, he watches a group of youngsters trying to learn English: they spout out words in Albanian while a girl, who stares as though entranced, returns the English word, the last of which is *nave*. Albania has been invaded twice by Italy – militarily in 1939 and, more recently, by television, teaching the Italian language and conveying a distorted image of a rich Italian society.[4] The scene cuts to the ship Partiziani, crowded with Albanian emigrants. Gino wanders around the ship, as dazed and expressionless as the Albanians on the train had been. He has become like them: an immigrant sailing to his native land as though for the first time.

Michele has also found his way to the ship. The ashamed Gino attempts to avoid him, but is thwarted by an Albanian and thus forced to confront his alter ego, as well as his "fellow" immigrants. Without bitterness, the kind Michele, his *paesano*, is happy to see Gino and, in a role reversal of sorts, tells him to have courage: they can travel together; they and all of these people will soon be in *America*, which is big enough for everyone. It is Gino's eyes that now function as the camera's lens, focusing on the smiling countenances of the Albanians who are presented as portraits filled with hope as were those faces of immigrants approaching Ellis Island in *Island of Hope, Island of Tears*. Still, Gino's eyes reveal neither the compassion for the Albanians exhibited by his alter ego Michele, nor the realization that he, the Albanian immigrants, and Michele are one. Gino does not answer Michele's questions as to whether or not Gino can speak American, or if they will find work in New York. While we can believe that Gino, through first-

---

[4] Gary Crowdus, Richard Porton, "Beyond Realism: Preserving a cinema of social conscience," *Cineaste* 21.4 (Fall 1995): 6.

hand experience, has become sympathetic to the reality of the devastating fate the Albanian dreamers will find in Italy, that he has discovered there is dignity in human suffering, and that perhaps he regrets his near taking advantage of others' misfortune, we cannot help but concede that Gino has failed to identify with his Sicilian ancestry. That is, until the protagonist's very last scene in which he joins Michele and allows the old man to rest his head upon the young man's shoulder – to become one with him.

Critics such as Ted Parks, who further extracted from the work the notion of life's fragility and the necessity of redemption even at the dawn of a new age,[5] failed to mention the importance of Gino's association with not only his postwar immigrant ancestry but, and maybe more importantly, with Italy's earlier wave of emigration which hailed in such overwhelming numbers from Sicily. Movie blurbs ignored it. Just as Michele's words fell upon the deaf ears of the dying Albanian boy, so perhaps has Amelio's message fallen on the deaf ears of the modern-day Italian. As a young Italian man recently told me, "The film was lost on the majority of Italians, who do not like to remember their history" (Desantis). And perhaps that is Gianni Amelio's real message.

REFERENCES

Agovino, Michael J. "Lamerica." *Migration World Magazine* 24.3 (May-June 1996): 49.

Lamerica. Dir. Gianni Amelio. Filmel/CICC/Fido Cinematografica (Rome), 1994. Videocassette. New Yorker Films Artwork, 1998.

Cardullo, Bert. "Lands of the Free." *Hudson Review* 49 (Winter 1997): 637-44.

Crowdus, Gary, and Richard Porton. "Beyond Realism: Preserving a Cinema of Social Conscience." *Cineaste* 21.4 (Fall 1995): 6.

Desantis, Emmanuele. Interview. Northampton, MA. Aug. 2000.

Di Donato, Pietro. *Christ in Concrete.* New York: Signet, 1993.

Island of Hope - Island of Tears. The Ellis Island Immigration Museum Film. Guggenheim Productions. Washington, D.C.

Kurzweil, Edith. "Films at the Festival: New York Film Festival." *Partisan Review* 63 (Spring 1996): 322.

Lyons, Donald. "New York." *Film Comment* 31 (Nov/Dec 1995): 76-77.

Parks, Ted. "Strange Bedfellows: Mixing the Spiritual and the Cinematic." *Sojourners* 29.2 (March/Apr. 2000).

---

[5]Ted Parks, "Strange Bedfellows: Mixing the spiritual and the cinematic," *Sojourners* 29.2 (March/Apr. 2000).

Italy and Greece, War, Culture, Religion.
Relationships and People in *Mediterraneo* and *Malena*

Mario Aste
UNIVERSITY OF MASSACHUSETTS, LOWELL

The Mediterranean Sea has been throughout the centuries the connecting link between Greece, Italy and the Hellenic civilization that followed in the territories that were known as Magna Graecia. The Greek cities of Akragas (Agrigento), Syracuse and other cities, in Sicily were the philosophical and scientific centers for studies in literature, philosophy and the sciences. The most famous Greek teachers and philosophers established these schools on the island, which seems to appear, on the map, to be in the center of the classical world. This becomes more obvious after the Roman conquest. Rome absorbed the culture, philosophy and arts of the Greeks when the Mediterranean sea became a Roman lake, appropriately called by them "Mare Nostrum." Through the maritime routes Rome brought law and order, peace, trade and communications between peoples. It is in homage to this historical event that this paper delves into the analysis of two contemporary Italian films, *Mediterraneo* and *Malena*, for the purpose of bringing to light the relationships between Italians and Greeks, not only in reference to the well known historical facts but also to make connections between the two cultures and the interpersonal relationships of the two peoples, who like to address each other "una faccia, una razza" as a form of greetings.

Salvatores' *Mediterraneo* and Tornatore's *Malena* are appropriate vehicles to analyze, in a historical-social and emotional context, the events and the interpersonal relationships of an interesting period of Italian history because the social and political world of Italy was going through a period of change. The general outlook, personal attitudes and the mentality brought by Fascism in Italy were slowly being replaced by the winds of social change and new political realities established by the parties belonging to the Committee of National Liberation, which operated in the close up background while establishing a new Italy. Salvatores' *Mediterraneo* addresses issues related to the Second World War and the discussions of Italian Soldiers literally and physically abandoned to their fate in a far away island that they are supposed to protect from a Turkish invasion in the Italian quest for an empire.

MEDITERRANEO

Gabriele Salvatore's *Mediterraneo* has a distinct antiwar message, as well as a multifaceted approach to a comparative analysis of the times and issues surrounding the historical period before and during WWII and the relevant aspects of the relationships between Italy and Greece. In *Mediterraneo*, the wartime period is represented through individual actions and perceptions, while the subject matter is delving into the poignant ethnic issues and peace-war themes between Italy and Greece, framed by Salvatores in a metaphorical approach. *Mediterraneo* emphasizes the ethnic tenor of the relationship between natives and invaders by blurring the lines of distinction between the two, thus implying that there is no difference between Italian solders and Greek locals. The interaction of the Greek natives, and their culture, with the war experience of the stranded Italian soldiers is transformed by Salvatores into a fertile ground of discovery with a comparative study of two cultures. The odd lot of Italian characters consists of eight soldiers: Montini, the cultural lieutenant, the orphan Farina, the two Muranon brothers (Felice and Libero), the unruly Lo Russo, the forlorn Strazzabosco, the pining Noventa and the shy Colasanti. While on the Greek side there is the local prostitute, Vasilissa, redeemed to the honorable state of wife by Farina, the local parish priest who convinces Montini to restore the frescoes of the church and the whole coterie of villagers. There is also a short appearance by a devious trading Turk.

These Italian soldiers are sent in 1941 to occupy the remote Greek island of Meghisti where they, while becoming increasingly isolated from the rest of the world, find pleasure in escaping the war and their national identity and eventually becoming "one" with the natives. The central theme of the film is precisely this erasure of national identity as the sea and the sun of the Aegean island wash out any traces of cultural and physical difference. In the first twenty minutes of the film, during the invasion, Meghisti seems to be empty of people, while the Italian soldiers are constantly involved in comic incidents that betray their apprehension of the (absent) natives. They also manifest their incompetence while establishing themselves as an occupying force. Their visible fears and lack of preparedness for the task undertaken lead to a series of self-destructive actions (such as shooting a mule and smashing a radio), thus isolating themselves from the outside world, the rest of the Italian army, and the war. They eventually lose also all traces of their military status, including uniforms and weapons. The viewers, in this context, will fully understand the disparaging comment, "Italians," made by the two British naval officers, at the end of the film, when they arrive at the island to return all the able-bodied Greeks, who fought in the war as partisans. These two officers will take back to Italy the stranded Italian soldiers, with the exception of Farina, who hides in order to remain on the island because of his marriage with Vasilissa.

The first encounter of the Italian soldiers with the locals occurs when the sentry is awakened by a group of Greek children who tease him. As panic takes over, the soldiers march in deadly silence and fully armed through the paths leading to the squares, streets and houses of a deserted, small village looking for the absent enemy. Suddenly they approach a washing line, with bright white sheets obscuring the view, and on parting them they discover the locals: playing children, women chit chatting and old men sitting in a café, drinking ouzo, discussing and playing backgammon. When they inquire where the younger men are, they are directed to the local priest who not only speaks perfect Italian but also reassures them that "Greeks, Italians, same face, same race." With the issue of difference settled like that, from this point forward, the film sets out to explore the universal themes of friendship, love, destiny, and the meaning of life.

In this new environment, most of the soldiers begin to relax, seduced by the island's leisurely ways and peaceful life. The two Muranon brothers, left on an outpost to guard the island, embark on a playful "ménage à trois" with a beautiful shepherdess; Farina, being an orphan, is instinctively led to appreciate Greek life and soon falls in love with Vasilissa, the local prostitute, who services all the soldiers according to a rotation plan devised by Lo Russo, the sergeant, who eventually finds an outlet to his macho posturing in Greek folk-dancing. The Italian soldiers have settled quite well on the island by becoming one with the natives, and they feel free and fulfilled with the exception of Noventa, who constantly longs to return home to his wife and family. He even goes, in the fulfillment of his wishes, to the extent of stealing a local fisherman's small row boat, and he tackles the long journey back to Italy, leaving the viewers wondering about his fate.

The stranded soldiers, in this new version of an earthly paradise, are put to another test: the arrival of a small fishing boat with a young trading Turk, who greets them with the – by now accepted – greeting, "Italians, Turks: una faccia, una razza." The Italians, not having many personal dealings with Turkey, invite him to share their quarters and a relaxed party ensues. They are perhaps too relaxed, but then the island gives them a sense and feeling of familiarity coupled with hominess, and so they let their guard down a bit. After all, what can happen in one's own back yard? They are confident and trusting, the local priest has assured them that Greeks and Italians are "una faccia, una razza," and so they too accept the Turk at face value, especially when he uses the same greeting, "Italians, Turks: una faccia una razza." The priest had seemed like a distant relative, so why not ease up a little bit and accept the Turk's invitation to a party? They enjoy his company, even though he does not say much.

The soldiers at the party are introduced to several types of drugs, and while everything seems to flow freely they open up their inner selves. Their discussion involves everything and anything from the meaning of life, love and war to their present situation. While dishing out the most intimate confessions about themselves and their interpersonal relationships, they also reveal well-hidden inner feelings about issues and things to the point of true confessions. After a night of drugs and endless talk, they fall asleep while the Turk steals their weapons and valuables before taking off to the open sea. The Italians quickly learned a valuable lesson: that although the Greeks could be trusted because of cultural affinity, the Turks are of a different breed. The priest, when he is told of their experience, reacts decisively: "You trusted a Turk?" as if it were the most amazing thing that he had ever heard. This statement should not come as a surprise, given the long history between Greeks and Turks, especially if the revolutionary war of Greek independence from Turkey, of the last century during the Romantic period, is taken into consideration, and especially if the multi-layered lack of trust between Turks and Greeks is also considered.

The Italian soldiers felt reassured by the concern of the priest and consequently they accept a higher form of affinity toward the inhabitants of the island and, since they could not return to their Italian villages, they adopt the Greek village with a sense of belonging while awaiting for the time when they can return home and reconnect with their families after the war. The only exception to this approach is the one of sergeant Lo Russo, who was a soldier by profession and thus believed in the values associated with the power coming from being a ranking member of the military. As the film progresses, the viewers become aware that the war has passed by. Since they are cut off from the world without a boat, radio, or other means of communication, they eventually "go native" and blend with the island's population. They start shedding their uniforms and begin to wear the more traditional and practical clothes of the natives. They take active part in the life of the community by going to church and help with the daily chores and in some cases by replacing the absent men of the village. They turn from soldiers and occupiers to cousins and inhabitants, thus making their life in the island much easier, thinking that, since they are going to be on the island, they might as well enjoy themselves as much as possible with pleasant and fulfilling life.

In this newly found reality their presence as an occupying force is slowly disappearing, especially when their interpersonal relationships with the natives move to new levels, e.g. Farina's declaration of his love for Vasilissa and his desire to marry her. With a loaded rifle, from the balcony of the brothel, he stops everyone from having sex with her. He marries her in an Orthodox religious ceremony, officiated, with almost fatherly understanding, by the local priest. Farina, however, is unable to fulfill another symbolic element of the ceremony: that of the breaking of the glass, and thankfully Lo Russo comes to his rescue and takes care of the business at hand by crashing the glass and thus allowing the festivities to continue with the wedding reception, in the village square, for everyone in the local community of Greek natives and the village's Italian invaders. Life continues on the island under every aspect of "normalcy." The Muranon brothers persist in their love relationship with the shepherdess, who appears to be several months pregnant at the end of the film when she greets them from the hill, above the village, on their departure for Italy. Strazzabosco finds a new mule, which he will take back to Italy, to the dismay of the same English officers, who make the famous comment, "Italians." It is sufficient to say that during their stay on the island the whole company accomplishes many of the tasks normally assigned to adult males, including entertaining the local senior citizens, playing soccer with the native children, and satisfying some of the lonely women.

One day, precisely during a soccer game, a Sicilian air pilot, on a single engine plane, makes an emergency landing and brings the news that Mussolini has fallen. The group is also informed that Italy is in a state of civil war and that Fascism is falling from political power. Some time later, English naval officers arrive on the island to bring back all the local men, who had fought, as partisans, against the Italian and German armies. The same English officers will bring the Italian soldiers back to Italy, including Strazzabosco with his donkey. Farina instead hides in a barrel of olives in order to stay with his wife, Vasilissa. Lo Russo, who went to look for him and finds him hiding, lets him stay and protects him from the Lieutenant's search. Several years later, an elderly Montini returns to the island, now overrun by tourists, to visit Farina on the occasion of Vasilissa's death, and to his surprise he finds in Farina's restaurant also the disillusioned Lo Russo. It seems that the sergeant's dreams of rebuilding Italy were in vain.

Vasilissa and Farina, after the war, were successful in opening the restaurant of their dreams and the three reunited men, while reminiscing of the war days and preparing eggplants for the daily menu, reflect upon the fact that life in Italy, after their perfect and ideal interlude, had failed to live up to their expectations. Perhaps the dedication at the beginning of the film, "To all those who are running away," must be understood in a new and different context: peace and tranquility can only be found in territories away from the major intercourse of civilizations and cultures. The characters express this theme over and over again, through their peaceful coexistence with the natives and the elimination of the violent and harsh reality of war. The film may be about conflicts, but in truth it is about the exact opposite: quietness and tranquility. *Mediterraneo* seems to emphasize that the ancient proverb, "Graecia capta, Roma capta est" ("Once Rome conquered Greece, Rome was captured by Greece"), still holds true in the twentieth century.

In this earthly paradise, the cultured Montini, after being invited by the village priest, restores the frescoes of the local Orthodox Church and helps Farina to woo the woman he loves, Vasilissa, by giving him a book of Greek love poetry translated into Italian. The poems captivate Farina and Vasilissa, and they fall in love and eventually get married. Their marriage may be interpreted as a union between two "peoples" by bringing forth the joys of peace and understanding. Farina, an orphan, had a troubled youth, but his turmoil comes to an end after he marries

Vasilissa. His life's long search for a truly personal intimate goal is fulfilled in marriage. Vasilissa's dream to open a restaurant on the island becomes a reality after her marriage to Farina, and it is to this restaurant, appropriately named "Vasilissa," that the lieutenant returns for his visit. Farina's character is fulfilled, after his marriage, because of his new found relationship based on love, while Vasilissa's character is reborn with new and personally exciting and fulfilling responsibilities, since, through love and marriage, she will escape "the profession." She will also achieve the most coveted and wished for conclusion to her earthly existence, fulfilling another dream, besides her respectable married life, that is, to open a restaurant. The union of Farina and Vasilissa is the metaphorical fulfillment of the peace strived for among two peoples and races, Italian and Greek. It highlights, in a positive way, the constantly repeated "motto": "una faccia, una razza," a motto that blurs the dividing lines of ethnic and cultural differences by indicating, through the metaphor of marriage, a more perfect union, of intent and purpose, between two nations: Italy and Greece, which have been so intimately associated in the history and civilization of the Western world.

Mediterraneo is not only a film about love's true values and authenticity, but also the expression of emotional interchange between friends and co-nationals. Above all it is a film about the exchange of communication, ideas and understanding with and about the other. It is also a film that addresses the common concerns and issues of the human family beyond the ethnic or the racial divide. These issues affect every human being and so Salvatores eloquently highlights them throughout the film, with the appropriately placed motto, "*una faccia, una razza*." Feminist scholars may wish that there were more women characters in the film; gay right activists also may have liked it if the only gay character had been taken more seriously, but overall the film's many statements are a sure affirmation of the deeper human values of love, loyalty, and friendship. *Mediterraneo,* if seen in this light, certainly conveys the true bonds of unity and understanding, especially when, on a more subtle level, it delivers the message of anti-violence and anti-war.

Non-violent, peaceful sentiments are emphasized in the epilogue of the film, set in the present. The island is no longer deserted but is still invaded by strangers, except that the new invaders are tourists arriving by ferry. The aged lieutenant returns to the island to visit Farina on the death of Vasilissa, and here, in the restaurant named after her and run by Farina, he encounters Lo Russo, who has left Italy because, according to him, "life was not great in Italy, they didn't let us change anything, so I said: 'You have won, but I don't have to be an accomplice,' so I came back here." This attitude reflects a condemnation of the political and economical systems established by the new Italy, after the war. The system was unsatisfactory to him and he escaped back to the island of Meghisti, where he found peace and tranquility, since he was truly disappointed with the course of events in Italian society. The film's dedication: "To all those who run away," has been the cause of some controversy in Italy, but Salvatores responds appropriately by saying: "Some saw it as an invitation to avoid commitment, which is not what I meant at all. You can escape and run away as an act of protest. If you escape from prison, it is not an act of defeatism. I don't think you can really escape from society, but you can run away from the general homogenization of society, from the atmosphere of indifference, from consumerism and brainwashing. It seems that many Italians were offended by the seemingly cowardly attitude of the film, which obviously was not what it meant to convey."

The good side of this film is that it can be enjoyed for what it is, a simple tale of the good side of humanity persevering for once in understanding the other and not looking for conflict with the other. It may look very unrealistic, but then it is highly entertaining and makes people feel good at the prospect of successful interpersonal relationships across the ethnic and racial divide. Differences exist in a dynamic and dialectic relationship of mutual interdependency, rather than of exclusion. In *Mediterraneo*, Salvatores engages in exploring the dialectic of similarity and difference and makes this exploration the basis for cultural border crossing and exchange.

On the level of the narrative the sequence functions as a reassurance for the invading and fearful soldiers that the invaded are not the hostile and dangerous "other" that a war enemy essentially is. On the level of the mise-en-scène, the disavowal of threatening difference takes the form of postcard-type shots of the villagers engaged in their peaceful and stereotypical Greek activities. This is further reinforced by the vaguely Greek-sounding music that dominates the soundtrack. Reassurance here takes the form of a representation of the native as a group of primitive, fun loving, simple and friendly people who only come to life under the gaze of Italian soldiers. The Greek villagers become an organic part of the wild but beautiful landscape that exists beyond history or conflict. The threatening but historically rooted difference of the enemy is replaced by a much more controlled difference, that of the objectified natives abstracted from historical reality and repackaged as local color. In this sense, the historically specific becomes eternal and the encounter of the two cultures an existential issue.

Conflicts around national and European identity, the representational regimes of this film and future strategies for a transcultural and transnational European cinema can be mapped around the notions of diversity/difference and dichotomy. The demand for, and celebration of, cultural diversity can be seen as essentially European in terms of the assertion of values, such as the democratic pluralism of culture and the freedom and the autonomy of artistic expressions. In liberal cultural relativism and culturalism, Europe discovers its enlightened uniqueness as well as a point of coherence in its fractured identity. *Mediterraneo* mobilizes these sensibilities by negating the specific historical context that defines the difference(s) between culture and conflict. The erasure of differences enables the film to capitalize on the assumed universality of its themes, since the film is "dedicated to all those who are running away."

Mediterraneo offers the comfortable "perspective" on the diversity of cultures by reducing differences into simple binaries. Crucially in this film, water plays an important role: the sea surrounds the island and gives its name to the film, Mediterraneo. Water is a material and visual manifestation of fluidity and fluidity involves first and foremost a renegotiation of identity. This entails a restructuring of the relationships between similarity and difference that support any identity. In this film, water has specific and narrative and symbolic functions representing distinctive ways in which cultural difference and exchange are conceived and constructed. Furthermore, in a geographical sense, water seems to reproduce this dynamic relationship between similarity and difference, union and separation: the sea is not only a physical frontier and marker of national boundaries, but also routes of communication linking and connecting ports, peoples and cultures.

In *Mediterraneo,* the cultural and historical difference between the Italian soldiers and the Greek natives is erased as the sea disconnects them from the flow of history and the fixity of national identity. But as the "first encounter" sequence demonstrates, this assertion of similarity, of the essential sameness of the human condition, negates difference by placing it within a discourse and a regime of representation that can only divide the world into "us" and "them," the same and the other. The function of the sea, then, despite the rhetoric and tone of sameness, is to separate, to protect the island from history, reality and interaction, to turn it into a "deserted island": where cultures exist in the totalizing loneliness of the utopianism rooted in the mythic memory of a unique collective identity.

MALENA

Tornatore's *Malena* skirts the issues of politics and dwells instead on the lives of men and women in a remote Sicilian hamlet during World War II. They are affected by the behavior of a beautiful woman: Malena, left alone by her soldier husband, who is serving in the Russian campaign. Malena is able though to condition her response to the locals. The plot and action of the film unfolds in the small Sicilian village of Castelcuto, among citizens who were dedicated admirers of Mussolini, Il Duce, around 1940-43. Tornatore's images allow the viewers to follow the span of several years of Renato's obsession about Malena, who lives with her aging father, since her husband, Nino, was called to serve in World War II. As Renato's fascination with Malena grows, he engages into a series of rather predictable youthful shenanigans, which are nonetheless entertaining. Among his several exploits there is the stealing of a pair of Malena's panties from the laundry line, fantasizing about her incessantly, and causing much consternation to his conservative Catholic family.

The citizens of Castelcuto seem to be unaware of the policies of Mussolini's grand-standing political gambles. While all the youthful shenanigans of Renato and his friends are taking place, the war efforts are slowly dominating the daily life of the citizens throughout Italy, including Castelcuto. Everyone is in dire circumstances of hardship caused by the war effort which affects every human being especially Malena, the protagonist. *Malena*, in this context, is not just the story of the shenanigans of the male residents of a small Sicilian village regarding their obsession for the other sex, but foremost it is the story of Malena, a woman whose life is destroyed because of the misfortune of having lost, according to military records, her husband during the Russian campaign of World War II. This circumstance forced her to return in Castelcuto and reenter the single state. By choosing this new way of life she created a situation that makes her desirable to the local men, who are looking for sexual favors. Being beautiful and attractive, during her daily routine while walking through town, she elicits the attention of the local male population, who ogle her and continuously make, in appreciative ways, comments about her physical charms. The scenes and action of this film, in this context, appear to be a continuous quotation of Fellini's films, and the adolescent boys who are affected by Malena's charms bring to mind Fellini's *8 1/2, Amarcord* and *I Vitelloni*.

Malena, as she passes by, is ogled by all those who allow their active imagination to run wild about her charms and their subliminal fantasies. She is the ultimate beauty and they can fantasize about her since they cannot imagine any other woman able to arouse such fantasies in their minds. Their inner desires of sexual gratification are not only aroused by continually dwell in their fantasies. All of the young men are affected by her languorous swaying passage and the male population of Castelcuo can hardly stop the appreciative glances while the minds of all these men continue to fantasize on over-time.

Malena, who is a school teacher and of at least average intelligence, must be aware of her effect on the collective male libido, but seems blissfully oblivious; her role is not so much dramatic as pictorial, a word used in the *Playboy* sense, but then she enjoys the attention given to her by the men of Castelcuto who support her with their business. Recalling Tornatore's previous works e.g. *Cinema Paradiso* and *The Starmaker*, Malena and Renato are cast in several appropriate roles in the realm of the fantastic, e.g. from several typical roles of classic Hollywood romantic films: "*Tarzan-Renato*" and Malena, "*Cowboy-Renato*" saves Malena from savage Indians and "*Gladiator-Renato*" proves his worth to "*Empress Malena*". In fact there is in *Malena* the suggestion that nostalgia is unobtainable but it can only be achieved with the images of an active imagination and through them and in them there is also the reinforcement of a non-existing relationship between and the characters, Renato and Malena.

The local women are suspicious of Malena and throughout the film clearly demonstrate that they do not like her. When she initially strolled through the town on her husband's arm, all of the women had something to say, but when her husband left for the war, they classified her as a "whore," because of her extra-marital activities in town. Malena totally disregards the local women, attitudes and, even though she continues to sells her body in order to survive, she hopes and eagerly looks forward to her husband's return and holds dearly to her determination. Convinced that it was her beauty that caused the village women's commotion, she disregards them and continues to go forward in her life. She finally makes the final and conscious decision to spend the years of the war by holding on to the hope that her husband will return safe and sound. Her goal was not to interact with the women but to go about her business of survival until the time that her life could return to normality again as it was before the war.

Malena is not only a lady who becomes a prostitute, but a human being who survives the horrors of war and beyond it. In a metaphorical sense, she is an allegorical character who is transformed into a political representation of Italy. In this context, she becomes a metaphor of Mussolini's Italy, perceived by some as Germany's prostitute. The ultimate result befalling Malena is her trashing by the local women in the public square, where they beat her, shave her head and banish her from the community. This political rite of passage of the Italian populace mirrors the one for Malena when, in the aftermath of the war, the country with a new republican vision of democracy forged a new form of government. This new political system, brought about by a coalition of anti-fascist parties, established a brand new democracy after decades of Fascism and the slowly dying horrors of World War II. This reborn vitality of the Italian People established and put into practice brand new ideas about politics, social concerns, political alliances and new visions for the citizens, coupled with a new role for Italy in a new Europe and in a new World.

Her relationships with the men of Castelcuto are not what they appear to be. Her activities are a means of survival while waiting for the safe return of her husband. The "profession" was a legal activity in this period of Italian history, so much so that brothels were controlled by government guidelines and directives for the sake of public safety. Her actions are not only an indication about her will to survive but also her most urgent need for independence in financial matters and companionship in a town where she feels more a stranger than an integral part of the community. The local rumor, that she had a man in her bed as soon as her husband left, speaks to the notion of longstanding and traditional forms of gossip reflecting cultural mores and taboos. The local dentist Cusimano does not help matters when he is caught lurking in the vicinity o her house and she must go to court to ask for some form of protection in order to defend herself. Malena was in constant fear of facing appropriate legal retribution in a situation where the law seemed to be more on the side of men, who prey on women like rabid animals and birds of prey. A local merchant offers her rationed sugar, coffee and other foods in exchange for sexual favors. Survival in war times is always difficult to appraise but in the case of Malena, men used their argument of helping her to survive the war to find a willing subject to fulfill all their needs as their sexual desires were concerned. Malena is obviously not only a beautiful woman, but also a woman in dire need while waiting for her husband to return.

Malena's good name is sullied by local gossip. Her descent in the world of back-talk and gossip requires her, in a very interesting way, to spend a great deal of time in scenes in which she is half-dressed before Tornatore's appreciative camera. She continues to shine brightly in Renato's eyes, however, even after his field of knowledge is broadened when his father takes him to the local bordello for the old "I give you the boy – give me back the man" routine. Tornatore certainly has taken a cue from several of Fellini's films, except that Fellini's films often involved adolescents inflamed by women who embody their carnal desires like in *Amarcord, Vittelloni* and *8 1/2*. While Fellini, beyond the story, sees the humor that underlies sexual obsession, Tornatore's *Malena* is only a simple story, in which a young man grows up transfixed by a woman without any action required by and for him.

Malena Scordia is the daughter of the Latin teacher, Professor Bonsignore, and she came to Castelcuto to care for her father while her husband is away fighting in the battlefields of World War II. Renato, the story goes, tells the viewers that she was destroyed by the misfortune of being beautiful and by having a nice set of "fun bags," a local nickname for female breasts. When she is outside the house every man's head turns; that is probably the reason why the women in town call her different names and she is a constant and continuous item of their daily gossip and subliminal hatred.

Malena's story and behavior are seen through the eyes of a thirteen-year-old boy who is growing up in a small village where everybody knows everybody else and nothing is hidden from the common view of the village's gossip. The secrets of everyone are well known to all, even though everyone involved or not involved in any of the issues give the impression of not being aware of what is going on. Malena is the returned local beauty and at the same time the object of desire of the local male population and the object of scorn of all the women of Castelcuto. She parades monotonously through streets and piazzas with cow-like indifference, followed by Renato and friends while adult males ogle her and fantasize about all the possible love encounters available to them in the secrecy of her love nest.

When the Germans arrive in town she finally reveals her persona and, in the eyes of all, she becomes what they thought her to be – a whore. Malena's physical and inner beauty is transformed into the craving calls of a vamp to attract male lovers. This becomes more evident when, in a not so subtle change, she dyes her hair blond, and continues to parade, now with clients. Once the war is over the villagers demand that she leave and, with images resonant of ancient actions from biblical times, throw stones at her. A true interpretation of these scenes allows the viewers to understand Tornatore's message: the need for society to find a scapegoat in order to explain all types of evil that unknowingly fall on the human family and the many interpretations and reasons why several types of evils, if not all, cannot be removed. They usually run their natural course even after tremendous struggle by the community.

Throughout the film, Tornatore seems to portray Malena as an innocent bystander while at the same time she is victimized by the rude gossip of the townsfolk. However when she finds out that her husband is a victim of the war she joins in the "profession," since she needs money to survive and longs for a warm plate of food and a place to live that she can call home.

The past of the leading female character in *Malena* is unknown, but it is clearly suggested that life in general has been difficult for her. During World War II and in it aftermath, when a period of economic depression was ruling the way of life for everyone, scarcity of food was normal, this situation meant that society and any individual, especially Malena, alone and with no one to care for her, would do anything to survive the horrors of the times. Renato, who may be willing to do something for her, is also going through adolescence and as he tries to grow up by achieving independence from his overbearing father and religious mother, discovers that there is little or nothing that he can actually do. His desires run the gamut from wanting to wear a pair of long pants to being in love with Malena, thus protecting her from all who could destroy her. Given his age, he only dreams and does nothing about it, except for bearing and accepting the village's ridicule and general gossip about Malena. It is patently clear that he has a teenage crush on Malena, which probably does not go beyond his desire for Malena as a sexual object. His attitude changes though, especially after Malena's final debasement by the village's women when they shave her head and leave her in the public square, bloody and bruised.

The relationship between Malena and the town's women can be seen as a political allegory. While Malena prostitutes herself to the German officers, the allegorical image of Italy as a German's prostitute is created, but things will change as soon as the United States Army liberates Sicily. At that point in time, the Sicilian women accomplish their awaited for revenge toward Malena. The women dressed in black, like birds of pray, capture Malena and they drag her into the village square, where they beat her, cut her hair and shave her head and finally, when all signs of public humiliation are accomplished, banish her from Castelcuto.

With the invasion of the United States Army, Mussolini and his forces are defeated and Sicily is finally liberated. Malena eventually returns to Castelcuto with her husband. On her return she holds her husband's arm and the two walk together toward their house and, as they stroll through the main street, the villagers part to allow the couple to proceed as they greet both of them.

The attitude of the local women, now is changed and they begin to treat her kindly in total contrast to their earlier actions when they banished her from the village. Even with their change of heart Malena's return becomes a constant reminder of the past in fact, for many of them, life in the present still continues as usual.

The nostalgia of the untenable is what drives the fantasy of everyone in Castelcuto from the school age Renato and the local boys in fantasizing about Malena to the women and men making judgments about her personal state of being and her social life. Malena's father is the local teacher and the students often play a game in school without him being aware of their shenanigans. The young men raise their hands as if asking permission to go to the bathroom, instead they are pointing at the door indicating that they want to go into the secret chambers with Malena, his daughter. The deaf man replies "yes" because he is unable to hear them. This is a constant joke in the classroom but eventually it grows stale, especially when the students discuss Malena amongst themselves. They often tell stories about how they talk to her, see her and she asks them to buy cigarettes for her. Everyone seems to have a form of psychological crush on her, but Renato is the one with the biggest one. He often sneaks away from home or school to spy on her, by peaking through the window and lusting after her. Often, while observing her, he sees her dancing to music and his desire is so strong that he want to join her and he behaves as if he is Malena's secret partner. He even buys the record with the music she usually listens to in order to fulfill his fantasy, and vicariously to make love to her.

Renato matures through Malena and his maturity is measured by the way in which he comes to understand Malena as a person beyond and above his consideration of her as an object of desire. Growing in his understanding of Malena as a woman, more than as an object of desire, he begins to sympathize with her. He is able to understand any type of evil that was done to her by the people of the town and, moved by this, he garners enough desire in his heart to protect her. He is the only person in town who knows the true and known story of Malena, mainly because of his interest in her. He is the reason, because of his interest, why Malena was able to reunite with her husband.

Malena and Renato represent traditional Italian social and gender relationships, as well as the political and cultural behaviors during the Duces' dictatorship of Italy. The success of *Malena* lies in how both Renato and Malena's bodies become national bodies and stories, and the personal negotiation of a delusional nostalgia for a primeval pre-Mussolini Italy in a post-World War II world. *Malena* addresses the issue of interpersonal relationships especially in the context of stereo-typing and, as Malena's case clearly shows, that women are more often than not, especially in those days, used as sexual objects for the grati-fication of men. Malena herself, because of her life, perhaps does not have the ability to understand the most fundamental commitments of human relationships.

Malena may give the impression that males do not respect persons of the other sex but we have to keep in mind the cultural milieu and the times that are highlighted in this film. It was common sixty or more years ago to consider women as sexual objects. The walk in the piazza of any woman, especially if she was beautiful, attracted the attention of male observers, who quickly would make laudatory comments on her passing by. Obviously we live in a different and more equal and just world as far as racial and gender relationships are concerned, even though we are still far behind where society should be on these issues.

The first time Malena walks through town is after her arrival and even then, with the escort of her husband, she receives a series of appreciative greetings by male bystanders. The same happens at the end of the film when she returns from exile to Castelcuto. Again, in this final scene, she is accompanied and escorted by her husband who has returned from World War II, who proudly holds his head high, while escorting his wife, Malena, as the village people part their way to allow the couple to proceed forward. Both walk with dignity and surety and by doing so they show their determination to impress all, especially the male population of Castelcuto with their everlasting love in the face of adversity and hardship. This is a clear warning from the couple to the townspeople that their marriage is strong, even though the husband may be absent for long periods of time, while working to support his family. By doing so the couple, shows the determination to impress all, especially the male population of Castelcuto, that they are determined to fulfill their lives with their version of everlasting love in the face of any type of hardship and by keeping a strong faithfulness in their marriage vows.

WORKS CITED

Aspden, Peter. "Mediterraneo" *Sight & Sound* 4 (1993) #50.

Baldassare, Angela. *The Great Dictators*. Toronto: Guernica, 1999.

Bondanella, Peter. *The Films of Federico Fellini*. Cambridge: Cambridge University Press, 2002.

____. *Italian Cinema: From Neorealism to Present*. New York: Continuum, 2001.

Carr, Jay. "*Mediterraneo* turns World War II into Club Med." *Boston Globe* 15 May 1992.

Dick, T.R.B. *The Greeks: How They Live and Work*. Newport, Gt. Brit.: Abbot, 1972.

Ebert, Roger. *Movie Yearbook 2003*. Kansas City, Andews Mc Neal Publishing, 2003.

Eder, Richard. "On a Greek Odyssey by Land, Sea and Poetry." *New York Times* 16 May 1992.

Elettriotris, Dimitris. "Cultural Difference and Exchange: A Future for European Film," *Screen* 41.1 (Spring 200), 92-100.

Gieri, Manuela. *Contemporary Italian Filmmaking: Strategy of Subversion*, University of Toronto Press, Toronto, 1995.

Haycraft, John. *Italian Labyrinth, Italy in the 1980's*, New York, Penguin Books, 1985.

Landgell, Cher. "Mediterraneo." *Magill Cinema annual* (1993): 244-45.

Landy, Marcia. *Italian Film*. Cambridge: Cambridge University Press, 2000.

____. *Cinematic Uses of the Past*. Minneapolis, University of Minnesota Press, 1997.

La Salle, M. :Tornatore Scores again in *Malena*, more emotional than *Cinema Paradiso*" *San Francisco Chronicle*, 25- 12 2000.

Marcus, Millicent. *Italian Films in the Light of Neorealism*, Princeton, Princeton University Press, 1986.

____. *After Fellini – National Cinema in the Post Modern Age*, Baltimore, John Hopkins University Press, 2002.

Martinetti, Cesare. "La Memoria, il regista ricorda il viaggio nell'isola greca dove e' Nato *Mediterraneo*." *La Stampa* 20 July 1992 #16.

Mignone, Mario. *Italy Today: At the Crossroads of the New Millenium*. New York: Lang, 1999.

Ryan, T. "Adolescent Fantasies" *The Age*, 28- 1-2001.

Stille, Alexander. "90's Movies Seen as 40's War through 60's Eyes." *New York Times* 3 March: 11, 25.1.

Thomas, K. "*Malena* emerges as an evocative beauty" *Los Angeles Times* 25-12-2000.

Young, Jules. "Mediterraneo." Video #47. 1993.

Zotos, Stephanos. *The Greeks*. New York: Funk and Wagnalls, 1969.

A Higher Level of Notation

Paul Marion
UNIVERSITY OF MASSACHUSETTS, LOWELL

> "If astronomy teaches us anything, it teaches that man is but a detail in the evolution of the Universe, and that resemblent though diverse details are inevitably to be expected in the host of orbs around him. He learns that though he will probably never find his double anywhere, he is destined to discover any number of cousins scattered through space."
> - Percival Lowell (1895)

On a Sunday morning in Lowell
the streets are wider, quiet – like the sky-colored river.
There's a rest in the song, a pause in the working rhythm.
And it's a chance to look hard,
to see what can be seen, to find what can be found.

Rolling down Salem and Market Streets
listening to Greek melodies on WLLH radio,
I feel the layers of occupation.
The matching weights of St. Patrick's
and gold-capped Holy Trinity pin down the Acre for good.
Like another Ellis Island,
this parcel bears tracks of those who have carried on.
The signs are an Embassy Row:
Club des Citoyens-Americains,Phnom Penh, Olympia.
The overlay sticks, links up in a set.
The census schedule is richer.

Truth hits home as my eye catches
gallon cans of olive oil gleaming in the window of an orange store
    [front.
Farther along the sidewalk men unload sacks of rice.
Old man crossing Worthen Street walks his dog toward the big brick
    [mill.
He stands for all scarred and decorated survivors, plus their line of
    [makers.
From a third story porch somebody's aunt
might be looking for Marion's Meat Market,
a solid, comer establishment that was erased
like the wrong price on a grocery bill in Little Canada.
At a stop sign I check the rearview mirror,

trying to stitch together in a moment
more than a century-and-a-half of life lived under a title, a surname,
"that great fact we call Lowell."
A name layered over Indian words.
I try to retain what I'm told, but the brain is weaker than I'd like.
I'm glad that remnants can be triggers
and grateful for discovery through preservation,
for the texture of diversity, this stained-glass history.

Looking back and looking at, I see the pattern is a turn,
with each turn wheeling in a world colored by long gone motions.
Our culture, the social protoplasm
in which we love, work, dream,
stirred by all this turning, animates each frame.
We are what we were as much as what we are.
What we will become is partly our choice.
We can always change and change again.

The Cultural Function and Trickster Figures of Aristophanic Comedy in Fred Gardaphé's *Moustache Pete is Dead / Evviva Baffo Pietro*

Paul Giaimo
HIGHLAND COMMUNITY COLLEGE

Twentieth-century Chicago's Little Italy and the Athens of fourth-century BC Greece are as superficially unlike each other as any two urban cultures can be; however, their comic muses seem to be relatives who resemble each other as much as Greek olives and Italian olive oils. I shall here argue that Fred Gardaphé's recent anthology, *Moustache Pete is Dead/Evviva Baffo Pietro,* performs a cultural function and presents trickster figures to the audience in a manner very similar to that which we find in the comedies of Aristophanes, the ancient Athenian comic playwright.

Gardaphé's text is a 1997 compilation of columns, which appeared in Chicago's *Fra Noi*, a monthly newsletter that was the cultural voice of Little Italy during Gardaphé's stint as Arts and Culture editor. The main character is a first-generation immigrant of Italian origin known as Moustache Pete. Like the wry social commentators invented by Mark Twain, this pasta-box philosopher offers his heavily dialecticized view on his new American world and the old world he remembers. As in Aristophanes's *The Frogs*, where the author's love of the tragic poet Aeschylus is revealed, as Aeschylus wins a contest against rival Euripides, the voice of Moustache Pete serves as an amplifier of many of his author's cultural views. Furthermore, to prove this Mediterranean resemblance, I will draw upon Laura Arnold's recent Reed College lecture, "The Cultural Work of Comedy," which serves as an outline of the cultural function of comedy and the role of the trickster figure found in Aristophanes's plays. Though some of the particular trickster characters I shall compare to the character of Moustache Pete are more Roman than Greek, in their roles as the opponents of culturally defined social norms and boundaries they act as Aristophanic tricksters. My analysis of Gardaphé's comic text will reveal that, just as in the ancient Athenian comedy, the issue of assimilation of the trickster figure becomes less important than the tensions and conflicts in the body politic, his role in the comic text reveals.

From Laura Arnold's Reed College lecture entitled "The Cultural

Work of Comedy," we can glean a conceptual framework for Aristophanic comedy. Her analysis of Aristophanic comedy states the claim that "comedy is about the assimilation of the individual into the polis or community, and it mirrors initiation rituals" (Arnold 10). This subject is precisely the primary concern of Gardaphé's narrative, as the first generation Italian American immigrant Moustache Pete attempts to come to terms with the pressures of assimilation into American society, and his comedic jibes will be towards that society. Arnold also helps us to see that "laughter insures that (comedy) presents multiple perspectives" and in terms outlined in well-known Russian literary theorist Mikhail Bakthin leaves these multiple perspectives "unresolved" (Arnold 4). Comedic plays of Aristophanes were used to heal the body politic by calling attention to problems therein, examining "problems in a less somber manner than tragedy" (Arnold 2). In short, the Greek comedy used humor to "question the established order." Arnold refers to Paul Radin's notion of the "trickster figure" in her discussion of Aristophanic comedies, describing the use of such figures "to add disorder to order and so make a whole, to render possible, within the fixed bounds of what is permitted, an experience of what is not permitted" (Arnold 3). This trickster figure, the "enemy of boundaries," behaves in ways "contrary to the established cultural norms" and participates in "burlesque of rituals, people in authority, and foreigners" (Arnold 3). Several examples of such figures can be found in Aristophanic comedy. One very relevant to Arnold's thesis is the character of Socrates from Aristophanes's play, *The Clouds*. As the "enemy of boundaries," Socrates turns the rebellious youth, Pheidippides, against his father Strepsiades, to expose the former's corruption as a part of "the larger problem of corruption in the city [of Athens]" (Arnold 7). Two more such Aristophanic figures fitting Arnold's analysis are the god Dionysius and his slave Xanthias, from the play *The Frogs*. As the disruptive "enemies of boundaries," they cross the river Styx from Earth to Hades to bring back the tragic poet Aeschylus, in order to redeem Athens from its aforementioned corruption. So, trickster figures in Aristophanes's plays question the established order in a comic fashion, and Arnold's analysis helps us to see this.

Other than the Aristophanic tricksters we will find, the second important motif that emerges as we study Baffo Pietro as a trickster figure is that of the Roman God Janus. Janus is the Roman god of doors and beginnings (K.E.T. 1). As such, the figure is appropriate for figures like

Pete, who lingers in the doorway to white American culture; they are ethnic figures who resist assimilation and the erasure of ethnic culture it brings. Janus is "the god with two faces. As he sat in his temple, he could see out both doors to see who was coming and who was going" (K.E.T. 1). Like Janus, the ethnic narrator in Gardaphé's text will present the reader with two faces, an affected persona for public consumption and another which presents the character's true perspective on the realities he encounters. Furthermore, the detailing of Janus as a motif can be seen in Gardaphé's narrative itself. In the January column, the narrator discusses Janus: "He's the one with 2 faces; one that looks forward and one that looks back" (53). In this context, Janus represents the self looking back upon its past, viewing life from different perspectives simultaneously, as the self in January reflects upon life to make New Year's resolutions: "This thinkin' about you life a little more than you do the rest of the year comes from (Janus). But is more than that. We should not just think about last year, but the whole of our past. Is a time to connect ourselves with where we come from and how we get to where we are today" (53). Janus is an appropriate figure to utilize in approaching Gardaphé's ethnic narrator, because Moustache Pete harkens the contemporary, assimilated Italian American reader back to a pre-Americanized, pre-assimilated past for the ethnic culture that the particular narrator represents. To summarize, we can describe the Janus trickster as the self looking from different perspectives simultaneously, reflecting back upon the past. When our ethnic narrator encounters or takes on the Janus perspective, his identity will appear to be multiple, divided between past and present, as well as public and private. So, as Moustache Pete experiences ethnic, social or class alienation, we will find the motif of Janus.

The Aristophanic "enemy of boundaries" is the first of our pair of Trickster figures to appear. It is significant that Dionysius's beverage wine is evoked in one of the first instances involving the motif: an episode of *Moustache Pete* that centers on the theme of wine consumption. In the September 1986 *Fra Noi* column, Pete bemoans the fact that "I doan know if so many people make wine in they bashument [basement] these days likea we use to, but I doan think so" (40). The quality as well as the quantity of homemade Italian wine is also declining: "I been livin' here for a long time an I never taste a good wine like in Italy" (42). The old Italian custom of a small glass of wine at dinnertime or meals clashed with the regulations of American society during "Prohibish" or prohibition days.

Pete refers to this cultural gap as he discusses the decline of Italian winemaking in the U.S.: "Wasa big problem with wine when we come to this country. Wasa no place to get the grapes, then to stomp them, and store the mash" (42). Here, alcohol is associated with the division and conflict between cultures. It is implicated in relation to issues of conflicting perception: while prohibition America demonized it, Moustache Pete's fondness for his homemade wine is a positive signifier of the boundary between Italian and American culture. Here, Pete's ethnic "otherness" is marked by the daily glass of Italian wine and the process (made difficult if not impossible during Prohibition) of Italian winemaking in the home (42). Furthermore, Pete begins playing his Dionysian role of obscuring ideological boundaries when discussing the issue of the use and abuse of alcohol. He thus defends drinking to the reader, "…when you young and you just testin out to see how much you can drink. Is good to get drunk then, you know, if you can remember, how much you can take" (41). Here Pete is an "enemy of boundaries," obscuring perception at the boundary between socially acceptable and unacceptable drinking. Ultimately, his views remain "other" to the Prohibition-era American view and its current versions, that all drinking is unhealthy, especially for the young.

However, Pete's defense of his daily glass of homemade wine (for which outsiders might call him a "wino") does contain some good advice for healthy consumption of alcohol: fill your stomach first (42). He does not resolve the issue he has raised. Rather, like Dionysius in *The Frogs*, he wanders along the boundary of the controversy stirring up some conflict. Despite the conflict, Pete is comfortable in this ambiguous space. He thrives in the cultural ambiguity, concluding the passage by saying, "So good luck and remember to drink with some friends. 'Chi non beve in compagnia o e'ladro o una spia.' Mean who doan drink in company is either a thief or a spy" (43). Thus, like the Aristophanic characters Dionysius and Socrates, the trickster here stirs up the conflict between multiple, divergent perspectives and concludes with these unresolved.

However, despite the occurrence of this Greek motif, it is the motif of the Roman God Janus who predominates in this narrative. One of the first instances of the motif of Janus is the point when Baffo Pietro rebels against the use of technology to define self-identity. Writing in 1986, Gardaphé treated the automation of personal identity in a manner prefiguring the contemporary identity problems of credit cards and Social Security numbers stolen from the Internet: "I have so many numbers in my life is no wonder they come up with computer. Soshsecurity, telephone, address, pension, identicaysh, is enough to drive an old timer like me craze. Is easy to get in big trouble if you doan keep track of all you numbers. If you lose you number you don't get anywhere" (29). Pete is here referring to the impact of technology on personal identity. He realizes the encroachment of the impersonal on the personal, which dehumanizes the individual and destroys privacy: "when evertin becomes a science I think maybe we got too much progress... Prett soon maybe we goan lose names and take on numbers. What you wann be called? Joe or 1731, Julie or 1219?" (30).

In addition, Pietro the ethnic narrator is experiencing a form of cultural alienation in the article; he is reprimanded for holding up the line of customers with numbers at a local bakery. When he is yelled at for talking too much and holding up the line, Pete responds, "Can't a man be friendly and make a little talk without having a number? Wasn't like this in the old days" (29). Clearly, the motif of Janus is operative here as Pete is viewing his current situation (the fact that numbers are encroaching upon his personal life) while simultaneously reflecting on a past ("the old days") when personal identity was not enumerated for technological consumption. Here Pete's identity is divided and in conflict. As a person accustomed to talking in the less hectic bakeries of the Old World, he experiences stress in the New World with its numbers in the bakery line. His private need to socialize rather than "stand around like a big jamoch" conflicts with the public self, which must conform to modernized American life. And as the Janus figure is reflective, here Pete reflects on the dangers of numbers, and moreover on the impact of technology on the people to whom the numbers refer: "I'm joosta say that behind the number is someat'ing human, someat'ing real and if you forget about that maybe you goan someday hurt somebuddy" (30). Just as Aristophanes, in *The Clouds* and *The Frogs,* applied his comic medicine to heal the Athenian body politic, so here Fred Gardaphé uses his trickster figure, Moustache Pete, to "question the established order" with its ever-growing encroachment of technology upon our lives. Our own body politic would do well to heed this trickster's warning.

Finally, the predominance of the Janus trickster is seen unmistakably in a later narrative sequence formed by a series of columns Gardaphé published. Seeking to become other than what he is, Baffo Pietro first enrolls in an ESL class, then drops out to make a return trip home to Italy. His reflections which lead him to decide to try school evoke the motif of Janus: "To get something new, you have to leave behind something old" (55). He attempts to replace the Janus reflections on the past by learning English, a symbolic break with his Italian homeland and culture: "All us oldtimers got to do with our minds is remember all the good and bad times we had. I was thinking that maybe now is a good time to start thinkin about other things" (56). Pete's Americanization is thus his attempt to de-Janus himself, to supplant the reflection he makes on the old country past with a new American language. Although at first he appears to be successful (the teacher remarks on Pete's having "become a writer," an ironic compliment only possible if one plays off Moustache Pete's role as the narrative voice for Gardaphé), the ultimate failure of this effort is foreshadowed in Pete's aphorism: " 'Whoever walks with the lame will learn how to limp.' And I think for too long I wasa limpin" (57). What Pietro means by this is that he feels "the lame" are those who do not burden themselves with the past. Learning English, he will no longer be "limping."

Ironically, however, his ESL experience reveals that it is the educators in this case who are limping, who are cut off from the past, and who are particularly cut off from Moustache Pete's own past. It is over the question of the reflection of the past that Moustache Pete falls out with his ESL teacher and ultimately drops out of school. The teacher focuses on Pete's pronunciation of English words: "Everytime you say a word, you put an 'A' in between. Like a thisa. Anda that'sa not righta" (62). But for Pete, and several other Italian Americans like him, this pronunciation is a way of learning English, of making "the language she flow smooth" (62), because Italian words tend to have such sonorous vowels in the ultimate syllable. Pietro's pronunciation is a relic of his past, which he needs; it is part of his Janus-like identity connected to both past and present. His response to her criticism reflects this identity: "that's joosta the way I am" (62). But the teacher's response is demeaning, "You tell me you've been coming here for all these weeks and you still can't tell that. You're still talking like you just got here." At this distortion of his own past, Moustache Pete loses his temper and states, "Listen, Miss Teach, you wasa not even born when I come here off the boat, so how do you know what I wasa soundin' like way back then" (62). He resents the implication that he has not worked at becoming an American; in terms of the past, he has been in America longer than she has. Ultimately, Baffo Pietro cannot let go of the past; indeed, he depends upon it to cope with his present learning of language. Thus, he is most like Janus in his double-faced, double-voiced identity, speaking an Ital-icized English (hyphen mine). We can see his failure at school in Janian terms, as a conflict between his public and private face of Moustache Pete, or rather his public and private voice, which will always show traces of Italy no matter how much he becomes part of the American public. Despite his encounters with Dionysius, Pete finally emerges as primarily a Janus figure.

As with the unassimilated trickster figures like Socrates and Dionysius in *The Clouds*, Gardaphé's protagonist, Baffo Pietro, remains unassimilated. However, this is in keeping with the cultural function and trickster characterizations typical of Aristophanic comedy. Like Aristophanes's plays, Gardaphé's columns are a comic medicine to the body politic, where successful assimilation is in the final analysis less important than the message to thoughtful citizens of a democracy. Italian-American Moustache Pete, like the Greco-Roman tricksters before him, disrupts cultural borders in his comic attempts to call into question the established order of the democratic body of which he is a member. As with our dominant trickster Janus, the text here created by Gardaphé reflects philosophically comedy's Mediterranean past.

WORKS CITED

Aristophanes. *The Clouds. The Complete Plays of Aristophanes*. New York: Bantam, 1988. 101-39.

Aristophanes. *The Frogs. The Complete Plays of Aristophanes*. New York: Bantam, 1988. 367-415.

Arnold, Laura. *The Clouds: The Cultural Work of Comedy*. Humanities 110 Lecture, Reed College. 24 Nov. 1999. 30 August 2000 <http://web.reed.edu/academic/departments/humanities>.

Gardaphé, Fred. *Moustache Pete is Dead! / Evviva Baffo Pietro!: The Fra Noi Columns 1985-1988*. West Lafayette, IN: Bordighera, 1997.

Kentucky Education Television, Distance Learning Website. *Janus*. 1996. 1 October 2000
http://www.dl.ket.org/latin1/mythology/1deities/gods/lesser/roman/janus.htm.

Aristotelian Tragedy in *Blue Italian* and *Night Bloom*

Mary Ann Mannino
TEMPLE UNIVERSITY

When Aristotle wrote his *Poetics* in the fourth-century B.C., areas that are now in southern Italy were part of Magna Graecia. These areas of Italy are deeply connected to the ideas and values of Greek civilization. The *Poetics*, possibly the most influential work ever written on the art of writing tragedy, delineated laws governing its structuring, and has remained an important text with whose rules writers and critics have grappled for centuries, interpreting and redefining Aristotle's mandates to fit the circumstances of their times. Like so many others, Italian/American women writers into the twenty-first century recognize the effects generated by following Aristotle's rules, and in their struggle to articulate Italian/American experiences both abide by and manipulate Aristotle's suggestions for plot and character development.

In the process of defining tragedy, Aristotle concluded that, unlike comedy, it produced an attraction/repulsion response in the audience by first arousing the painful emotions of pity and fear and then with the catharsis of these emotions leaving a sense of pleasure with the audience. In the *Rhetoric,* Aristotle defined fear as "a pain or disturbance arising from a mental image of impending evil of a destructive ... sort" and pity as "a sense of pain at what we take to be an evil of a destructive ... kind, which befalls one who does not deserve it, which we think we ourselves or someone allied to us might likewise suffer" (Aristotle, *Rhetoric* 2, 5, 1; 2, 8, 2). For Aristotle, then, tragedy is action that causes members of the audience to mourn for the character's undeserved losses and to realize that the same circumstances could happen to them.

For Aristotle, it is the action structured by the plot that has the greatest effect on the arousal of both pity and fear in the audience. Aristotle suggests that the plot or the structuring of events is the "goal of tragedy, and the goal is the greatest thing of all" *(Poetics* 26). He tells us that plot "is the basic principle, the heart and soul, as it were, of tragedy" (*Poetics* 28).

When delineating the elements that should be taken into account by the writer of a tragic plot, Aristotle argues that the writer should never be an historian and report what happened in life but rather he should be "a maker of his plots," an inventor of the possible *(Poetics* 34). Aristotle also insists that the plot should be unified by clearly defining the beginning, middle and end of one aspect of a character's existence and that it should not tell everything that happened to a character but only those things that are relevant to the action the writer has chosen to focus upon. Plots should not be episodic, but there should be a design and logic for the placement of events.

In addition, a plot should have some element of irony. To illustrate his point, Aristotle gives an example of a statue of Mitys at Argos killing "the man who had been the cause of Mitys's death by falling on him while he was attending the festival" (*Poetics* 35). This situation is also an example of another Aristotelian element of tragedy, peripety, which Aristotle defines as a "shift in what is being undertaken to the opposite" i.e. a reversal of fortune from good to bad. When combined with peripety, "recognition" which is a character's shift from ignorance to awareness "is most integrally a part of the plot" for it "will excite either pity or fear…" (*Poetics* 37). Another important element in Aristotle's theory is pathos, which is "a destructive or painful act such as deaths on stage, or paroxysms of pain, woundings" (*Poetics* 37). For Aristotle, then, the story line, peppered with ironic twists, must take the tragic character from good fortune to bad. The bad luck must be serious, preferably life threatening, and the character must be aware of what is occurring and be unable to reverse it.

Although the plot is central to Aristotelian tragedy, Aristotle also offered guidelines to writers for the kinds of characters who would best support the plot he outlined. Aristotle's ideal character is someone "who is neither a paragon of virtue and justice nor undergoes the change to misfortune through any real badness or wickedness but because of some mistake; one of those who stand in great repute and prosperity, conspicuous men from families of that kind" (*Poetics* 38). A suitable tragic hero would be a person who was good because he had made good or moral choices, his qualities would be appropriate to his position in life, and finally his behavior would be consistent. His fall would occur because of a small mistake or error in judgment that a member of the audience himself might make.

Two recent books by Italian/American women, *Blue Italian,* a novel by Rita Ciresi, and *Night Bloom,* a memoir by Mary Cappello, both conform to and deconstruct the Aristotelian elements of tragedy. Both texts arouse the readers' emotions because they depict pain and suffering, which befall protagonists who, while good, are not remarkably virtuous, and yet, whose misfortunes do not seem in any way to be deserved. Although both books contain many elements that Aristotle listed as essential to structuring the tragic plot such as irony, peripety, recognition, and pathos, each writer includes these in a way that reflects her unique Italian/American identity and not an Aristotelian worldview.

The first two sentences of the Prologue of Ciresi's *Blue Italian* set up the novel's plot and also suggest a tragic ending: "Gary Alan Fisher had cancer. He was thirty-one and he was going to die" (*Blue Italian* 3). There can be no doubt that this novel will arouse "fear" and "pity" in readers because they will easily identify with a young couple who are facing a potentially fatal but common illness.

Later, on the first page Ciresi suggests the way in which the reader should understand the pain and suffering depicted in this text, and it is in a pleasurable way. By revealing that Gary Fisher's childhood response to an earthquake, "the scariest thing that ever happened to the Fishers," was that it "also was oddly comforting" because it made him feel "surprised the sun was still shining and they were all still alive," Ciresi invites the reader to experience the novel in a similar way. Ciresi has established the Aristotelian ambiguity of tragedy: all those who experience the catharsis of painful emotions have their "souls lightened and delighted" (Bl, 3 *Politics* 134a5). The readers of the novel will identify with the characters' suffering and feel a sense of joyful relief that they themselves have been spared a similar fate.

I want to suggest that Rosa Salvatore, Gary's wife and the novel's protagonist, has many of the qualities Aristotle suggests in identifying a tragic hero. She is a moral person, a hospital social worker, who, nonetheless, makes certain choices that contribute to the losses she suffers.

Rosa has long wished to escape the Italian/American neighborhood, Pizza Beach, where she grew up. She feels at odds with the values of her parents and other relatives, who would limit her by insisting that she follow tradition, marry and have children with someone from her ethnic background and continue to live in Pizza Beach. Since childhood, Rosa has been uncomfortable with many neighborhood and family habits of being that would restrict her because of her gender. She was particularly annoyed by the practice that allowed the men to leave the dinner table and go outside to smoke cigars while her mother and grandmother "stood at the sink, watching the world go by as they washed dish after dish" *(Blue Italian* 237). Rosa had no interest in continuing that practice by marrying one of the neighborhood men whom she saw as unintelligent, crude and offensive. She wanted to attend college so she could elude that fate and find a man whom she would describe as refined: "College men did not deign to lower their pants on East Rock. They did not wear black leather belts with silver studs; they did not drive delivery trucks; they did not eat pizza with their mouths open. They said *please* and *thank you* and never said *bitch* or *cunt* or bragged about their big ten-inch" *(Blue Italian* 147).

When Gary Fisher begins to date Rosa, her fortune improves, but not without stress and conflict. Rosa loves Gary; he is not like the men from her neighborhood and while that pleases her immensely, it also makes her uncomfortable because in dating him she must break taboos. Because Gary Fisher's family is both Jewish and rich, he and his parents have a perspective on life that is very different from Rosa's family's. His world is both appealing and frightening to her. When their first date leads to their first sexual encounter, Rosa gladly acquiesces. However, as she is falling asleep, she imagines that she has checked into a hotel in Rome and that the concierge has asked if she has a marriage license (*Blue Italian* 57). Rosa both resists and conforms to parental values.

Rosa's attraction for Gary is often laced with feelings of transgression that manifest as illness. As their relationship develops, Rosa feels pressured by her mother to bring Gary home for Sunday dinner. Although Rosa realizes that Gary represents all that is different from Pizza Beach, she also recognizes that her mother will see him as a threat to that environment. In the car on the way to her parents home, Rosa develops symptoms: "a throbbing headache, an aching bladder, a sore throat, and the initial abdominal rumblings that always signaled the prelude to a spastic colon attack" *(Blue Italian* 70).

Their courtship continues to bring both happiness and conflict to Rosa. Although Rosa is comfortable with Gary and glad to have a boyfriend who is intelligent and caring, their cultural differences continually produce anxiety and symptoms. Her first visit to Gary's family finds Rosa locked in the bathroom with stomach pains. Gary's family's wealth highlights Rosa's poverty, their ease, and her disease. Rosa's journey away from the constrictions of Pizza Beach and all it represents is filled with self-doubt caused by the awareness that she is a pioneer and a transgressor of parental and community codes.

Despite these difficulties, eventually she becomes engaged to and then marries Gary. Rosa settles into her new role as wife, but when she becomes pregnant accidentally because she once neglected to reinsert spermicide for a second sexual encounter, feelings of conflict and transgression arise over the issue of baptizing the baby. At lunch in a restaurant, Antoinette, Rosa's mother, points out the ways Rosa has rebelled: "You gotta be different. You gotta have a job. You gotta pay twenty-five dollars to get your hair cut. You gotta shop at Macy's. Caldor isn't good enough for you" (*Blue Italian* 204). Finally, after pointing out that Rosa had to be different and marry a man from New York who drives a foreign car, Antoinette says, "You gotta have a baby and-and-not even baptize it" (*Blue Italian* 205).

When Rosa asks how her mother knows this, Antoinette reveals that she has asked Gary. While Rosa denies the accuracy of her mother's information, she admits to herself that, "If Gary didn't let her baptize the baby, it might die and float around in Limbo for the rest of eternity, and Rosa herself would go straight to hell or be condemned to twiddling her thumbs for thousands of years in the gray area known as Purgatory" (*Blue Italian* 205). To prevent all this from happening, Ciresi tells us, "Rosa was planning to douse the baby with water the moment the cord was cut" (*Blue Italian* 205).

Just as Rosa begins to take some pleasure in the pregnancy, her luck shifts. Very suddenly, she has a miscarriage and is alone in the hospital for some time because Gary cannot be found. While she is still recovering from her procedure, Gary develops a very virulent form of prostate cancer that is surprising in someone so young. For months, Rosa watches Gary grow weaker and weaker and eventually die. When he is very sick, she discovers that while she was in the hospital having the miscarriage, he could not be found because he was having an affair with a woman Rosa had seen once, at the party they had attended the night before her miscarriage. In a very short time, Rosa has lost her husband, baby and belief in her husband's faithfulness. The world away from Pizza Beach she longed to enter, which required her to separate from the tenets of her family, has brought her not security but loss.

The plot of *Blue Italian* contains many of the aspects of Tragedy as outlined by Aristotle: the action of the plot is unified around Rosa's attempt to escape from Pizza Beach by marrying an outsider, Gary Fisher. Something serious happens; Gary, a young law student, dies from prostate cancer, and his unborn child dies as well. When Gary dies, the story ends. There is a sudden reversal of circumstances, and some ironic incidents. When Rosa's life suddenly turns from lucky to unlucky, she is aware of what is happening and is unable to change it.

Ciresi creates a character, Rosa Salvatore, who both acquiesces to and rebels against Aristotle's suggestions for tragic heroes. Rosa differs from Aristotle's ideal because she is both a woman and a member of a working class family. Nonetheless, like Aristotle's male heroes, she is a moral person who consistently attempts to fulfill her responsibilities, in her case, as wife and daughter. Aristotle believed that the moral dimension that defines a person's essential nature develops exclusively from actions revealing that moral makeup. Ciresi establishes Rosa's morality by detailing her actions before and after Gary's diagnosis.

Rosa often finds that her own needs conflict with the wants of those around her. Rosa's humanity is manifested by her choice to sometimes take care of her desires first. This healthy selfishness, which must be respected and admired, can also be read as her tragic flaw because it causes her pain and suffering. For example, it is Rosa's desire to leave the family and its values, which leads to her marriage to Gary Fisher. It is her reluctance to get up from bed to use the spermicidal, which results in her pregnancy. It is her questions to Gary about his affair that leads to his confession.

In many ways, the things that happen to Rosa result from her attempt to push beyond the limits of her prescribed fate and to construct a richer life. Her punishment, the death of her husband and baby, is undeserved. Ciresi's novel implies that when Italian/American women attempt to leave home and break all the cultural taboos that that choice implies, they should be prepared for monumental losses.

It may seem that a memoir such as Mary Cappello's *Night Bloom* violates Aristotle's dictate that tragedy not report on events that actually happened but be the invention of the writer. In the same way that Ciresi shaped her novel around Rosa's attempt to escape from Pizza

Beach through marriage, Cappello is selective in what information she reports. I want to argue that because Mary Cappello structured her memoir to discuss one theme, the destructive effect of immigration on the immigrant's children and grandchildren, it is as unified and as inventive as Aristotle demanded.

What Cappello has chosen to focus on are the ways that three generations of her family are affected by the undeserved suffering of the original immigrant. He is portrayed as a moral and just man, a tragic hero, suffering because he must live in abject poverty simply because he is an immigrant. Cappello's memoir delineates actions by her grandfather, her mother and herself, which demonstrate how immigrant suffering leads to inheritable habits of being such as fear as a way to view the world which must be addressed anew by each generation.

It is the action of John Petracca, recorded in his journal or remembered and recorded by his daughter or granddaughter, which reveals him to be a moral and good person whose circumstances produce fear and pity in the reader. On January 2, 1945, John Petracca writes that the house in which he is living is too cold for his family. His mother, wife, and daughters are cold. He too is cold but instead of complaining, he writes "…although I feel bitter about the whole thing, I am laughing and dancing… Trying to keep warm and inspire gaiety so that the rest could snap out of their grimace and become happy and warm…"*(Night Bloom* 30). Time after time John Petracca records the effects of poverty: "Headaches, pains, empty pockets, the roof leaks, need coal, mate needs eyeglasses and I need everything. Life is for the rich… The poor only exist; although they bear everything, they get very little" *(Night Bloom* 32). Another day he writes, "I feel worst than I ever did! Will I survive? Who knows? Yet I am working and shall keep on" *(Night Bloom* 34). On yet another day, he pens, "To see my family in such dire need and me, tied to the star of torture, impotent to procure what is of absolute need makes me despair" *(Night Bloom* 46). Petracca inspires empathy in the reader because he is more concerned with the effects of poverty on his family than on himself and because his journal reveals physical and mental pain that seem unjust. In October of 1941 he writes, "I am working and starving. This is almost unbelievable in this country of great wealth and democracy" (*Night Bloom* 38).

John Petracca attributes his suffering to his immigrant status: "The answer to my suffering and to my lacking power is that I was raised in

Italy and am living in America and trying to be both I am none" *(Night Bloom* 37). If we see John Petracca as a tragic hero, then his flaw is his desire to immigrate and improve his chances of survival. This determination to escape the limits of his societal placement is the same determination that motivates Rosa Salvatore to attend the university and move away from Pizza Beach, and like Rosa his choice is fraught with suffering. Cappello's memoir implies that John Petracca's suffering has effects not only on himself but also on his progeny. She says: "And yet there are ways that we inherit the pain or deformation caused by the material or laboring conditions of our forbears ... of habits of being that cause one to lie, rest, love, move, speak on one's body in certain ways" (*Night Bloom* 43).

Cappello outlines the way her mother and then herself have inherited fear as a habit of being. Because John Petracca's life as an immigrant was marked by loss of homeland and all that means, and his marginalization by poverty, he and his family lived in constant fear of further losses: "fear of invasion of their house, of displacement from their home and of an estrangement, not 'merely existential,' but legally enforced. The house [could] be invaded at any time" *(Night Bloom* 35). If he could not pay his bills, strangers could enter his home and turn off his gas or electricity, making his existence even more precarious and shaming.

The immigrant's fear about real issues reappears in his daughter's life as a series of phobias, among them, agoraphobia. Cappello believes that her mother's childhood "living with the threat of losing one's heat, water, electricity and not having enough food to eat can easily engender states of terror" (*Night Bloom* 127).

When Cappello's mother tells her about a frightening dream in which she is a child and can't leave her house because gunmen are waiting outside to kill her father and perhaps herself, Cappello suggests that the dream connects her mother's agoraphobia to the material conditions of the immigrant household: "My mother's agoraphobia might be a sign that something terrible was happening in the immigrant household: to go outside would be to announce it, but its expression is prohibited" (*Night Bloom* 133). Cappello's mother's body was somehow marked by John Petracca's poverty and outsider status.

Cappello tells us that the actual events of her own childhood are a "backdrop" or "padding" for what she sees as her "inheritance" of fear.

Cappello claims that the source of her childhood fears was "material inheritance" (*Night Bloom* 86). On childhood walks Cappello absorbs her mother's fear of dogs and with it the habit of being afraid. As an adult she continues to respond to life with fear. She claims that she is as much afraid of getting tenure as of not getting it because both possibilities engender loss. If she does not acquire tenure then her education has not come to fruition. However, if she does become a tenured professor, she sees that achievement as separating her from her working class family.

The lives of Cappello, her grandfather and her mother in many ways mirror the struggles of Rosa Salvatore in Ciresi's novel. They, like Rosa, struggle to establish themselves in a secure location in American society, but like Rosa they are plagued by feelings of inadequacy, guilt and outsider status. I would argue that the emotions generated by the immigrant's determination to improve his lot and his subsequent displacement continue to haunt his children and grandchildren and appear in the writing of Italian/American women in the telling of tragedy.

Heroes in the works of these Italian/American writers are people who push against those societal structures that would limit their lives. Society read as both the family and the larger world oppress and suppress brave women who continue to resist. However, Ciresi and Cappello suggest that pain, suffering, loss and a legacy of fear are often the results of these heroic moves, and thus the writing of Italian/ American women frequently tells a story of tragedy.

WORKS CITED

Aristotle. *The Rhetoric*. Trans. Lane Cooper. New York: Appleton Century Crofts, 1932.

Aristotle. *Poetics*. Trans. Gerald F. Else. Ann Arbor: U of Michigan P, 1970.

Cappello, Mary. *Night Bloom*. Boston: Beacon, 1998.

Ciresi, Rita. *Blue Italian*. Hopewell, NJ: Ecco, 1996.

Where It All Began: Tracing the Origins of Cinema to the Mediterranean and the Baroque

Joseph Garreau
UNIVERSITY OF MASSACHUSETTS, LOWELL

The aim of this essay is to show that cinema, in its very essence, can be defined as the logical sequence of a set of representations, whose origins can be traced to the basin of the Mediterranean. These representations have attempted, through time, to reproduce reality with more and more precision. Furthermore, this paper will show that the baroque, by prefiguring this essential element of cinema that is the illusion of movement, has provided a privileged stage in this evolution, before its actual realization in the late nineteenth century. And finally, that this exceptional period that was the baroque, reactivated in the twentieth century, has influenced various filmmakers and thus constitutes the very source of their works with a mark on their originality.

I will briefly illustrate this last point in my conclusion by focusing on Max Ophüls's film, *Lola Montès,* first presented in Paris in 1955, in which he recounts the life and loves of the Spanish-Irish cabaret-dancer, who became the mistress of Franz Liszt and Ludwig I, Maria Dolorès Porriz y Montez, countess of Lansfeld, known as Lola Montès, a film from which I will only repeat, at present, the definition that Lola gives of herself: "La vie pour moi, c'est le mouvement." Life is movement, movement is desire, and desire, as Ophüls said, is cinema.

Allow me to begin by quoting the late Fernand Braudel, author in particular of *The Mediterranean: Space and History* and of *The Italian Model:* "Before becoming a place, the sea obviously was an obstacle [...], however the Mediterranean, first and foremost, is a space-movement."[1] On the literary plane, a perfect illustration of Braudel's statement would be the founding text of the Mediterranean, namely Homer's *Odyssey.* Homer's epic can be considered both as the praise

---

[1] *La Méditerranée et le monde méditerranéen (*Paris: Colin, 1982) and *Le Modèle italien* (Paris: Arthaud, 1985). Quoted by Pedrag Matvejevic, *Le Bréviaire méditerranéen (*Paris: Fayard, 1992), 242.

and the anti-praise of traveling, since, at the end of his adventurous voyage – I would prefer the Greek term of _____, which we have kept in the Romance languages – Odysseus finds himself at the very place where he had started. In fact, some feminist commentators are now suggesting that the main character of the *Odyssey* is not Odysseus but Penelope. The whole poem, they argue, is constructed with Odysseus's return in view, not to Ithaca, the homeland, but to Penelope, the spouse, who, by unweaving every night her quilt, allows for the wanderer to return home. Thus, although presented as an epic poem, when everything is said and done, Odysseus finds himself where he had started without any other reward for himself than the proof of the indefectible fidelity of his spouse.

Here is my first point: when we search texts, or when we look into beliefs and legends, a major contradiction in Mediterranean thought appears. On the one hand, we see clearly the attraction for all that is mobility, voyage, exchange and, at the same time, it is as clear that this *élan* must be curbed, given the fact that seafaring expeditions are especially perilous. On the other hand, there is the mention, for instance, of those mysterious "peoples of the sea," about whom we don't know a great deal, but whose escapades we suspect. A case in point is the one undertaken by those Sardinian master builders who emigrated from their island to populate faraway Scotland and who taught the Picts the art of building the mysterious towers made of dry stones that are found on its northwest coast and in the Orcades islands, which are called brochs and strikingly resemble the Sardinian nuraghe.[2]

We cannot forget to mention as well the Phoenician ships that rallied for the first time the Cape of Good Hope, or even Alexander the Great, who went as far away as the Indus River, but who, as we know, did not return. Let us salute also the valor, the curiosity, and business acumen of the Venetian Marco Polo and his China expedition.

Said otherwise, the Mediterranean, if I could retain Dominique Fernandez's French play on words between the homophonic *mer* (the sea) and *mère* (the mother), *Mère Méditerranée*[3] – which is the title of his study – behaves like a possessive "mama," questioning all reasons

---

[2] See Frank Renwick of Ravestone, *Scotland, Bloody Scotland* (Edinburgh: Canangate, 1986).

[3] Dominique Fernandez, *Mère Méditerranée* (Paris: Grasset, 1965).

in her children for leaving her safe haven, and yet she seems to be encouraging in them all types of adventurous dreams.

I could mention in passing that other peoples around the Mediterranean were not as fond of navigation as the ones I've just mentioned: the Jews, for example, did not trust those bold navigators that were the Philistines, and those whom they globally called "the peoples of the sea." The Romans, on the contrary, developed all forms of land travels with their superb *viae*: via Appia, via Flaminia, via Aurelia, and others. Marguerite Yourcenar, for instance, in her *Mémoires d'Hadrien,* has the emperor declare: "[La route], le plus beau don peut-être que Rome ait fait à la terre" ["The road, perhaps the most exquisite gift that Rome has ever given to the world"].

It is revealing as well that the first cartographers of the Mediterranean, such as Eratosthenos or Ptolemy, had a tendency to reduce the size of that *Mare Internum,* which still holds true when you examine the Catalan atlas of 1375. We'll have to wait until the seventeenth century to have a more accurate geographic representation of the Mediterranean.

Therefore, with such a lack of breathing space in his surroundings, what other means did the Mediterranean man have to find an escape? Paradoxically, he found one in movement, but again a form of movement that did not necessarily force him to displace himself physically. And, if I may jump over centuries, taking the *Quattrocento* as my second focus point, we may wonder whether Brunelleschi's *perspectiva artificialis,* illustrated by Masaccio, theorized by Alberti, and codified by da Vinci, was not born from the same profound desire to escape from too confining a space by means, this time, of a visual subterfuge.

This new pictorial system, namely the monocular perspective, which originated in Florence in the fifteenth century, was going to conquer the Western world. And for the sake of this exposé, I need to mention at this juncture for the cinema to exist, more precisely for the first photography to be created, the importance of the *camera obscura.*

Early credit goes to Aristotle, whose works in optics were probably taken up in the ninth century by Arab scholars. On his side, Lucretius, in his *De natura rerum,* described the phenomenon of the persistence of vision, allowing the human brain to reconstitute movement thanks to a succession of fixed images. Credit ought to be given as well to da Vinci, already mentioned, who discovered that the *camera obscura* was modeled in fact on the human eye. In the eighteenth century, with the addition of lenses, this *camera obscura* became the magic lantern. A century later, in 1822 to be exact, Joseph Nicéphore Niepce, a Frenchman, captured the first photograph. True, it was a *nature morte*, a "still life," not yet a "motion picture."

We know also that credit must be given, not so much to the American father of the movies, Thomas Alva Edison, but to Edison's director of the motion picture project, William Kennedy Laurie Dickson, who invented the camera and the viewer, called the kinetograph (etymologically "motion writer"), for which Edison simply took credit. We owe the fancy name of *cinématographe* to the Lumière brothers, who shot their first film in 1895. Do I need to add that, in many countries today, the movies are simply known as the cinema, and shooting is known as cinematography? However, I seem to anticipate...

For there is another major element that Italian Renaissance, in addition to the monocular perspective, has given to the cinema: the *quadro,* from the Latin *quadrus,* of course, meaning *square,* translated into English as *frame.* Despite its etymology, however, the *quadro,* in cinema parlance, quickly took the shape of a rectangle, dictated probably by the phenomenon of human vision, wider in range than high in scope. It is interesting to point out as well that, as early as 1539, the verbal form *quadrare* already means, "to fit well with something." I may want to add that the technician we call in English a cameraman, in French, for example, is aptly named a *cadreur.* What needs to be emphasized is how this *cadre* or frame, inherited from Italian Renaissance painting, is one of the most important constituents of cinema. As Jean Mitry notes in his *Esthétique et Psychologie du cinéma*: "The shots and the angles that are the result of a specific choice, or of a cut performed on the outside world, have a common denominator, namely the frame of the image, which is the basic condition of the filmic form."[4]

The next illusionist stage toward the creation of cinema, as announced in my preamble, is the baroque. Whether we derive the word baroque, by which I mean the Italian – Roman more precisely – baroque of Bernini and of his rival Borromini, from the Portuguese *barrôco* or the Spanish *barrueco,* meaning in both languages the irregularly shaped pearl found in an oyster – and not its pejorative derivation

---

[4] (Paris: Editions Universitaires, 1963, vol. 1, 165.) [My translation].

of bizarre – what characterizes this novel art form is the movement or, more exactly, the continuous opposition between the movement and the decorative detail.

There is no doubt that Italian architects, sculptors, and painters considered themselves the upholders of the Renaissance, and no doubt they found the immediate source of their inspiration in the *cadaveri eccelenti* of Imperial Rome. However by re-utilizing the column and the pediment, the oval and the decorative detail, they were given a new life, adding to these dead and massive stones an impression of mobility. Art historian Heinrich Wölfflin has this concise explanation of the baroque, which needs to be repeated: "The picturesque is based on the impression of movement. Effects of mass and movement are the principles of the baroque."[5] Now, this attempt to represent the movement in the inert, or what is called the illusion of movement, which could not be achieved technologically in the *Seicento,* became possible some two centuries later, thanks to Edison's kinetograph and the *cinétographe* of the Lumière brothers.

If there is need to repeat *hic et nunc,* in a city that prides itself on being the birthplace of the American Industrialized Revolution, I will reiterate that the nineteenth-century's inventive mind created machines for work as well as its necessary complement, machines for entertainment. Allow me to make a brief, albeit chauvinistic, parenthesis about our city. It may be well known that in the 1840s, on a trip to America, Charles Dickens paid Lowell a visit. Much less known probably is Victor Hugo's reference to our Merrimack Valley. He has the revolutionary student, Grantaire, ask: "Otez *Time is money,* que reste-t-il de l'Angleterre? Otez *Cotton is King,* que reste-t-il de l'Amérique?" This chapter of *Les Misérables* was written in 1861, exactly at the time when there were some fifty looms in the twelve Lowell mills functioning in this very neighborhood, at a time when, in New England, *Cotton was King.*[6]

To add substance to my point, namely the unique and privileged stage that the baroque constitutes for the advent of cinema, I will add two voices – incidentally two French voices– whose authority however

---

[5] *Renaissance et Baroque* (Paris: Livre de Poche, 1967). Quoted by Pierre Pitiot, *Les voyageurs de l'immobile* (Montpellier: Climats, 1994), 98.
[6] Arthur L. Eno, Jr., ed., *Cotton Was King: A History of Lowell, Massachusetts* (N.p.: New Hampshire Pub. Co., 1976).

is uncontested in both art history and the history of the cinema. The first is that of André Malraux, who wrote the following in *Les voix du silence:*

> Once the era of discoveries in the technique of representation came to an end, painting began to cast about with almost feverish eagerness for a means of rendering movement. Movement alone, it seemed, could now impart to art that power of carrying conviction, which had hitherto been implemented by each successive discovery. But movement called for more than a change in methods of portrayal; what Baroque – with its gestures like those of drowning men – was straining after – was not a new treatment of picture but rather a picture sequence. It is not surprising that an art so much obsessed with theatrical effect, all gestures and emotion, should end up in the motion picture.[7]

The second is André Bazin, who in *Qu'est-ce que le cinéma?* credits Italian painting for what has been called "a paternity at least conceptual"[8] of the cinema:

> Since perspective had only solved the problem of form and not of movement, realism was forced to continue the search for some way of giving dramatic expression to the moment, a kind of psychic fourth dimension that could suggest life in the tortured immobility of the baroque art.[9]

The next question that we can raise, which will be my last point, is the following: Is all cinema baroque? It may be interesting to point out, for instance, that a good number of directors originate from parts of the world where the baroque of the seventeenth and eighteenth century had developed, not only in Italy and Spain, but we cannot fail to also notice the strong presence of filmmakers from Vienna or from the Rhineland, or the importance of Italo-Americans, Coppola and Scorcese, just to name two. Do I need to point out that France, however, except in mu-

---

[7] *The Voices of Silence*, trans. Stuart Gilbert (New York: Doubleday, 1953), 121.
[8] Pierre Pitiot, *op. cit.* "André Malraux et André Bazin [...] surent créditer la peinture italienne de cette paternité au moins conceptuelle" (115).
[9] *What is Cinema? Essays Selected and Translated by Hugh Gray* (Berkeley: U of California P, 1976), 11.

sic, kept her distance from the baroque? In his finest poem, "Heureux qui, comme Ulysse, a fait un beau voyage," the Renaissance poet, Joachim Du Bellay, after his meditations on the vanished glories of ancient Rome, concluded his *Regrets* (published after his return to France in 1558) with these famous verses: *"Plus que le marbre dur me plaît l'ardoise fine, / Plus mon Loire gaulois que le Tibre latin, /Plus mon petit Liré que le mont Palatin. / Et plus que l'air marin la douceur angevine."* Yet, as Fernand Braudel so rightly said: "The baroque, that Italy extending beyond Italy, [the baroque,] the last great cultural export of the Mediterranean."

Although many are the filmmakers who, from Wells to Fellini, or from Visconti to Losey, have borrowed from the aesthetics of the baroque, I have chosen to focus on Max Ophüls's last filmic creation, *Lola Montès*, which, on the one hand was dismissed as boring and incoherent because of his excess of décor, mise-en-scène and narrative convolution. On the other hand, by reason of this same excess, it was hailed as a masterpiece of the baroque. From the first reel, we recognize the filmmaker's touch, namely the architectural overcharge, his fondness for the unusual, not to mention the Vienna morbidity of the tone, in addition to his first use of color and Cinemascope, which, among other things, allowed him such a freedom of movement, *mutatis mutandis* similar to what Fellini called *fantasia*, which translates quite well into our word fantasy.

Now, allow me to bring the film into context. Although Gamma Films advertised a super-production based on the life and loves of the most scandalous woman of all times, featuring Martine Carol, France's foremost sex goddess at the time, and an all-star supporting cast headed by the flamboyant Peter Ustinov as Monsieur Loyal, Ophüls chose instead to take aim at the very mechanism that Gamma Films was using to market the film: lurid publicity. In an interview with François Truffaut, he cites the fate of Judy Garland and Diana Barrymore, which he blamed on the public's appetite for scandal and on the entrepreneurs who shamelessly exploit scandals: "We must kill publicity... I find it dreadful, this vice of wanting to know everything. This irreverence in the face of mystery. It is on this theme that I have built my film: the annihilation of the personality through the cruelty and indecency of spectacles based on scandal."[10] Commenting upon the scandal provoked by the film's initial release, his son, Marcel Ophüls, said: "What was not understood was that the film is a denunciation of exhibitionism in show business and a denunciation of spectacle within the spectacle."[11]

As summarized in *CineAction,* the diegetic present of the film is a circus wherein will be performed the 'most sensational act of the century' which contains "spectacle, romance, action and history," and which will deliver to us the "whole truth of an extraordinary life," the "scandalous career," the rise and fall of a femme fatale: Lola Montès. Lola's life is re-enacted by the entire company with the ringmaster as choreographer. Complete with whip and provocations, the ringmaster calls upon the audience to ask Lola the "most intimate questions" which he facilitates and edits until he manages to evoke the one question which the design of the show depends upon: "Combien d'amants?" ["How many lovers?"]. During this parade of suitors, Lola is motionless upon a rotating platform, a circumstance which reaches its apotheosis in the finale, of both the film and the circus act, when she is utterly contained within a cage after her perilous fall.[12]

Ophüls used the framing device of a mammoth circus set in New Orleans circa 1880 to distance the spectator from the events of Lola's life presented in flashback. If life for Lola is movement, then in the circus she is effectively dead, for it is precisely her capacity to move that is impaired. She is more often moved (generally in circles) than moving. And when she does move during the performance (as on the tight rope), it is with great difficulty.

We can't help but notice the profusion of circular motions and, in particular, the travelling that turns around Lola exposed at the center of the track, herself placed on a pedestal pivoting in reverse. This sequence shot, namely the opposed double circumference, is another illustration of the baroque, which is to be understood as the visual translation of the reciprocal gravitation and inner thoughts of Lola and of the

---

[10] Article on Max Ophüls, *International Dictionary of Films and Filmmakers – 2 Directors* (2nd ed., 1991).
[11] Interview with James Blue, Rice University Media, March 7, 1973, in "Max Ophüls and the Cinema of Desire," *Style and Spectacle in Four Films, 1948-1955,* by Alan Larson Williams (New York: Arno, 1980), 38.
[12] Susan Lord, *CineAction* (Winter-Spring 1990): 60 (passim).

world that surrounds her. We notice as well the circus pyrotechnics and Ophüls's obsession with monochromy, exemplified by the mineral glows of the lighting gas turning to absolute red when Lola remembers her past.

A French critic, Philippe Collin,[13] has insightfully remarked that, although other films have borrowed aesthetically from the baroque, Lola Montès solely, however, is a film which is ethically baroque, in the sense that each sequence-shot questions the meaning of the preceding ones, and the whole film offers the aspect of a vast array of questions and answers which annihilate and recreate each other indefinitely. An eloquent illustration of this is offered to our eyes in the last scene, when we see Lola climb higher and higher up the rope ladder, preparing to jump without the safety net, ready for a plunge which, she realizes, could be her death.

The next day, however, everything starts anew. Nothing is solved, nothing is explained. Life itself is both consoling and cruel, both Sphinx and Oedipus. Or to borrow a last image from that other essential Mediterranean man, Albert Camus, one could conclude with these often quoted words from the *Myth of Sisyphus*: "La lutte elle-même vers les sommets suffit à remplir un coeur d'homme. Il faut imaginer Sisyphe heureux" ["The very struggle toward the mountain top is enough to fulfill a man's heart. We must imagine Sisyphus happy"].[14]

---

[13] "D'une mise en scène baroque," in *Baroque et cinéma. Etudes cinématographiques* 1-2 (vol. 1, Paris: Minard, 1960). "D'autres films ont fait des emprunts à un baroque esthétique, mais seul *Lola Montès* est un film éthiquement baroque; chaque plan remet en question la signification des précédents et l'ensemble offre l'aspect d'une multitude d'interrogations et de réponses qui se détruisent et se re-créent indéfiniment les unes les autres. (…) Rien n'est résolu, rien n'est expliqué" (97).

[14] *Le Mythe de Sisyphe*. Paris: Gallimard, 1942. [My translation]

Pirandello e il cinema

Maria C. Pastore Passaro
CENTRAL CONNECTICUT STATE UNIVERSITY

In un'intervista apparsa in "Les Nouvelles Litteraires," a Parigi (1-15 novembre 1924), Pirandello afferma: "Io credo che il Cinema, più facilmente, più completamente di qualsiasi altro mezzo d'espressione artistica possa darci la visione del pensiero."

Luigi Pirandello è forse tra i primi autori del diciannovesimo secolo a scrivere seriamente e con chiaroveggenza sull'appena nascente industria cinematografica. Già nel 1903,[1] aveva ideato il romanzo *Si gira*, che, come è noto, ha per soggetto il cinema, il suo ambiente fatuo e le sue istanze tecnologiche. Ma dall'intervista è evidente che il suo interesse per il cinema va al di là delle considerazioni mondano/sociali. Il cinema rappresenta una novità espressiva e la sua caratteristica è di dare ciò che Pirandello chiama "la visione del pensiero." È una fenomenologia.

Aperto a tutte le novità coeve nel campo intellettuale, Pirandello, già padre del teatro rivoluzionario moderno, mostra immediatamente grande curiosità per le forme innovative della cinematografia. Anche se, in un primo momento, è costretto a questa forma di arte da necessità finanziaria,[2] ben presto riesce, ad apprezzarne il valore artistico, il "sogno di una rivoluzione" che è contenuto in esso: "Vorrei se potessi, e son certo che potrò, portare anche nel campo cinematografico la rivoluzione ch'io sogno."[3] Cos'è questo "sogno di una rivoluzione"? In che modo questo sogno si rapporta al Futurismo? Per il momento è il caso di sottolineare che l'evoluzione letteraria di Pirandello coincide

---

1. In una lettera da Roma (19 gennaio 1904), indirizzata ad Angelo Orvieto, Pirandello parla del romanzo *Filauri*, il cui titolo diventò *La tigre* (1913), e fu poi cambiato in *Si gira* (1914). Il romanzo uscì a puntate in sei numeri del quindicinale "Nuova Antologia" (Roma, 1 giugno-16 agosto 1915). Fu poi pubblicato in volume (Milano: Treves, 1916) e ristampato dallo stesso editore col titolo *Quaderni di Serafino Gubbio operatore* (quarto ed ultimo titolo a partire da Filauri) e con nuovo editore (Firenze: Benporard, 1925). Francesco Callari, *Pirandello e il cinema. Con una raccolta completa degli scritti teorici e creativi*, Venezia: Marsilio, 1991, 11, 18-21.
2. Gaspare Giudice, *Vita di Pirandello*, Torino: Ulter, 1963, 511.
3. Da un'intervista a Enrico Rocca su "Il Popolo d'Italia," Milano, 4 ottobre 1928. Francesco Callari, *Pirandello e il cinema. Con una raccolta completa degli scritti teorici e creativi*, 10.

con la scoperta del linguaggio cinematografico e con i primi timidi tentativi di adibire il film a veicolo artistico-culturale.

La genesi laboriosa di *Si gira*, più tardi trasformato in *Quaderni di Serafino Gubbio operatore*, è forse il primo romanzo della letteratura universale a descrivere il mondo del cinema dall'interno. Cinema e letteratura – ormai fin troppo di moda nel mondo accademico americano – sono messi a confronto in questo romanzo. Particolarmente notevole è la struttura del testo che precorre le scoperte del *nouveau roman*. Come nei suoi altri testi teatrali, e nei romanzi, anche qui il drammaturgo siciliano mira a porre in conflitto la vita e l'arte, la vita e le forme, e la vendetta di quella su queste. Serafino Gubbio – nome che ricorda l'angelo, il messaggero di una nuova forma d'arte, ma anche gli angeli che ardono, che bruciano come il fuoco – sta girando un film intitolato "La donna e la tigre." Egli contempla – come fanno i serafini tra le gerarchie angeliche – dal di fuori quello che avviene sulla scena. La dimensione tematica del film riflette specularmente l'esperienza dell'operatore. In questa struttura autoriflessiva i personaggi del film si confondono con quelli del romanzo: una falsa caccia alla tigre, con falsi cacciatori e con una falsa belva. Le circostanze, intanto, portano sulla scena una vera tigre che non è uccisa. Anzi, sarà la belva a sbranare l'attore-cacciatore. Serafino, operatore per mestiere più che per vocazione, diventa, testimone e pontefice di una realtà nuova e inattesa che prorompe sulla scena e sopraffa la finzione.

La tecnica narrativa mette a fuoco il rapporto – sul quale il Futurismo italiano aveva meditato e auspicato – tra uomo e macchina. Siamo in un universo tecnologico moderno, e Pirandello ne indovina le nefaste complicazioni esistenziali.

Marinetti si esalta nell'immaginare il mondo delle macchine nella convinzione che, grazie ad esse, le percezioni umane giungeranno a ritmi frenetici. L'uomo futurista è un superuomo. Pirandello coglie gli aspetti ironici di questa innovazione tecnologico-rivoluzionaria. La metafora della macchina da presa si rivela tanto più efficace in quanto Serafino riesce ad identificarsi con essa e la fa funzionare prestandole gli occhi e girando una manovella. La contrapposizione dello "sguardo" o occhi e della "mano" fa di lui l'emblema privilegiato della scissione che oppone nell'uomo contemporaneo, la soggettività di uno spettatore immobile nella impassibile contemplazione di un flusso di immagini alla reificazione della propria corporeità oggettivata, alla mano, che è ridotta al meccanismo di un gesto automatico. Infatti, Serafino è diviso tra due poli egualmente negativi: l'immobilità di uno sguardo impassibile e la cecità di un movimento assurdo, la cui velocità si conforma a quella dell'azione che si svolge davanti alla cinepresa. Di conseguenza, il corpo-macchina, privo d'interiorità, divora la vita e l'anima dal di fuori, e la restituisce poi all'uomo in una ripetizione frammentaria. La macchina di Serafino, assume i caratteri di una bestia artificiale, mostruosa e famelica, connessa alla tigre, vista in gabbia, come innocente belva, da esser sacrificata. Infatti, nella scena centrale del film in produzione, mentre la tigre divora il corpo, la cinepresa divora l'anima. In breve, l'operatore Serafino Gubbio, girando la manovella della macchina da presa – trasformando, cioè, il mondo in finzione cinematografica – si configura come una specie di esecutore che uccide e spoglia gli attori della loro realtà. La sua funzione di operatore è parcellare, frammentando e disgregando l'integrità vitale dell'organismo vivente, trasforma la "vita" in "forma." Nella dinamica delle forme che proietta sugli schermi dei cinematografi, anche la soggettività di Serafino Gubbio si dissolve: "io ero fuori di tutto, assente da me stesso e dalla vita..."[4]

Con questa metafora cinematografica è ovvio che, in un primo momento, il discorso di Pirandello si rivela come critica dell'apparato di ripresa, e che il cinema è visto come un fatto commerciale. Ben presto, però, l'esperienza di Pirandello come spettatore cinematografico e come visitatore assiduo di stabilimenti cinematografici, se non altro per andare a trovare i suoi amici cineletterati, nel periodo di assestamento del cinema come industria e organizzazione dello spettacolo (1905-1914), contribuisce a cambiare la sua posizione verso il cinema. Egli, infatti, si orienta verso questa espressione d'arte che condensa il suo pensiero sul carattere effimero dell'oggettivo e del soggettivo, già trattato in alcune opere precedenti e sviluppato poi nel suo teatro. In *Quaderni di Serafino Gubbio operatore* si vedono gli stessi personaggi apparire in scene diverse, e in momenti diversi. Olga Ragusa ci fa notare come Pirandello riesca a creare "the kaleidoscopic effect of life which is not structured by any *unifying concept.*"[5] Di conseguenza, nel

---

4. *Pirandello: saggi, poesie e scritti vari*, a cura di M. Lo Vecchio, Milano: Musti, 1960, 153.
5. Olga Ragusa, *Luigi Pirandello*, New York: Columbia UP, 1968, 21.

cinema, Pirandello trova la soluzione al problema che impegna tutta la sua opera: la vita che scorre e cambia; l'arte che sembra essere finzione ma che si rivela realtà; l'arte che ferma e fissa le mutevoli situazioni e i personaggi della vita in atteggiamenti definitivi ed eterni.

Il presente studio si iscrive nella lunga e complessa storia dei rapporti tra cinema e letteratura. Ha scritto Alberto Asor Rosa che "è difficile indicare a livello mondiale un'altra cinematografia in cui si verifichi, come in quella italiana, una presenza altrettanto forte dell'ispirazione letteraria come base dell'invenzione e della sceneggiatura cinematografica."[6]

Pirandello come soggettista e sceneggiatore cinematografico ha ispirato "un totale di 44 film (se si contano complessivamente cioè calcolando produzioni separate, come di fatto sono, la triplice versione di *La Canzone dell'amore*, la duplice di *Ma non è una cosa seria* e *L'Homme de nulle part*." Francesco Callari aggiunge che "ad essere esatti, i film diventerebbero 64 qualora si considerasse che il no. 21, *Questa è la vita* comprende quattro episodi da altrettante novelle; il no. 25, *Il Mondo di Pirandello* è adattamento di tredici novelle in cinque episodi; e il no. 37, *Kaos*, è composto di cinque episodi tratti da sei novelle."[7] Sarà la Francia ad imporre Pirandello all'attenzione internazionale con il primo capolavoro cinematografico di Marcel L'Herbier, anche adattatore e scenarista, nonchè condottiere della "Nouvelle Vague" di quell'epoca e futuro fondatore del noto Institut des Hantes Etudes Cinematographiques. La sua versione del *Feu Mathias Pascal* (1924-25) tratta dal romanzo *Il fu Mattia Pascal* (1904), fu emulata più tardi da Henry Bigot (1910). Questa versione capeggia la lista dei film stranieri pirandelliani finora realizzati (tredici) e di quelli di cui si conserva copia; è anche il primo film che Pirandello vide con favore ancora prima che fosse realizzato. Del *Pascal*, abbiamo due successive edizioni cinematografiche: *L'homme de nulle part* (1936-37) di Pierre Chenal, con Pierre Blanchar, che, come quella di L'Herbier, è fedele all'epoca in cui si svolge la vicenda narrata da Pirandello cioè all'inizio del secolo; e *Le Due Vite di Mattia Pascal* (1984-85) di Mario Monicelli con Marcello Mastroianni, coproduzione italo-francese la prima,

---

6. Alberto Asor Rosa, 'Il neorealismo o il trionfo del narrativo,' in *Cinema e leteratura del neorealismo*, a cura di G. Tinazzi e M. Zancan, Venezia: Marsilio, 1983, 82.

7. Francesco Callari, "Pirandello soggettista e sceneggiatore del cinema," in *Pirandello e la cultura del suo tempo*, Milano: Mursia, 1984, 177-246.

italo-francese-tedesca (e televisivo-cinematografica) la seconda.[8] Questo terzo adattamento del *Pascal* trasporta la storia ai giorni nostri, con tutte le conseguenze che un aggiornamento cosi drastico comporta. Del romanzo è stato preso solo lo spunto, che è attualissimo, il resto viene da esigenze cinematografiche (più immagini che parole e descrizioni) che prevalgono su quelle letterarie. La prima e importante variante è proprio quella del titolo. Il regista Mario Monicelli elimina "Il fu" e lo sostituisce con "Le due vite." Secondo variante è il compromesso tra il personaggio e l'attore. Mattia Pascal è descritto da Pirandello con un occhio che "tendeva a guardare per conto suo, altrove."[9] È un dettaglio attraverso il quale Pirandello mette in luce il ruolo della percezione oculare. Ma Mattia è anche rappresentato con "un barbone rossastro e ricciuto, a scapito del naso piuttosto piccolo, che si trovò come sperduto tra esso e la fronte spaziosa e grave."[10] Marcello Mastroianni, l'attore che interpreta Mattia Pascal, era lungi dall'essere un ometto basso e piuttosto brutto. Al contrario del personaggio descritto da Pirandello, Mastroianni, con la sua aria simpatica e seducente affascinava. Monicelli riconosce il compromesso tra il personaggio e l'attore e dichiara che proprio per questo la sua scelta per la parte va benissimo: "...lui cosi ironico, cosi sornione, cosi spietato e crudele, uno che malgrado l'apparenza dolce, non si lascia schiacciare da nessuno, semmai schiaccia lui tutti gli altri."[11] Il protagonista del noto romanzo pirandelliano va in cerca della sua identità. È un personaggio contraddittorio e angosciato; è la figura dell'uomo moderno. Nel film del Monicelli, molti dialoghi sono rimasti cosi come sono nel testo. Il regista rispetta lo sviluppo narrativo, gli scatti psicologici del protagonista che rimane figlio di benestante, che non ha mai fatto nulla e non riesce ad adattarsi alla realtà della miseria provocata da Malagna, l'amministratore disonesto che lo deruba di tutto.

Come è ben noto nel film, che segue la narrativa, Mattia è figlio di un ricco agricoltore. Alla morte del padre, si scopre povero a causa della disonestà dell'amministratore. Come nel romanzo, Mattia va a Montecarlo, e al tavolo da gioco vince molti soldi. Nel testo, il prota-

---

8. Francesco Callari, *Pirandello e il cinema. Con una raccolta completa degli scritti teorici e creativi*, 33.
9. *Il Fu Mattia Pascal romanzo di Pirandello*, Milano: Mondadori, 1965, 21.
10. *Il Fu Mattia Pascal romanzo di Pirandello*, 21.
11. Francesco Callari, *Pirandello e il cinema*, 418.

gonista, in treno, sta facendo ritorno al suo paese (forse in Sicilia), apprende da un giornale la propria morte. Un cadavere di un misterioso suicida viene identificato come lo scomparso Mattia Pascal. Nel film il personaggio torna a casa (l'ambientazione finzionale è la Liguria e non la Sicilia) e si rende conto che è dato per morto. Approfitta della sua finta morte per reinventare la propria vita: allontanandosi dalla moglie, dalla suocera, dai debiti e dalla greve realtà quotidiana in cui è costretto a vivere, Mattia scorge la sua possibile rinascita nella più piena libertà. La sua è la tragedia del ribelle che tenta di sottrarsi alle maschere e alle convenzioni sociali per essere, con un altro nome, esclusivamente e liberamente se stesso. Ben presto, però, il suo sogno fallisce. Mattia cerca di crearsi una seconda vita, ma questo diventa impossibile sia per fattori psicologici che burocratici.

Nelle uniche pagine di *Il fu Mattia Pascal* in cui si parla di sentimenti e di tenerezze, si leggono quelle dedicate alla morte della madre e della figlia di Mattia. Il protagonista è un uomo cinico, non riesce ad amare. Quando teme di essere coinvolto con Adriana, la ragazza della pensione a Roma, si inventa una seconda morte per suicidio. Nel film, grazie a Mastroianni, l'attore che interpreta il ruolo di Mattia Pascal, il protagonista riesce a diventare simpatico, malgrado la sua natura cinica e fredda.

Il film, *Le Due Vite di Mattia Pascal*, dimostra una vasta ricercatezza stilistica da parte del regista, e ci dà un esito notevole sia dal punto di vista della tecnica cinematografica, sia nel rispetto per l'opera letteraria che l'ha ispirato.

Nel 1984 alla XLI Mostra del cinema di Venezia, il film *Kaos*, che era stato prodotto dai fratelli Taviani per la televisione, veniva giudicato dalla maggior parte dei critici come il miglior film italiano. Suddiviso in sei parti – un prologo, quattro episodi e un epilogo – *Kaos* – nome che si riferisce al reale luogo di nascita di Pirandello e, allo stesso tempo, parola greca che indica il disordine dell'esistenza – si ispira a sei novelle contadine di Pirandello raccolte in *Novelle per un anno*: "Il corvo di Mizzaro," "L'altro figlio," "Male di luna," "La giara," "Requiem aeternam dona eis, Domine!" e "Colloqui coi personaggi." I registi toscani, che desideravano fare un film sulla Sicilia, spiegano la loro scelta dei testi pirandelliani in *Kaos*: "Abbiamo cercato l'omogeneità del film attraverso il Pirandello che svolge le sue storie nei campi tra la terra, tra i contadini."[12] Ma perchè il film porta il titolo di *Kaos* e non "il corvo," "la luna," o "la giara"... Già dal titolo, lo spettatore capisce che il film tratta di un viaggio della memoria; di un ritorno all matrice originale; di una risalita della coscienza fino alla fonte primitiva di ogni vita. Nella produzione dei fratelli Taviani, i temi ricorrenti sono: la vita dei campi, la passione per la storia, per la letteratura, per la musica.

La visione pirandelliana dello scenario siciliano assume un'importanza fondamentale. Della novella "Il corvo di Mizzaro," i registi sono essenzialmente interessati ai brani che permettono di visualizzare la Sicilia. Le immagini costituiscono il commento visuale alle frasi di Pirandello in cui fa riferimento all'immensità del cielo: "Il corvo di Mizzaro, nero nell'azzurro della bella mattinata, suonava di nuovo pei cieli la sua campanella, libero e beato."[13] Il paesaggio, assieme alla musica, assume una funzione strutturale. La Sicilia ariosa della cornice, vista verticalmente, dal cielo, inquadra quella orizzontale dei racconti. È una Sicilia mitica, simile a un immenso palcoscenico teatrale sul quale recitano gli attori a campi medi e a figura intera davanti alla cinepresa che, intanto, fa da spettatore. Con poche linee grafiche i registi dipingono il mondo dei contadini che, con le braccia tese verso il cielo, implorano le forze di una natura deserta e ostile, e rielaborano la ricchezza delle descrizioni che Pirandello fa della vita dei campi. I Taviani danno un'immagine più umana dei contadini poveri e deboli.

In "Mal di luna," Batà non è più quell'uomo vecchio descritto da Pirandello, e in "L'altro figlio," Ninfarosa, la giovane donna che fa finta di scrivere lettere per Mariagrazia, non è la donna arrogante del testo letterario. La stessa Mariagrazia, che vive di speranza e di amore per i figli lontani, assume una bellezza rara e innocente. Nel rappresentare le donne, i Taviani usano sapientemente l'estetica femminile. Come se stesse li a contemplarle, spesso la loro cinepresa rimane immobile davanti a queste donne bellissime. Il senso dell'estetica appare anche nel viso sorridente e nel corpo sensuale della moglie di Don Lolò, un personaggio, che, anche se essenzialmente pirandelliano, è stato inventato dai registi. In *Kaos*, il ruolo della madre assume la stessa importanza

---

12. S. Borelli. "Cosi la Sicilia ritrova la storia. Arriva 'Kaos.' C'e' anche un episodio nuovo." *L'unità*, 16 marzo, 1986.
13. Luigi Pirandello, "Il corvo di Mizzaro' (1919), *In Silenzio*, vol. II, tomo I, Milano: Mondadori, 1987, 183.

di quello della madre terra, la Sicilia. Le tre madri, Mariagrazia, la madre di Batà e la madre di Pirandello, incarnano l'intensità emozionale e mitica del mondo siciliano. Esse apertamente raccontano la loro storia, e rivelano le loro emozioni e i loro più intimi segreti. La madre di Pirandello, morta, riappare agli occhi del figlio sia per impartirgli una lezione di coraggio, che per il piacere di poter narrare. In questo viaggio della memoria, Pirandello ritorna in Sicilia (un viaggio che non esiste nella narrativa). Soltanto tornando nella terra natia egli riesce a ritrovare la sua identità. Ma il suo viaggio è anche un viaggio nel tempo quando, cioè, sua madre era ancora viva. Il tempo passato è rieccheggiato nella musica discordante, nell'odore del limone che entra dalla finestra del salone. I ricordi, le emozioni sono cosi forti e intensi che per qualche istante – e la scena ricorda il pascoliano "sogno" – egli vede la vecchia casa rianimarsi e la madre rivivere. La vede seduta nel posto che era solita occupare e l'ascolta mentre racconta la storia che lui vuol tanto sentire. Cerca la ripetizione dell'emozione creata dal racconto; un racconto che l'autore non è 'mai riuscito a scrivere' ma che i registi riescono a realizzare. Mentre la madre racconta ancora una volta la sua storia al bimbo-Pirandello, lo spettatore ne sente la voce, ma non vede la donna. L'affabulazione, il piacere del racconto, si articola in una dimensione tematica che regge lo svolgersi sia del film che del testo letterario.

Malgrado le difficoltà e la pena di vivere che percorre il film, i fratelli Taviani concludono *Kaos* con un messaggio di speranza che è direttamente ripreso dal testo letterario. La madre di Pirandello rivela al figlio la ragione per cui lo ha richiamato nella terra delle sue origini: "Impara a guardare le cose con gli occhi di quelli che non le vedono più. Ne proverai dolore certo. Ma quel dolore te le renderà più sacre e più belle." La morte – o lo sguardo postumo sul mondo – come a suo modo anche Mattia Pascal aveva intuito quando sceglie di vivere come uomo morto e rinato alla vita, si pone come prospettiva da cui l'arte della contemplazione e della scrittura ha origine.

In questo saggio ho cercato di illustrare due temi. Il primo è il rapporto di Pirandello con il cinema. Il suo è un rapporto conplesso di uno scrittore che coglie le possibilità estetiche nuove di questa forma d'arte moderna. Il cinema – arte che dipende dalla macchina – è arte che divora la realtà e rischia di divorare l'artista. Da questo punto di vista, Pirandello prende le sue distanze dall'ideologia dei Futuristi che si esaltano ed esaltano la meccanizzazione moderna della vita.

Il secondo tema di questo saggio tratta del rapporto del cinema con Pirandello. Come si è mostrato, il cinema europeo (francese e italiano) si ispira all'arte di Pirandello. Eppure, esso trascura gli aspetti più inquietanti del suo pensiero (le forme, la vita, l'arte, ecc.). Il cinema europeo di matrice pirandelliana coglie gli aspetti più naturalistici e mitici della Sicilia.

In effetti, esiste un grande divario tra Pirandello e l'esperienza cinematografica successiva. C'è da concludere che, proprio come Pirandello lucidamente aveva anticipato, il cinema consuma e "divora" il mondo dell'arte autentica.

The Italian American Press and the "Woman Question," 1915-1930

Bénédict Deschamps

In the aftermath of World War I, the feminist movements intensified their struggle for the improvement of the condition of women. As has been widely documented, during the conflict, women had displayed qualities of strength, courage, and efficiency that contrasted with the attributes of frailty, gentleness and inconsistency with which the female gender was usually credited. The general labor shortage resulting from men's mobilization in the army had led munitions factories and heavy industries to employ women, thus giving the latter an opportunity to show they were quite able to perform tasks that had been previously reserved to male workers. Moreover, the involvement of women on the front as nurses had proved that the stereotype portraying them as weak creatures was wearing out and was no longer appropriate.[1]

In the United States, the participation of women in the war effort contributed to shedding a new light on the feminist claims, and it lay the foundation for major changes in American society. In fact, at a time when the creation of a Women's Bureau within the Department of Labor opened the way for a formal reflection over the working conditions of wage-earning women, the 19th Amendment helped redefine the role female citizens were supposed to play in the public arena.[2] Meanwhile, the flappers, whose quest for equality was not limited to job opportunities but was also extended to sexual emancipation, offered a new model of womanhood that was both disturbing and fascinating to young American females.

Southern Europeans looked upon the emergence of a "new American woman" with mistrust, as the metamorphosis of obedient housewives into "full-fledged individuals" capable of molding their own lives certainly challenged their traditional approach to femininity.[3] New immigrants were indeed confronted with an image of womanhood that most of them were at least uncomfortable with. In Italy, although such

---

[1] See, for example, Carol Hymowitz and Michaele Weissman, *A History of Women in America* (New York: Bantam, 1978), 262-63.

[2] See Mary Anderson, *Women at Work* (Minneapolis: U of Minnesota P, 1951), 102-04.

[3] Dorothy Dunbar Bromley, "Feminist – New Style," *Harper's Monthly Magazine* 155 (Oct. 1927): 560.

feminists as Gualberta Beccari had started fighting for the legal reform of women's status as early as the mid-nineteenth century, old Latin schemes still prevailed and women were supposed to derive their power essentially from their positions as mothers.[4] In this context, Italian immigrants were not ready to welcome the evolution of American society, nor were they willing to let those new models influence their daily lives. In fact, Southern Italy's family customs generally required women to stay home and perform household duties. Whether in the United States or in Italy, Italian girls were raised to be housewives first, even though the economic insecurity they were faced with in America forced them to break the Italian rule by working in factories.[5]

Italian-American journalists adhered to those traditional patterns and defended a very Italian definition of women's role, precisely in the name of their cultural heritage. Among other things, they feared that the American environment would pervert the "sweetest and weakest half of the human kind," to quote the New York City-based daily *Il Progresso Italo-Americano*, the most influential Italian-language newspaper in the country.[6] For example, the new dressing codes the flappers had adopted in their own quest for independence were regarded as highly threatening. Thus, in 1925, *Il Progresso Italo-Americano* implicitly backed the Vatican's campaign against the dangerous transformation of female attire, giving voice to the Pope's disapproval of the "excesses of women's fashion" which "had gone from bad to worse as necklines had lowered and sleeves had been eliminated."[7]

By allowing their bodies to move freely in a more fluid kind of clothing, women were trying to break free from an oppressive Victorian heritage. In the process, they tended to endorse a behavior that was

---

[4] Judith Jeffrey Howard, "The Civil Code of 1865 and the Feminist Movement in Italy," in *The Italian Immigrant Woman in North America*, ed. Betty Boyd Caroli, Robert F. Harney, and Lydio Tomasi (Toronto: Multicultural Society of Ontario, 1978), 14-22; Donna Gabaccia, *From the Other Side: Women, Gender, and Immigrant Life in the U.S., 1820-1990* (Bloomington: Indiana UP, 1994), 16.

[5] Humbert S. Nelli, *From Immigrants to Ethnics: The Italian Americans* (New York: Oxford UP, 1983), 137, 144; Donna Gabaccia, *From Sicily to Elizabeth Street: Housing and Social Change Among Italian Women, 1880-1930* (Albany: State U of New York P, 1984), 101; Judy Smith, "Italian Mothers, American Daughters: Changes in Work and Family Roles," in *The Italian Immigrant Woman in North America*, op. cit., 206-21.

[6] Francesco Gaeta, "Alla difesa delle donne-," *Il Progresso Italo-Americano* 8 July 1923: Sunday supplement, 2-S.

[7] "Una nuova campagna contro le esagerazioni femminili," *Il Progresso Italo-Americano* 20 July 1925: 1.

labeled as typically "male" and was therefore resented by many Italian immigrants. The Italian-American newspapers reflected this concern for the "masculinization" of women and seized every opportunity to emphasize what they saw as the perversions and contradictions of feminism. In an article dedicated to the suffrage movement, editorialist Emilio Cecchi expressed, in *Il Progresso Italo-Americano,* a viewpoint that epitomized such continuous attempts to ridicule women's claims for equal rights:

> One could expect feminism to be a form of sublimation of women and femininity. But, it must be acknowledged that feminism is really a distortion of femininity and that it acclaims and extols women not as women, but as men or only as potential surrogates of men.[8]

When discussing the woman question, the Italian-American periodicals almost systematically failed to mention the struggles led by the existing feminist organizations in Italy. However, this was not an unintentional omission. In their efforts to focus on the American analysis of a phenomenon that was also developing in Europe, they sought to restrict the problem of female emancipation to the United States. This strategy let them limit the extent of the debate and helped them discredit feminism by presenting it as one of the numerous oddities of a country where everything, even the inconceivable, could happen. Therefore, according to *Il Progresso Italo-Americano*, it was the changes affecting American society and the loss of key family values that were the unmistakable sources of feminist agitation. As this Italian-language daily put it:

> The problem of American society is the little inclination for marriage, especially ever since women replaced men during World War I. This is why nobody will be able to stop women on their way to political and social achievements. He who tells women – as Prof. Quinby does – 'you must go back to your homes' must first offer female rebels a flock of young men who are ready for the sacred rite of marriage. Because, ultimately, the female crisis – that is a crisis of discontent and adaptation to a new state of things – is nothing but the consequence of the marriage crisis. The quest for public involvement is nothing

---

[8] Emilio Cecchi, "Il voto e le donne," *Il Progresso Italo-Americano* 5 Aug. 1923: Sunday supplement, 2-S.

but a substitute for the unsuccessful quest for a happy marriage. This substitute, though, is just like any substitute. It falls short of full-fledged satisfaction.[9]

The Italian-American newspapers assumed the self-attributed position of guardians of Italian traditions which they endeavored to protect from any possible corruption. In particular, they advocated a return to what they thought embodied women's true virtues: beauty, motherhood, compassion, sacrifice, and gentleness. For instance, *La Gazzetta del Massachusetts*, the Boston-based leading Italian-American newspaper in New England, made a point of reminding its female readers that child-bearing was their sacrosanct duty. As this weekly argued, "women must be free, but they must not forget that nature assigned them an extremely noble task: motherhood."[10]

The conservative idea that basic differences in the nature of men and women justified their respective positions in society was widespread among Italian-American journalists. It is doubtful that any editorialist would have dissented with *Il Carroccio* when it claimed that "Italy wants its women to be different from men." Actually, in an article that this New York City-based pro-fascist magazine published in 1923, an Italian interviewee argued that:

> In my country, we want women to be different from men, and women prefer it themselves that way, too. We don't believe they are equal, we believe they are superior, and it is woman who rules the world, anyhow. But it is through her individual influences on the individual man. We're not at all in favor of these Western theories which would give womanhood an erroneous idea of her sphere in life.[11]

In her study of the Sicilian peasants' migratory experience in America, Donna Gabaccia explains that the "myth of male dominance" was mostly a "compensatory belief."[12] In fact, it seems that Italian-American men tended to be all the more chauvinist as their dominant position within the families they had formed in the United States was

---

[9] "La crisi femminile," *Il Progresso Italo-Americano* 6 July 1925.
[10] Antonio Renzi, "A proposito dei diritti delle donne," *La Gazzetta del Massachusetts* 1 Oct. 1921.
[11] C. Drexel, "Italy Wants Its Women to Be Different from Men," *Il Carroccio* 8.2 (Aug. 1923) (reprinted from the *New York Evening Post*).
[12] Donna Gabaccia, *From Sicily to Elizabeth Street*, 113.

threatened by economic difficulties that compelled numerous women to find a job outside the household. Therefore immigration proved to be a significant factor in Italian-American men's attempt at regaining a power that they feared they were losing. The same motivations led Italian-language newspapers to defend the male viewpoint with all possible means: flattery, paternalism, irony, condescension, and mockery.

Il Lavoro, one of the official organs of the Amalgamated Clothing Workers of America (ACWA), was among the few Italian-American periodicals to offer a more complex image of womanhood. As part of a press campaign launched by the Amalgamated, *Il Lavoro* incited women to organize, encouraged them to get involved in the proletarian struggle, and welcomed contributions by such leading activists as Theresa Serber Malkiel, Bessie Abramowitz or Dorothy Jacobs Bellanca.[13] Considering that Italian women accounted for sixty-eight percent of the female labor force employed in the men's garment industry – where the ACWA was recruiting its members – such endeavors to attract "sisters" to the union were essential to the development of the organization.[14] However, within the Amalgamated, Italian male unionists were often reluctant to give up their prejudices against women workers, who they thought were responsible for lowering wages.[15] Frank Bellanca, *Il Lavoro*'s editor, was fully aware of the situation and published articles that denounced his peers' ordinary misogyny.[16] He wanted readers to understand that female workers had a part to play in the future of the ACWA and that "the time when Italian women were thought to be refractory to the Organization [was] over." Bellanca and

---

[13] For more information on how the ACWA dealt with women workers, see Jo Ann Argersinger, *Making the Amalgamated: Gender, Ethnicity, and Class in the Baltimore Clothing Industry, 1899-1939* (Baltimore: John Hopkins UP); for details on the ACWA press, see Earl D. Strong, *The Amalgamated Clothing Workers of America* (Grinnell, IA: Herald Register, 1940), 210-13.

[14] Miriam Cohen, "Italian-American Women in New York City, 1900-1950: Work and School," in *Class, Sex, and the Woman Worker,* ed. Milton Cantor and Bruce Laurie (Westport: Greenwood, 1977), 122.

[15] For an account of male chauvinism within union organizations, see for instance: Alice Kessler-Harris, "Organizing the Unorganizable: Three Jewish Women and Their Union," *Labor History* 17.1 (Winter 1976): 5-23; and Colomba M. Furio, "The Cultural Background of the Italian Immigrant Woman and its Impact on her Unionization in the New York City Garment Industry, 1880-1919," in *Pane e Lavoro: The Italian American Working Class,* ed. George Pozzetta (Toronto: Multicultural History Society of Ontario, 1980), 81-98.

[16] See Frank Bellanca, "La questione delle donne," *Il Lavoro* 25 May 1918.

his friends believed women should use the qualities that allegedly characterized their gender for a better purpose:

> Italian women [...] have the virtue of bearing suffering without complaining. But they must also have the virtue of holding their heads up and looking ahead toward the future. It's about time they were done with resignation and humility.[17]

Poet and unionist Arturo Giovannitti shared similar views. Drawing a parallel between workers' subjugation to capitalism and women's submission to their male relatives, he insisted that "women should be liberated from the domestic servitude."[18] Nonetheless, in spite of Bellanca's undeniable efforts to support the women's cause, *Il Lavoro*'s editorialists were unable to free themselves completely from the influence of powerful stereotypes. Admittedly, *Il Lavoro* instructed women to rebel against male oppression, and advised men to choose a spouse that would not be just a "housekeeper" or a "cook" but also a "companion" and a "friend." Yet one could conclude from the following quotation that, even for *Il Lavoro,* women's emancipation was due to have some limits too:

> At home, graciousness, gentleness, patience, and sacrifice are much more valuable than all personal seduction or intellectual qualities. Those virtues contribute more to happiness and are the real source of mutual understanding because the wife who loves understands better and sees farther than an intelligent woman without a heart. A good wife rules her husband by obeying him with intelligence.[19]

However much enthusiasm *Il Lavoro*'s contributors may have displayed in spurring female workers to join the open fight against capitalist exploitation, their campaign in favor of a greater involvement of women in public affairs did not include suffrage. A simple explanation was provided to justify the journal's standpoint in that matter:

> The woman question is interwoven with the social question and, consequently, the women's movement is necessarily a component of the

---

[17] R. Canudo, "Per grande famiglia dei sarti da uomo," *Il Lavoro* 22 Apr. 1916.
[18] Arturo Giovannitti, "Ai margini del grande sciopero," *Il Lavoro* 13 March 1919.
[19] "Mogli e mariti ... felici," *Il Lavoro* 11 Sep. 1920.

labor movement. Problems exclusively related to women, including the right to vote, [...] can be used within our propaganda as accessory issues to clarify women's position, but they must always be considered as nothing but mere argumentative devices. Agitation in favor of such claims would be inappropriate because, even though we admit that women would be fighting for legitimate rights, they would spend much energy without improving the condition of the proletarian woman, whereas – whatever the stage of the labor movement – there will always be more urgent problems which will be of interest to the whole working class and not only to women.[20]

Both Sally Miller and Elisabetta Vezzosi have discussed the socialists' ambiguous attitude toward women in general and the suffrage problem in particular.[21] *Il Lavoro*, which openly supported the Socialist Party, was no less ambiguous. It presented the right to vote as an ancillary right, not as a priority. At any rate, its editors maintained that female suffrage was not a goal that ought to supersede the struggle for the emancipation of workers, nor did they think that it was worth risking class collaboration through an alliance with the bourgeois suffrage movement. Interestingly enough, on the issue, though for different reasons, *Il Lavoro* sided with the Italian-language commercial press.

In the years that followed the passing of the 19th Amendment, the Italian-American press showed great hostility toward feminist achievements. As sexist prejudices within Italian institutions had always defeated the Italian women's organizations, the Italian-language newspapers carefully avoided reporting the debate over female suffrage that had been launched in Italy. Nonetheless, a reform of the Italian electoral system started by the Fascist regime in 1923 aroused the interest of the Italian-American press in this issue. Benito Mussolini, who

---

[20] "Tesi sul movimento femminile," *Il Lavoro* 25 Nov. 1922.

[21] For the tendency of the Socialist-oriented Italian-American press to share a traditional view of women and its grudging support of feminist claims, see Elisabetta Vezzosi, "Italian Immigrant Women: In Search of a Female Identity in Turn-of-the-Century America," *RSA: Rivista di Studi Anglo-Americani* 3.4-5 (1984-1985): 528-30; Elisabetta Vezzosi, *Il socialismo indifferente: Immigrati italiani e Socialist Party negli Stati Uniti del primo Novecento* (Rome: Lavoro, 1991), 129-30; Elisabetta Vezzosi, "Immigrate italiane e socialismo agli inizi del Novecento," *Il Veltro: Rivista della Civiltà Italiana* 34.1-2 (Jan.-Apr. 1990); Sally Miller, "Other Socialists: Native-Born and Immigrant Women in the Socialist Party of America, 1901-1917," *Labor History* 24.1 (Winter 1983): 84-102; Sally Miller, "Socialism and Women," in *Failure of a Dream, Essays in the History of American Socialism*, ed. John H. Laslett and Seymour Martin Lipset (Berkeley: U of California P, 1984), 291-317.

understood the benefits he could derive from rallying women to the fascist cause, promised that his government would propose a bill which would "grant the right to vote to certain categories of women, starting with the administrative level."[22] In August 1923, while Italy's feminist organizations seemed to have very little chance to succeed, *Il Progresso Italo-Americano* mocked such an allegedly ridiculous effort to change the political status of women. As this Italian-language daily commented:

> What remains to be shown, quite luckily, in the question of female suffrage is the statement that women actually feel the need to vote. Nothing else really matters. The debate over whether this vote could be granted in political and administrative elections or, for the time being, only in administrative elections, is of no real interest to those who care for concrete elements. It all comes down to the interpretation of a quite unacceptable and unsubstantiated concept: the theory that women would actually care for this right or, with all due respect, that women who care most for this right are actually women.[23]

However, by the end of 1923, the Italian-American newspapers changed their minds and suddenly began supporting Italy's electoral reform, as they realized that Mussolini was indeed seriously considering the idea of keeping his word. *Il Progresso* based this surprising reversal of editorial policy on a new approach to the problem, the purpose of which was to oppose the United States to Italy. According to the New York daily, Italian women were gifted with specific qualities which set them apart from American women and justified the fact that *they* could be trusted – within reasonable limits – with a distinctive civic mission conferred to them by the right to vote. In December, *Il Progresso Italo-Americano* explained that:

> The Italian woman is far from being dogmatic and limits herself to a maternal and fraternal understanding of society. Her participation in the electoral process can establish an intimate connection between

---

[22] Benito Mussolini, *Opera Omnia*, ed. E. and D. Susmel, v. 19 (Florence: La Fenice, 1951-1980), 215, quoted by Victoria de Grazia, *Le donne nel regime fascista* (Venice: Marsilio, 1993), 63.
[23] Emilio Cecchi, "Il voto e le donne," *Il Progresso Italo-Americano* 5 Aug. 1923: Sunday supplement, 2-S.

life and politics, between the household and the world of ideas, between the mind and the heart.

Italian women could be granted the right to vote in local elections precisely because they knew what their real place in society was, and accepted it. *Il Progresso* further stated that:

> When – as it is the case in our motherland – women want to remain women, which is not the case elsewhere, [...] when the arguments women use to show the humanity of their intentions tend to prove that their participation alongside men in the elections, means the collaboration of mothers, wives, sisters and daughters toward a fairer and more efficient selection of the Italian people's representatives, then, a bill acknowledging the female right thereof, as defined in those terms, deserves to be not only accepted but also enlarged in its spirit and enriched by further developments.[24]

Il Progresso Italo-Americano's viewpoint was in complete harmony with that of Italian fascist women's magazines, which claimed that female suffrage would celebrate the "victory of good industrious femininity and holy maternity, and not of gross feminism."[25] Agostino de Biasi, *Il Carroccio*'s editor, was eager to support the same theories, and he loved to depict Italian women as active and sensible mothers who knew they were the guardians of society's moral values. In an article evoking various Italian women's organizations supposedly involved in the improvement of the nation, de Biasi gave his own account of the attributes he believed best characterized his fellow countrywomen:

> There is also a suffrage organization which however does not enthuse large numbers. Many of the best thinking women of the day are not altogether in sympathy with the movement. But it must be said for truth's sake that the Italian woman in her efforts to broaden her sphere of life and action [...] retains, however, a larger portion of her feminine attractiveness and assumes generally less masculine airs

---

[24] "Il voto alle donne in Italia," *Il Progresso Italo-Americano* 16 Dec. 1923.
[25] Fanny Dalmazzo, "Femminismo e azione femminile," *La Donna Italiana* 1.1 (1924), quoted by Sarah Follacchio in "Conversando di femminismo, *La Donna Italia*," in *La corporazione delle donne: Ricerche e studi sui modelli femminili nel ventennio fascista* (Florence: Vallecchi, 1988), 176.

than one is wont to see in women of other countries along the same lines.[26]

It is difficult not to recognize in the description of those "women of other countries" who assumed more "masculine airs," a scornful portrayal of American females who had achieved, by the mid-1920s, a greater freedom both in terms of fashion and legal rights. In opposition to the American model, *Il Carroccio* praised Italian women who revered their child-rearing duty. It was through their offspring that women could influence the fate of their nation, argued the pro-fascist magazine, and no example could better illustrate this theory than the accomplishments of Mussolini's mother. No one could deny that:

> ...some of these marked characteristics which make of [the Duce] a much admired and very unique figure in the present day, are the heritage of a strong-minded woman [...] from whose early schooling Mussolini has forged his powerful character.[27]

Therefore, the Italian-language press made a distinction between the American women, who were seen as corrupt, and the Italian women, who were reliable because they were attached to the value of motherhood. In other words, Italian women could be trusted because they were willing to assist men and did not nurture the inappropriate desire of competing with them.

On November 22, 1925, Mussolini finally granted women the right to vote in local elections, though not for long, as the law was repealed a year later. Eligible for the suffrage were only women over twenty-five years of age who knew how to read and write and had been officially recognized for their actions to the benefit of their nation as mothers or wives.[28] Since this law involved only a very limited number of women, the Italian-American newspapers did not perceive it as a possible threat. In this perspective, the social pattern that was developing in Italy could still prevail and inspire Italian immigrants in the United States.

---

[26] "The Italian Women: Their Part in the Making of a Greater Italy," *Il Carroccio* 14.3 (March 1924).
[27] Alice S. Rossi, "The Italian Woman," *Il Carroccio* 9.2 (Feb. 1924).
[28] Act of 22 Nov. 1925, no. 2125, now in Commissione Nazionale per la Realizzazione della Parità tra Uomo e Donna, *Donne e diritto: Due secoli di legislazione, 1796-1986* (Rome: Istituto Poligrafico e Zecca dello Stato, 1987), 1:1296.

As years passed by, the Italian-language press tried to persuade women to remain confined within the limits in their domestic world. In the late 1920s, while *Il Progresso*'s editor acknowledged that a newly found access to education qualified women as potential readers, he created a specific page for Italian females entitled "*Per Voi Signore,*" which purposefully narrowed down the range of topics to fashion, cooking, and romance. *Il Progresso Italo-Americano* was probably one of the fiercest opponents of feminism and spared no effort to criticize the model of the emancipated woman that American females embodied. As late as the mid-1930s, a columnist resorted to words that were undeniably emblematic of this daily's everlasting rancor when he wrote:

> Many theories about women have been nothing but statements of perversion and, as such, they should be energetically corrected if not eliminated. [...] I would be the first person to approve a proposal by the League of Nations that would recommend, for instance, that political women and demagogic feminists in general be deported to a tropical or Australian island inhabited by snakes and savage cannibals.[29]

It would be too tedious to draw a list of all the Italian-American newspapers that attacked the women's movements. It is also possible that some Italian-language dailies and weeklies were supportive of women's rights. Yet, what was specific in the way the Italian-American press reported on the woman question was how journalists transformed the debate over feminism into an ethnic debate. While they could have opposed "emancipated" women to "traditional" women, they deliberately chose to contrast "American" women with "Italian" women.

---

[29] Dot, "Il femminismo causa di deformazione e di rovinoso traviamento sociale?" *Il Progresso Italo-Americano* 9 Sep. 1934: Sunday supplement, 4-S.

Virgillia, or the Contribution of Italian Americans to the United States through Intermarriage

Marie-Christine Michaud
UNIVERSITÉ BRETAGNE-SUD, FRANCE

INTRODUCTION

In November 1995, the Center for Migration Studies of New York was given an unpublished autobiographical novel by Gilda Ciani Sferra, an Italian immigrant, because she felt that her work could contribute to Italian-American studies, as a testimony of immigrants' lives, giving a human dimension to sociological or statistical analyses. She wrote in a letter she included with her gift: "I want to contribute *Virgillia* to the CMS for it is a true story of an Italian family who lived in the tenement and I watched them all through my childhood... I suffered much sadness for my three daughters fell in love with non-Italian men... and the mothers in law did not want Italian American girls for their sons. The two oldest were divorced very young... I finally come to the conclusion that most races are not as civilized as the Italian race." Marriage/ intermarriage represents an essential element in community life for her and, in fact, it is the main topic of the novel she gave to the CMS.

Marriage is a reference point in the Italian-American collective consciousness, and intermarriage could be a destabilizing element in the organization of the community, particularly when Italians settled abroad. On the other hand, intermarriage can also be seen as an instrument in the process of integration. It is a driving force for the second generation, and the example given in *Virgillia* is significant. Like all autobiographies, it is a probative and worthwhile illustration of what individuals could have felt and experienced. It gives a personal and intimate point of view that complements scientific research. Thus, it shows the function of marriage among Italian Americans and the role of intermarriage in their contribution to the American society.

THE NOTION OF MARRIAGE AND ITALIAN IMMIGRANTS

Endogamy has always been one of the strongest norms in all societies as it represents the backbone of the concept of the family. It is the basis of family cohesion, and for the Italians, the *famiglia* has always had precedence over the individual and has been the central institution in the organization of the group (Tomasi 1972). It is the notion of amoral familism, that is, it is the interest of the family and not the ethic provided by the society as a whole, that has to be taken into account. Therefore, individuals have to sacrifice themselves for the interest of their family and marriage is a means to protect them. Marriage is a social process that should guarantee stability and improve the interests of the family. It imposes restrictions and codes that regulate the community. Consequently, it is commonplace to have weddings arranged by parents who appraise the acceptability of possible spouses for their children (Messina 191). Love is not necessary as marriage is seen as a social contract uniting families through the union of young spouses. Individuals are given social status from their families, which is particularly true for young women who only get a social status when they are married. Thus endogamy is a means to reinforce families' cohesion and power to face outside forces.

Such a traditional view of marriage was exported to America when the Italians immigrated. The rate of endogamy had always been very high among first-generation immigrants. It constituted a remedy to social alienation due to the immigration in the new environment. As Francesco Vina, Virgillia's father, put it, marriage was synonymous to stability and shelter, "just as a steamer anchored in port" (24). In fact, it was a means to perpetuate one's ethnic identity. On the contrary, exogamy seemed to jeopardize the organization as well as the identity of the colony. Endogamy relied on distrust and prejudice toward outsiders, and campanilismo urged individuals to find suitable mates "next door," in the same village or at least the same province, proximity resulting in a sharing of values and solidarity. At the turn of the century and until the 1920s, when Italian immigration was the largest and when *Virgillia* takes place, more than 95% of marriages involving an Italian were endogamous. Nevertheless, the rate kept decreasing as generations grew and their integration to the host society progressed. In 1930, the rate of endogamy *only* reached 86% (Kennedy 234). Yet, immigration had not changed the significance of marriage in the Italian community, since endogamy remained the essential norm in marriages. It meant family cohesion and security against outside and unknown influences from the new environment. Such is the case for Francesco and Maria Vina. They were first-generation immigrants who came from the same village. Once in the United States, they tried to marry their daughters according to their community tradition. Marriage was deeply linked with the maintenance of Italianness as it structured the family. In addition, it kept intact the Italian identity that was still based on campanilismo and amoral familism. In the 1920s, when the process of assimilation was still at an initial stage for first-generation immigrants, marriage still had a strong part to play in the organization of their colonies. Therefore, it was the parents' responsibilities to find a suitable spouse for their daughters, *i.e.*, "a good Italian American husband" (5) who would give them respectability, security, and a fair social status. Thus, Francesco appealed to matchmakers to find a spouse for Virgillia, and the Longobardos' son was chosen as an appropriate mate since the Longobardos came from the same village as the Vinas and had a good position. The place of birth remained the main reference point in the selection of the mates, as it perpetuated ethnicity. While examining the situation of Italians in Chicago in 1920, Humbert Nelli noticed that many Italians tended to marry mates from the same province (31%), and 19% married an Italian born in another province, which means that 50% married Italians born in Italy. Six percent married non-Italians (Nelli 197). The rest of them married a mate born in the United States with Italian origins, that is, second-generation immigrants. Thus, it is obvious that marriage – and endogamy – stood for a fundamental stability provider, but its function lost ground with younger generation immigrants. Such a difference of attitude is shown through Francesco and Maria's attempt to get mates for their daughters and Virgillia's wish to choose her spouse.

VIRGILLIA AND THE SIGNIFICANCE OF INTERMARRIAGE FOR THE SECOND GENERATION

The decline in the rate of endogamy among second-generation Italian immigrants testifies to a decline of ethnicity and reveals a growth in their contribution to their host society. Broadly speaking, the percentage of exogamy between first and second generations increased by 10% within the Italian American community (Russo 14). Marriage had adopted a new significance. Among second-generation Italians, love would be a prerequisite to the choice of their spouse over their parents' selection. In fact, they intended to choose their mates, whereas according to Italian tradition, spouses were to be chosen in the interest of the family, with no attention to feelings. As illustrated in *Virgillia*, second-generation females were ready to date men without a chaperon. Such an attitude is typical of the desire for emancipation of those young women as well as the impact of American society on the Italian young generation who were exposed to it (Michaud 1994). By the time of the story related in *Virgillia* – the 1920s – new forms of leisure were spreading. The movies and the availability of automobiles permitted the youngsters to have a new way of courtship, which gave rise to more romanticism, and to live romances such as that of Virgillia and Donald, who met at the theatre or went for a ride on their own in New York. The choice of mate went along with more freedom in dating and opposition to the repressive parents' authority attached to tradition. Virgillia is torn apart between her desire not to upset her parents, the interest of the family, and her wish to live her life, as she said : "I am an individual, papa, and must express myself in my own way; don't you understand, papa?" (4). Her attitude is typical of the second-generation immigrants who were becoming Americanized and who contemplated realizing their dreams. Besides, didn't their parents come to America in order to allow their children to live out their dreams? The emancipation of young Italian females is part of the process of integration, of their Americanization, and is a prerequisite to their contribution to American society. They did not want to remain "the victims of their parents' migration" (17). Such a behavior is qualified as a rebel attitude by Irving Child (1943), who distinguished three types of attitude among the second-generation immigrants concerning their acceptance of or resistance to Italian traditions (apathetic, in-group, or rebel reactions). The youngsters who were the most likely to adopt the values of the foster society and quickly integrate were those who had a rebel attitude about their parents' background and wanted to replace some of their ethnic values with American ones. So, urged by those American models, they faced family authority at the risk of becoming marginalized, because they did not want to sacrifice themselves for the interest of the family any longer. They wanted to be considered as individuals. At the beginning of the novel, Virgillia's rebellion is asserted. While feelings are superfluous in the arrangement of marriages because they did not necessarily respect the principles of amoral familism, the novel opens on the affirmation of the importance of love for Virgillia. The fact that the novel begins with a short but decisive sentence, "Virgillia was in love," has a fundamental dramatic purpose. It foretells her rebellion, her determination to put forward her individuality, and her likeliness to overcome ethnic yokes, which would be part of her integration into American society. Such a situation can also be seen through the character of Octavia in *The Fortunate Pilgrim,* by Mario Puzo, for example. Both Virgillia and Octavia adopt a rebellious attitude in their manner of reacting toward marriage. Marriage represented a way to express their identity and an indication of the progress of Americanization, since they were adopting American values to the detriment of part of their parents' heritage. While Octavia told her mother that the purpose of life was to be happy and not only to be alive (Puzo 13), as her mother thought, Virgillia wanted to express her individuality as she felt "deprived of her right to fall in love with whom she pleased" (17). For second-generation immigrants – and girls especially – marriage crystallized personal feelings and no longer family interests. Marriage was acceptable only if it went along with love. Therefore marriage lost its social function among second-generation Italian-Americans and, naturally in the United States, which was characterized by the heterogeneity of its population, intermarriage was part of the evolution of their ethnic identity and socialization in their host society.

During the 1920s, as immigrants concentrated in metropolitan areas such as New York City, many people of the same origins could be found in the neighborhood, which maintained high rates of endogamous unions. Virgillia's two older sisters had found their husbands in the Italian neighborhood. Nevertheless, the selection of mates would also depend on the unconscious readiness of immigrants on their way to being Americanized. They would select individuals out of their community, available in large metropolitan areas, who would facilitate their integration.

Such is the case of Virgillia, who works as a secretary outside her immediate surroundings. She is the Vinas' first daughter to be born in America and to have a job. It seems that her process of integration is more advanced than that of her older sisters. In addition, she falls in love with Donald, her American boss, who symbolizes the young American businessman and American modern society. Her attraction to him is representative of her psychological and social integration. In addition, her meeting Donald coincided with a promotion at the workplace (chapter 5), which symbolically meant that social mobility and integration may also correspond to emotional integration. Her tendency to leave her group is also exemplified in her unexpected attitude towards Donald and in her desire to underline her femininity, by using make-up or by wearing a negligee (3). It goes along with her desire for independence and recognition. Obviously her readiness to marry outside the Italian community – since she agrees to marry Donald at the end of the novel – accelerated the process of integration and meant that marriage was no longer a family consensus but a personal decision. Brought up in a heterogeneous society, youngsters were more able to cross ethnic boundaries and accept other cultural heritages. Consequently, intermarriages were more likely to take place. Moreover, they went with individual desires, since they revealed an intimate decision to break with expected attitudes. Therefore they would convey a greater likelihood to contribute to the outside community, that is, to join mainstream America. Furthermore, Donald's coming to Virgillia's house while her parents were away epitomized the intrusion of American values within Italian colonies (chapter 15). It is supposed to be the uncovering of her world by Donald's appraisal. This invitation was significant of the possible mixture and interpenetration of ethnic heritages that melt when intermarriages take place, of the possible contribution of minority groups to the core society.

VIRGILLIA, OR THE ITALIAN CONTRIBUTION TO AMERICAN SOCIETY

It seems that intermarriage is "a good measure of the immigrant's willingness to cross over national lines in choosing a spouse."[1] It is even more than that. It represents an advanced step in the process of Americanization, as it displays a tendency not only to accept but also to contribute to one's spouse's ethnic and biological heritage. But the irony of the book is that, technically speaking, there is no intermarriage, *i.e.*, the union of two people belonging to two different groups. Donald had been brought up in an Italian family and had an Italian cultural background. His parents were Americans. He was American-born but he was adopted by the Longobardos after they had lost their infant while they were immigrating to the United States. He was an

---

[1] T. Krontoft, "Factors in Assimilation, a Comparative Study," *Norwegian-American Studies* 26 (1974).

Italian by adoption (chapter 18). On the other hand, Virgillia was an Italian and she was becoming American by adoption. Such an ironical situation can be interpreted in two different ways. Either intermarriage was not really possible and the Italian "race" had to be protected – the author's opinion – or belonging to one particular group did not matter, as discrepancies can easily be overcome in love affairs.

It is possible to say that there was intermarriage, considering the fact that Donald was born American and Virgillia had Italian parents. Because his cultural heritage was Italian, however, there was no cultural blending, as opposed to intermarriages when the mates belong to different ethnic groups. Thus, he was familiar with Virgillia's values, and the alleged crossing of national lines referred to earlier is but a deception in the novel. While Donald did not belong to the "Italian race" that G. Sferra mentioned in her letter, he could be considered as a second-generation immigrant, since he had been brought up by Italian immigrants as their son. Nevertheless, his way of living was American: his social status, his values, his friends – and he had even been engaged to an American girl – made him a real American. So, at first, the reader is drawn to believe that Virgillia and Donald would intermarry. In the last chapter in the novel, the reader becomes aware of Donald's background, as if it was time for the writer to acknowledge that people felt attracted only if they shared cultural heritage. A kind of *deus ex machina*, working for the maintenance of Italianness, had saved "the Italian race" (to quote Sferra) from outside forces and was maintaining biological equilibrium among groups. It seems that immigrants could recognize mates with the same ancestry and such a *natural genetic attraction* was the guardian of their ethnic identity, which was praised by G. Sferra in her letter relating her daughters' experiences.[2] Ethnicity seemed to play a kind of magnet that kept groups apart. The presence of this *deus ex machina* opposes the idea that the United States had been built thanks to the contribution of immigrants, that the Melting Pot is a basic factor in the construction of the American identity.

Nevertheless, a controversial point of view can be adopted, since throughout the book the idea of the Melting Pot resulting in the high contribution of immigrants to American society was proceeding. The struggle that characterized the incoming American society at the turn of

---

[2] See introduction.

the century, between the integration of immigrants through the acquisition of some American values – through intermarriage in particular – and the desire to maintain one's ethnic identity – through endogamous marriage – is prevalent in *Virgillia*. Moreover Virgillia and Donald's courtship is reminiscent of Vera and David's romance in *The Melting Pot,* by Israel Zangwill (1909). In both works, lovers belonged to different groups but they readily overcame the ethnic boundaries that characterized their heritages and believed in the birth of a new generation of Americans born out of love and the amalgamation of all ethnic qualities. Both Donald and David gave a definition of what the new American is, a definition based on the concept of the blending of groups.[3] In chapter 13, Donald proposed to Virgillia to "take a trip with (him) around the world" (126), that is, to go for a ride in New York City, the city where many immigrants had settled and where the coexistence of groups may be the most obvious. This allegorical passage, which can be seen as an initiatory journey for Virgillia, who discovered the ethnic reality of New York City, such as the image of Zangwill's symphony, praises the contribution of immigrants to the forming of American identity and future. Virgillia and Donald united in spite of their different ancestries and social discrepancies and should give birth to a new generation of Americans. The fact that they overcome alleged national boundaries reveals the progressive decline of ethnicity among second-generation immigrants who are hyphenated Americans. In other words, the possibility of intermarriage affected their contribution to American identity as it changed the biological and cultural characteristics of the United States, as well as those of ethnic communities. Intermarriage would give birth to a new man, a new American. The Americanization of second-generation immigrants, apparent in their rebel attitudes facing their parents' ethnic heritages, added to their contribution to the core society, since it was representative of the weakening of group solidarity at the same time as a new American identity emerged. Since the coming of the first waves of

---

[3] Israel Zangwill, *The Melting Pot*: "The Great Melting Pot... Celt and Latin, Slav and Teuton, Greek and Syrian, - black and yellow - Jew and Gentile... Here shall they all unite to build the Republic of Man and the Kingdom of God" (act IV).

G. C. Sferra, *Virgillia*: "I am an American. There is a bit of English, Scotch, French and Indian in me, and when we have our children, they too will be Americans. Their background will not be one nationality, but many nationalities rolled into one – that is an American" (164).

Italians to the United States during the nineteenth century, which went along with the spread of prejudices and discrimination because they were said to be unassimilable,[4] their contribution has shown that they were assimilable and that they could be members of mainstream America. The rate of in-group marriages reached more than 95% among first-generation immigrants, whereas it decreased to 65% among their grandchildren, which shows that prejudices and ethnic barriers had dropped and that integration was in progress. The contribution of young Italians is shown in the novel through Virgillia's attempt to get rid of ethnic yokes, her adoption of American values, and her readiness to marry outside the Italian community and give birth to the new Americans. Therefore, intermarriage appeared to accelerate like a mainspring the participation of immigrants, as it implied amalgamation, the mixture of cultural, social, and above all biological, traits and the evolution of American identity.

CONCLUSION

To show the contribution of the Italian community to mainstream America, intermarriage is one of the best examples. It accelerated the Americanization of foreigners as most intermarriages involved an American spouse. By the end of the 1920s, in New York City, not even 4% of Italian immigrants had married a non-Italian immigrant spouse, because to marry another foreigner was of "no interest" (Lindmark 52). As a matter of fact, intermarriage essentially involved an American as if, even though unconsciously, to marry outside the ethnic group was a kind of strategy to accelerate one's Americanization and social mobility. It seemed easier to accept American values through one's spouse, as they constituted the reference points of the society when other immigrants' values were still marginalized. In the novel, Virgillia was compelled to adopt American values, as they meant integration and emancipation. So, it is not surprising to read that she married an American businessman.

The blending of people belonging to different groups quickened the mixture of social and cultural values, which has given the United States its specificity and its identity as a nation of nations. The Italian community has contributed to mainstream America in the sense that,

---

[4] Salvatore LaGumina, *WOP!* (San Francisco : Straight Arrow, 1973).

like some other groups, it has helped form a multicultural society based both on the coexistence of several cultural heritages and the mixture of ethnic backgrounds through intermarriage. *Virgillia* provides an example of the process of Italian contribution, since the protagonist acquires some American characteristics. But the novel remains an ironic illustration of the issue, since no intermarriage actually took place and Virgillia married a man who had received an Italian heritage. Does that mean that love is more powerful than any genetic or ethnic consideration and prejudice? Such might be the moral of the novel, whether G. Sferra likes it or not.

REFERENCES

Belfiglio, Valentine. *Cultural Traits of Italian Americans which Transcend Generational Differences*. New York: AIHA, 1986.

Child, Irving. *Italian or American? The Second Generation in Conflict*. New Haven: Yale UP, 1943.

Kennedy, Ruby J.R. "Single or Triple Melting Pot." *American Journal of Sociology* 49.4 (Jan. 1944).

LaGumina, Salvatore. *WOP!* San Francisco: Straight Arrow, 1973.

Lindmark, Sture. "Swedish America." *Studia Historica Upsaliensia* 38 (1971):

Messina, Elizabeth. "Narratives of Nine Italian American Women: Childhood, Work and Marriage." *Italian Americana* 10.2 (spring/summer 1992):

Michaud, Marie-Christine. "L'américanisation: voie d'émancipation." *Migrations Société* 6.35 (1994):

Nelli, Humbert. *The Italians in Chicago*. New York: Oxford UP, 1970.

Puzo, Mario. *The Fortunate Pilgrim*. 2nd ed. Reading, UK: Mandarin, 1992.

Russo, Nicholas. "Three Generations of Italians in New York City: Their Religious Acculturation." *International Migration Review* 3.2 (Spring 1969):

Tomasi, Lydio. *The Italian-American Family*. New York: CMS, 1972.

Zangwill, Israel. *The Melting Pot*. 3rd ed. New York: Arno, 1975.

Maria Elisa Ciavarelli

Athens

Athens glistens, white, modern,
under the white, marble Acropolis.
Ancient governors, your whispers of empire
lay strewn among the poppies.
Athens can't high rise.
City of light, stay close to the arms of
your mother mountain.
The Acropolis sighs above you
breathes the air of mortal gods
into every flawed stone.
Athens, white, modern, you need not
scrape the sky.
The sky bows to Acropolis,
Antique before men's minds
Yet carved by human hands
blooded, boned, and warm
As the white sunned heat of Athens.

Atene

Atene risplende, bianca, moderna,
sotto il bianco Acropoli di marmo.
Antichi governanti, i vostri sogni d'impero
giacciono dispersl nel mezzo dei papaveri
Atene non può estendersi in alto.
Città di luce, resta vicino alle braccia della tua montagna madre.
L'Acropoli sospira su di te
soffia aria di dei mortali
in tutte le pietre incrinate.
Atene, bianca, moderna, non puoi
grattare il cielo.
Il cielo s'inchina all'Acropoli,
Antico già prima della mente degli uomini
Eppur scolpito dalle mani dell'uomo
insanguinate, ossee, ed ardenti
Come il bianco soleggiato calore d'Atene.

Sicily

Each day, under the huge bowl
of Sicilian sky, we ride
through this landscape:
the mountains form a ring around us: their colors,
the colors of soil –
red, ochre, deep brown.
We pass small farms,
scattered, like handkerchiefs,
on hillsides. We visit villages
with twisted streets,
narrow and cobblestoned,
the houses, rough-textured fieldstone
with wooden doors so ancient
we are awed.

Past the dizzying vista of mountains
and sky, the peaks draped in mist
light as a gauze shawl,
we see a town that cascades
down the hillside like a waterfall,
balanced and beautiful as a Japanese garden.

Each night I dream my mother
is speaking to me. Is it her courage,
I find in the primitive and elemental hills?

Sicily, you speak to me
in the faces of your people ....
>   two old men sit on crates
>   in a dooryard on a cobbled street.
>   Square-faced, stoic,
>   the sharp planes of their high cheekbones
>   their blue eyes
>   suspicious, and squinting
>   against the intense and pitiless sun.

Sicily, I see your faces
and am moved.
Your women have the strength of the hills
on their countenances.
When they walk, there is a sureness to them,
as though they heard some inner music:
their skin is a silken dress
in which they move.

And the men, their gentian eyes
startling against tanned skin.
They are men together.
I see them on street corners and in cafés,
arguing politics, cantankerous
and passionate. Their sharp eyes
miss nothing, and are pleased.

Sicily, I hear your intense music,
in the words of your poet, Nat Scamacca
in his name, hard as fist,
in his face,
the slash of color across prominent cheekbones,
the fine contours,
ascetic and handsome,
and in the face of Nina, his wife,
proud and audacious,
chiselled as if sculpted
from stone,
the face of these mountains,
 the land, passionate and fierce,
which has seen everything
yet survives.

Sicilia

Ogni giorno, sotto l'immensa coppa
del cielo di Sicilia, attraversiamo
questo paesaggio:
le monatagne formano un anello
intorno a noi: i loro colori,
i colori della terra-
rosso, ocra,bruno scuro.
Traversiamo piccoli poderi,
sparpagliati, come fazzoletti,
sui flanchi delle colline. Visitiamo borghi
dalle viuzze tortuose,
strette e acciottolate,
le case, rozza struttura di pietra
con porte di legno si antiche
da destar riverenza.

Oltre la vertiginosa vista delle montagne
e del cielo, le vette drappeggiate di nebbia
leggera come scialle di garza,
vediamo un paese che scivola
giù per le pendici della collina come una cascata, armonioso e bello
come giardino giapponese.

Ogni notte sogno che la mamma
mi parla. È il suo coraggio,
che trovo nelle primitive ed elementari colline?

Sicilia, tu mi parli
nei visi della tua gente ...
       due vecchi siedono su casse
       sulla soglia d'un cortile d'un'acciottolata via.
       Visi quadrati, stoici
       gli acuti piani dei loro alti zigomi sporgenti
       occhi azzurri
       diffidenti, e strabici
       sul fondo d'un sole intenso e spietato.

Sicilia, vedo i tuoi visi
e mi commuovo.
Le tue donne hanno la forza delle colline
sul loro volto.
Quando camminano, c'è in esse una sicurezza,
come se avessero sentito una musica interiore:
la loro pelle e come un vestito di seta
in cui si muovono.

E gli uomini, dagli occhi di genziana
impressionanti su pelle abbronzata.
Sono uomini in crocchi.
Li vedo agli angoli delle vie e nei caffè,
discutendo di politica, irascibili
e appassionati. Ai loro occhi acuti
non sfugge nulla, e son soddisfatti.

Sicilia, sento la tua intensa musica,
nelle parole del tuo poeta, Nat Scamacca
nel suo nome, duro come un pugno,
nel suo viso,
la sferza del colore sui prominenti zigomi,
le delicate linee,
ascetiche e belle,
e nel viso di Nina, sua moglie,
audace e fiero,
cesellato come se scolpito
dalla pietra,
il viso di queste montagne,
la terra, ardente e cruda,
che ha visto tutto
e tuttavia sopravvive.

DREAM POEM

I miss my grandmother
As I walk along Italian streets,
Old men sit hunched on steps,
Their words tumble like skipping stones,
In a dialect I cannot understand.

I walk past them, the cold air
Tastes foreign in my mouth.
Across the street, the house
Sways in and out of sunset light-
Dizzying my flight-a brown girl on
Skateboard whizzes through patches of black and
White, her braids burn my cheek in the metallic air.

I knock on wood. Two black dogs, handsome as men,
Snarl and wag at the door.
I scold them in the old men's language and they
Whimper in retreat.
My old comare knows why I have come: her doe eyes
Are like glass before my eyes, reflecting the street
Outside. She kisses both my cheeks, grasps my hair in
Peasant hands, turns me to the door:

>   And there I see her,
>   Grandma with flying braids
>   Looks up at me elfish and gay
>   In the urban sun.
>   Her eyes are older than time.

POESIA SOGNO

Sento la mancanza della nonna
Quando. cammino per le vie italiane,
Uomini anziani seduti rannicchiati sulla soglia,
Le loro parole ruzzolano come pietre saltellanti,
In un dialetto che non riesco a capire.

Passo accanto a loro; l'aria fredda
Mi causa un sapore d'estraneo in bocca.
Dall'altro lato della via, la casa .
Si dondola entro e fuori la luce del crepuscolo-
Sconcertando il mio volo-una ragazza bruna con
Monopattino sibila attraverso chiazze di nero e
Bianco, le sue trecce mi bruciano le gote nell'aria metallica.

Tocco ferro. Due cani neri, belli come uomini,
Ringhiano e scodinzolano alla porta.
Io li rimprovero nella lingua degli anziani e loro
Uggiolano indietreggiando.
La mia vecchia comare sa perchè son venuta: I suoi occhi di daina
Sono come vetro davanti ai miei occhi, riverberando la via
Al di fuori.

Mass at the little church

in Quercegrossa
was different
that day
one priest, so bent
he looked comical
the other taking over the more
strenuous
prayers and incantations

We went to church early
our first full day in Italia
walked from farmhouse
to village
sat in the back
 prayed amid stuccoed walls

St. Anthony and his candles
on the right
at the door large heavy drapes
keep out heat
attract coolness
on the corner
 old men gather
at the bar
watching women
walk homeward

Messa nella chiesetta

a Quercegrossa
era differente
quel giorno
un sacerdote, sì curvo
sembrava comico
l'altro
occupandosi delle attività
più faticose
preghiere ed incantesimi

Siamo andati in chiesa presto
la nostra prima giornata intera in Italia
abbiamo camminato dalla cascina
al paese
ci siamo seduti dietro
abbiamo pregato tra le pareti di stucco

sant'Antonio e le sue candele
a destra
alla porta
grandi tandaggi pesanti
tengono fuori il caldo
attraggono il fresco

all'angolo
i vecchi si raccolgono
al bar a guardare le donne
che vanno verso casa

The Graeco-Roman Influence in Sicily

RoseAnna Mueller
COLUMBIA COLLEGE, CHICAGO

If you were to visit the website, "More Italy than Ever," and click onto the section for Sicily, here is what you would read: Do you want to learn about Greece? So come to Sicily. It is a paradox, for sure, but only to a certain extent. The Greek cities of Sicily – Agrigento, Selinunte, Segesta, Syracuse, to mention the most important – were among the most beautiful of the Hellenic world. Nowadays, to visit the Valley of Temples in Agrigento or to watch a summer performance in the great Greek Temple in Syracuse is to plunge yourself into the remote Hellenic past. Sicily is extremely rich in classical Greek remains, hardly less than Greece itself, with about 40 classical sites.

Sicily was also known as Trinacria, the Greek word for "three promontories." It was in Sicily that Greece expanded her colonies, among them Naxos, Syracuse, Catania and Messina in the eighth and seventh centuries BC. The island of Sicily has linked East and West, Europe and Africa, and the Latin and Greek worlds in her role as go-between in the Mediterranean. This strategic position in that "wine-dark sea," in the words of Homer, bequeathed on the island a rich cultural mix. Sicily has been the Mediterranean's richest prize throughout most of her history.

More than a colony, Greek Sicily was and felt itself to be fully Greek. There is evidence of continuous traffic between Sicily and Greece. Sicilian patrons summoned Greek skilled craftsmen to work on the island. No fewer than nine temples were built in the Greek colony of Selinunte between 580-480 BC. The early Greek settlements were focused on the southeast of Sicily, especially at Syracuse, which was founded in 733 BC. Naxos, on the east coast of the island, was founded in 735 BC. The Greek cities in the west were prosperous. These temples were bigger than those at home, and the art was more ornate. Artists and philosophers could be lured from Greece with rich commissions and lecture tours. In founding the Greek colonies in Sicily, the choice of location had to be both strategic and economic. A defensible position was preferred and cultivatable land was necessary to support a growing community. And so it went for many years, the triangular island providing breathtaking sites for temples and theaters, her fertile soil producing the grain that fed the motherland and the colonists. When the Greek world lost its hold on the island, and its colonial influence gave way, the memory of Greeks in Italy and Sicily survived in the form of myths and in the stories of Odysseus's wanderings. The break in contact after 1200 BC was almost complete.

Greek vases came in a variety of shapes. The most common type of clay vessel was the amphora, used to store oil and wine. Artists and potters specialized in this craft according to shape. The decorations on these vessels remind us both of everyday life in Sicily and its rich heritage of Greek history and myth.

Among the many Attic kraters and Greek vases in Cefalu's Museo Mandralisca is the fourth-century vase depicting a tuna fisherman filleting his catch. Other vases depict Aphrodite admiring herself in a mirror, and a scene that tells the story of Theseus and the Minotaur.

Greek theaters such as the ones found in Eraclea, Segesta, and Morgantina and on the island of Filicudi were conceived as part of a plan to take advantage of a natural stage. Steps were carved into the slopes and lead to the stage. Whenever possible, the builders availed themselves of the spectacular views, so that drama could be found in the natural background scenery all around and behind the stage as well as on it. Most of the Greek theaters in Sicily were modified or completely rebuilt when Sicily belonged to Rome. A good example is the theater at Taormina, with Roman stage and columns added to the original Greek plan. This theater is still in use. It was first erected in the Hellenistic period and almost entirely rebuilt under the Romans. It is next largest to Syracuse's theater and, like the one in Syracuse, it is formed from excavated wedges in the hill. It has a remarkable view of the sea, and Mt. Etna often puffs away in the distance.

Segesta, in western Sicily, is the finest example of a hilltop site of which the Greeks were fond. Segesta's hill site has a small theater and a magnificent temple. Segesta has the best preserved of all the Hellenic Sicilian theaters of the third century BC. The Romans later used the city for its strategic vantage-point.

The "generic" Doric temple flourished about 600 BC. According to Janson, "the elements are constant in number, in kind, and in their relation to each other, resulting in a narrowly circumscribed repertory of forms" (125). This repertory of forms, as Janson calls its, played itself out throughout Sicily.

The principal elements of the Doric temple consist of a stepped platform, columns resting on the platform which support the entablature, made up of architrave, frieze, and cornice.

The stone blocks were fitted together without mortar and the roof was made of terra-cotta tiles supported by wooden rafters and beams. These components, according to Janson, "achieve a structural logic that make the temples look stable because of the precise arrangement of their parts" (138). The impressive exterior of the temple is what mattered most, which was just as well, since few people were allowed inside it. Religious ceremonies took place out of doors, with the temple facade providing the backdrop. The temples always faced east.

Syracuse was the richest of the Greek cities. The Corinthians founded it in 734. Syracuse rivaled Athens as the largest and most beautiful city in the Greek world. In fact, the increasing power of the Syracuse republic provoked the jealousy of the Athenians, who dispatched a hostile expedition in 415; a reinforcement from Sparta saved the city. Syracuse was home to Archimedes, Theocritus, the father of idyllic poetry, and Moschus, another pastoral poet. Plato visited the city several times and advised Dyonisius II how to rule his kingdom. Cicero noted that Syracuse knew no day without sun, and its splendid theater still hosts performances of classical Greek plays.

The oldest temple was that of Apollo, or of Apollo and Artemis, built in 575 BC. This structure was a pioneer building featuring enormous, heavy Atlas figures. The Duomo (Santa Maria Delle Colonne) was constructed from the Doric Temple of Athena. The facade of the church is Baroque. In an effort to transform the open Greek temple into a walled Catholic church, the spaces between the columns were walled in. Unless one mentally strips away the filler between the Doric columns of this Greek temple, and uses one's imagination to remove the facade, it looks like any other of the Sicilian churches who succumbed to seventeenth-century Baroque-mania.

Agrigento's Valle dei Templi lies in undisturbed countryside with groves of almonds and olive trees. The site really should be visited several times during the day, and especially at night, when the temples are dramatically floodlit. The Valley is also home to a Paleochristian necropolis, with tombs cut into the rock and catacombs. The misnamed

Temple of Castor and Pollux is really part of the Sanctuary of Chthonic Divinities. The four columns have been used as the picturesque symbol of Classical Sicily and more specifically as an emblem for Agrigento. But they incorporate elements from more than one building near the site, and were reassembled in 1836.

The Temple of Hera (Juno) resembles the Temple of Concord in form but is slightly smaller and older, having been built in 450 BC. The Temple of Concord is the best-preserved Greek Temple in Sicily. This is partly because it was converted into a Catholic church by San Gregorio delle Rape (turnips), who was bishop of Agrigento in the fifth century AD. It was then restored to a Greek temple in the eighteenth century.

The most remarkable Sicilian Greek building was the temple of Olympian Zeus, the largest of all Doric temples. Begun in the fourth century BC, it was never finished. The Temple of Olympian Zeus is now a heap of ruins whose stones laid the foundation of nearby Porto Empedocle. This is the largest Doric temple known, but little remains in position. There was also a Temple of Heracles, a building famed for its statue of Hercules, which shows traces of a fire.

Selinunte marks the westernmost end of Greek colonization of Sicily and the city sits on the edge of the sea on a terrace. Selinunte was colonized from Megara Hyblea as early as 651 BC. Its name comes from *selinon,* the Greek name for wild celery. Selinunte allied itself with Syracuse against Carthage. The city was very consciously laid on a rectangular plan, and at least nine temples were constructed here during the peaceful period between 580-480 BC.

Of all the Greek cities in Sicily, Selinunte is the only city to have decorated its temples with sculpted metopes. These are now housed in the archeological museum in Palermo. In *Art and Architecture of Sicily*, Helen Hills claims that "this is perhaps the most impressive of the Greek cities in Sicily, since the ruins have never been built over in modern times" (150). Some of the temples still have plaster, and sacrificial altars are beside most temples. Earthquakes have toppled some temples; an especially destructive one occurred during Byzantine times. The eastern group of temples contains the three largest ones, and the city also has an acropolis.

The Roman Villa at Casale, or the Villa Romana, is a luxurious country mansion that must have belonged to one of the wealthiest men in the Roman Empire, possibly Diocletian's co-emperor Maximinian. The villa consists of four distinct, though connected and related, groups of buildings and appears to have been built in the fourth century AD. The villa was probably built over another dwelling that existed in the second century. The splendid mosaics, some of the finest to have survived Roman antiquity, are of the fourth-century Roman-African school. Here we are reminded of the close links between Roman Sicily and Africa. The villa includes an entrance, an atrium, a grand latrine, cold and warm baths, colonnades, and gardens. It is probably best noted for its Sala delle Ragazze. This room has mosaics of ten young women performing gymnastic exercises. They wear black bras and low-cut panties, and tourists and guides commonly refer to these female athletes as the "Bikini Girls."

The villa was partially uncovered in 1761, but systematic excavations began in 1950. There is attention to detail in all the mosaics and everyday activities are portrayed. There are scenes that include household attendants, soldiers, hunters, and fishermen. There is a scene of wild animals being loaded on a galley to be transported from Africa to Italy. In a dormitory, a nearly naked female kisses a youth; her cloak is slipping off, revealing her bottom. These lush and detailed mosaics form the floors of the various rooms of the villa. We have no idea what the walls looked like.

SOURCES

http://www.piuitalia2000.it/uk/regioni/sicilia.htm

Langdon, Helen. *The Knopf Traveler's Guides to Art: Italy*. New York: Knopf, 1984.

Janson, H. W. *History of Art*. New York: Prentice Hall, 1995.

Macadam, Alta. *Blue Guide: Sicily*. New York: Norton, 1999.

Sapienza, Teresa. *Sicily: Art History and Beauties*. Officina Graffica Bolognese, 1998.

Valdes, Giuliano. *Arte e Storia della Sicilia*. Florence: Bonechi, 1994.

Printed in the United States
30588LVS00002B/55-510